"In a cultural context dominated by stories of deconstruction and de-conversion, *The Reconstruction Project* is a breath of fresh, encouraging air. Travis and Shepardson marshal their ample knowledge, social understanding, and rhetorical skills to winsomely and persuasively address twelve of the most common critiques of the Christian faith and the church. From science to sexuality, and evolution to evil, *The Reconstruction Project* faces challenges head-on, acknowledging legitimate accusations and questions while pointing readers to resources and answers that enable readers to recover the truth of the Christian faith. Highly recommended, particularly for students who have doubts, concerns, and objections to the faith they currently inhabit."

—**Tawa J. Anderson**, associate professor of philosophy and apologetics and director of the Institute for Christian Apologetics at New Orleans Baptist Theological Seminary

"You've heard the charges. Maybe you've even made some yourself. Christianity is anti-science, anti-woman, and anti-LGBTQ+; but pro-slavery, pro-Crusades, pro-colonialism. It can't explain the problem of evil, is filled with hypocrites, and is too often abusive. Evolutionary theory has ruled out the possibility of God, while modern lifestyles have ruled out the need for God. No one book could ever adequately address all of these charges, much less one that is barely 200 pages. But Shepardson and Travis work a minor miracle by consistently homing in on the most important responses to these kinds of complaints and do so in succinct and readable fashion. A valuable resource indeed."

—**Craig L. Blomberg**, distinguished professor emeritus of New Testament, Denver Seminary

"Have you been looking for a resource you can hand to people whose Christian worldview is unraveling? If you are a care warrior with a friend or family member doubting, deconstructing, or even de-converting, this book is for you . . . and for them. Melissa Cain Travis and Andrew Shepardson do a masterful job anticipating and answering the most popular objections among deconstructionists. They do this by first dignifying the questions—no straw manning here—and then answering both the evidence and the heart behind it. It turns out that the trendy intellectual exits from the faith are all dead ends. The authors don't back down from the tough truth either. Christianity isn't easy. The gospel is life eternal, but it's also death to self. Simon Peter said it this way, responding to Jesus as his followers were scattering: "Lord, to whom shall we go? You have the words of eternal life" (John 6:68 NIV). This book is for people who want hard truth, tough love, and real rather than soft, sweet lies."

—**Dr. John D. Ferrer**, speaker with Crossexamined.org and Mama Bear Apologetics

"Many in our post-Christian culture long to frame their lives around something bigger than themselves but are disillusioned with traditional religion. In *The Reconstruction Project*, Melissa Cain Travis and Andrew I. Shepardson provide a compelling defense of the truth, beauty, and goodness of the Christian faith that addresses this concern. It is rigorous and well argued yet engaging and accessible. I highly recommend it."

—**Keith A. Hess**, associate professor of philosophy and apologetics, Oklahoma Baptist University

"Apologetics in the twenty-first century has seen a significant sea change. It used to be that the primary accusation against Christianity was that it was not true. Today, the main accusation is that it is not good. *The Reconstruction Project* answers that charge and then some. Shepardson and Travis demonstrate that the Christian faith is true, good, and beautiful."

—**Kenneth D. Keathley**, research professor of theology, Southeastern Baptist Theological Seminary

"Christians are called to offer reasons for their convictions (1 Peter 3:15), but in every generation, the objections change. In our postmodern age, people are no longer asking, 'Is Christianity true?' They're asking questions like, 'Why are Christians such bigots?' In this book, Andrew Ike Shepardson and Melissa Cain Travis take on today's most controversial questions and equip readers with solid, biblical answers."

—**Nancy R. Pearcey**, professor of apologetics and scholar in residence, Houston Christian University

THE RECONSTRUCTION PROJECT

RECOVERING TRUTH AND REBUILDING FAITH

THE RECONSTRUCTION PROJECT

ANDREW I. SHEPARDSON
AND MELISSA CAIN TRAVIS

The Reconstruction Project: Recovering Truth and Rebuilding Faith

Published by B&H Academic®
Brentwood, Tennessee

ISBN: 978-1-4300-8838-7

Dewey Decimal Classification: 239
Subject Heading: APOLOGETICS \ CHRISTIANITY-
-APOLOGETIC WORKS \ THEOLOGY

Cover design by Gearbox

Printed in the United States of America

30 29 28 27 26 VP 1 2 3 4 5 6 7 8 9 10

CONTENTS

FOREWORD

Douglas Groothuis, PhD, Distinguished University Professor
of Apologetics and Christian Worldview,
Cornerstone University and Seminary

If an individual thinks that Christianity is *bad*—that it is anti-science, anti-woman, proslavery, colonialist, and more—then one will not consider whether it is *true*. The nonbeliever or the doubting Christian will then not be interested in pursuing the evidence in its favor. Because of this, much of the constructive evidence for Christianity—science, history, philosophy, and human experience—goes unheeded. Why investigate something that is intrinsically corrupt in several ways? Why taste rotten fruit? Why should anyone care about the reliability of the Bible, for example, if what it teaches is objectionable? What can be done to break this apologetic logjam?

This carefully argued, winsomely written, and thoroughly documented book helps resolve the problem and free people up to discover the positive evidence for the Christian faith. The authors take seriously the charges they address and give nuanced responses to each criticism of Christianity. They admit that Christians have sometimes been on the wrong side of moral and intellectual issues, but also argue that Christianity itself (the biblical teaching) is not what is misguided. For example, while some Christians have been racists and have even supported slavery, many did not. In fact, many believers actively opposed slavery. Most important, the Bible itself does not support racism or slavery. Further, Christianity is far from misogynistic; it values highly both women and men as made in the divine image and equally capable of serving God and neighbor.

This book makes a cogent case that the major objections against Christianity are simply not true. (To use a technical phrase, it "defeats defeaters" against Christianity.) Along the way, it also offers constructive evidence for the truth of the Christian worldview, such as the argument that a Christian view of nature was fundamental to launching and sustaining the scientific revolution.

The book is calm in spirit and careful in exposition. You will find no rushed conclusions, no clichés, no slogans, and no easy answers. However, you will find reasonable, factual, and persuasive answers to the charges addressed. The issues are urgent and not trivial since Christianity teaches that Jesus Christ is the only way to find forgiveness of sins, objective meaning, and eternal life (see John 3:1–18; 14:1–6; Acts 4:12; 1 Tim 2:5). This statement forms the Bible's nonnegotiable message, and that message should become more believable to skeptics and doubting Christians after reading this exemplary work of apologetics. The convinced Christian will come away fortified and encouraged that their Christian faith is able to withstand the toughest objections.

INTRODUCTION

Over the past quarter century, attitudes and conversations about religious faith have evolved in unexpected and fascinating ways. In early 2001, when I (Melissa) first began an independent study of Christian apologetics to improve my interactions with biotech industry colleagues, the so-called New Atheism had yet to fully materialize. Later that year, the 9/11 terrorist attacks generated a storm of anti-religion polemics and, as Alister McGrath puts it, "turned out to be the intellectual and moral launchpad" of the movement.[1] Even so, it was not until the 2004 publication of Sam Harris's book *The End of Faith: Religion, Terror, and the Future of Reason* that what we now call the New Atheism began to emerge. Richard Dawkins's *The God Delusion* (2006) was a major catalyst in its development, as were Daniel Dennett's *Breaking the Spell: Religion as a Natural Phenomenon* (2006) and Christopher Hitchens's *God Is Not Great: How Religion Poisons Everything* (2007). When Harris, Dawkins, Dennett, and Hitchens gathered in 2007 for a recorded roundtable discussion they called "The Four Horsemen," the satirical label stuck; these revered atheist evangelizers were thereafter referred to as the Four

[1] Alister McGrath, "Introduction: The Ambiguity of Richard Dawkins" in *Coming to Faith Through Dawkins: 12 Essays on the Pathway from New Atheism to Christianity*, ed. Denis Alexander and Alister McGrath (Kregel, 2023), 12.

Horsemen of the New Atheism (or, of the New Atheist Apocalypse). When I began graduate work in science and religion in 2009, well-known Christian philosophers and apologists were avidly responding to the New Atheists and even engaging with them in highly publicized formal debates.

Contrary to the perception of the time, New Atheism did not come armed with devastating new evidence against the existence of God; rather, it restyled perennial objections in the regalia of seething hatred of religion (the alleged root of all evil) and religious zeal for science. The rhetoric was aggressively mocking and their (typically fallacious) talking points were eminently quotable, and this guaranteed the movement's online virility. Followers of the New Atheists multiplied, but there were some high-profile secular thinkers who, even early on, regarded New Atheism as intellectually shallow and embarrassing. Dr. Michael Ruse, an atheist academic, was a vociferous critic. In an essay titled "Why I Think the New Atheists Are a Bloody Disaster," which he wrote before the release of his 2010 book, *Science and Spirituality: Making Room for Faith in the Age of Science*, he pulled no punches: "These people do a disservice to scholarship. Their treatment of the religious viewpoint is pathetic to the point of non-being. Richard Dawkins in *The God Delusion* would fail any introductory philosophy or religion course. Proudly he criticizes that whereof he knows nothing. . . . I am indignant at the poor quality of the argumentation in Dawkins, Dennett, Hitchens, and all of the others in that group."[2]

Several skeptics similarly distanced themselves from the New Atheism, but others hopped onto the coattails of the Four Horsemen and published books of their own.[3] Lecture and book tours contributed

---

[2] Michael Ruse, "Why I Think the New Atheists Are a Bloody Disaster," Beliefnet (2009), https://www.beliefnet.com/columnists/scienceandthesacred/2009/08/why-i-think-the-new-atheists-are-a-bloody-disaster.html.

[3] Physicist and philosopher Victor Stenger (1935–2014) is one example. He even authored a book titled *The New Atheism: Taking a Stand for Science and Reason* (Prometheus, 2009).

to the momentum of the movement and sparked the formation of atheist student groups on college campuses across the nation. This was a deer-in-the-headlights moment for many Christians who had never heard the arguments put forth in the atheist media tidal wave.

Fortunately, the onslaught of New Atheism ignited a veritable renaissance in Christian apologetics and philosophy that spread well beyond the academy. In early 2012, famous atheist-turned-Christian Lee Strobel predicted that Christian apologetics was about to enter a "golden era."[4] This was a thrilling thought for those of us working in the field, and it turned out that Strobel was right. As British radio broadcaster and author Justin Brierley puts it, "New Atheism has revitalized the intellectual tradition of the Christian church in the West. [It] arrived with a whole bunch of awkward questions about science, history, and religious belief–questions the church had not had to think about for a long time. But now, with the four horse-men at their heels, the church was forced to put down its tambourines and guitars and pick up its history and philosophy books again."[5]

Over the ensuing years, scores of apologetics books were published. A multitude of conferences devoted to making a case for Christianity were held in churches, seminaries, and universities across the US and beyond. Films, YouTube channels, podcasts, online magazines, academic journals, classroom curricula, campus groups, and university courses in apologetics rapidly proliferated.

New Atheism persisted for a few more years, during which rallies and debates were held and more books and blogs were written, but it is now widely regarded as defunct. Its decline was not all that surprising

---

[4] Alex Murashko, "Lee Strobel: We're on Cusp of Golden Era of Apologetics," *Christian Post* (January 22, 2012), https://www.christianpost.com/news/lee-strobel-were-on-cusp-of-golden-era-of-apologetics.html.

[5] Justin Brierley, *The Surprising Rebirth of Belief in God: Why New Atheism Grew Old and Secular Thinkers Are Considering Christianity Again* (Tyndale, 2023), 30.

considering its philosophically flawed talking points, its misconstrual of history and theology, and the abrasive (sometimes juvenile) verbal tactics of its proponents. The revival in Christian philosophy and apologetics undoubtedly contributed in crucial respects, but the falling away of disillusioned advocates of New Atheism was another factor. "The cultural mood began to shift," writes McGrath, "as many who had initially embraced the New Atheism found that it failed to deliver the secure knowledge they longed for or a sustainable vision of the 'good life.' . . . Many began to look for better answers, wondering if there were alternatives that might be more credible, attractive, and satisfying."[6] The realization of how existentially thin the movement truly was seems to have produced, quite ironically, a new wave of spiritual seekers and Christian converts who credit the New Atheism for inspiring their journey to faith. Take, for example, human rights activist and former politician, Ayaan Hirsi Ali, whose conversion from atheism to Christianity in 2023 made headlines. In her essay, "Why I Am Now a Christian" (a nod to the famous essay, "Why I Am Not a Christian" by Bertrand Russell), she writes, "I ultimately found life without any spiritual solace unendurable—indeed very nearly self-destructive. Atheism failed to answer a simple question: what is the meaning and purpose of life?"[7]

All of this is to say that there has been a notable change in conversations surrounding the truth and viability of Christianity. Public intellectuals such as Canadian psychologist Jordan Peterson and British historian Tom Holland (not to mention pop culture celebrities like Joe Rogan and Russell Brand) have effectively reopened the God question in surprising new ways. And various objections, including some that were previously trumpeted by the New Atheists, are receiving more insightful

---

[6] McGrath, 16.

[7] Ayaan Hirsi Ali, "Why I Am Now a Christian: Atheism Can't Equip Us for Civilisational War," UnHerd (November 11, 2023), https://UnHerd.com/2023/11/why-i-am-now-a-christian/.

and academically rigorous treatment than ever before. Interestingly, many (perhaps most) of these concern the *goodness* of the Christian worldview: Is it detrimental to science, society, or individual human flourishing? Can it account for the human condition and fulfill our intense longings for meaning, significance, and purpose? Atheistic alternatives have certainly failed to satisfy, and many thoughtful people are searching anew. In short, the God question in general, and Christianity in particular, have gained a fresh hearing in unlikely circles, and thus the conversation is evolving in important and unique ways.[8] This presents the church with an enormous opportunity for influence in today's public square, and that is the main motivation for this book.

Many of the issues covered in these twelve stand-alone chapters are often cited in various "deconstruction" stories—autobiographical accounts of former Christians who began systematically questioning and discarding facets of their worldview until, by their lights, it collapsed like a destabilized Jenga tower. While the vast majority of these individuals seem to have *begun* questioning the goodness of Christianity for painful personal reasons–church abuse, struggles with their own sexuality or gender identity, or experiencing the fallout of unchecked hypocrisy (all topics covered in this book), objections related to the natural sciences and the history of the church sometimes play a role in a latter phase of their journey. As a professor and as a pastor, I (Ike) have known, counseled, prayed for, and loved many dear people who have wrestled with these topics. Some emerged with a strengthened trust in God, while some, tragically, walked away from Christianity altogether. If you are (or if someone in your life is) dealing with the pain and confusion of doubt or full-blown deconstruction, perhaps this material will prove helpful.[9]

---

[8] Brierley's book, *The Surprising Rebirth of Belief in God*, is a fascinating exploration of this dynamic.

[9] Dr. Jana Harmon's podcast, *eX-skeptic*, is devoted to personal stories of adult conversions and returns to the Christian faith. Many of these former

At its heart, this book is a work of apologetics, a defense and commendation of the Christian faith as rational, good, true, and relevant to every aspect of human life.[10] This single-volume, accessible treatment offers readers the opportunity to take their knowledge to a depth beyond what is typically found in popular-level resources that cover similar ground. Yet, we acknowledge that it will not address every single philosophical and emotional difficulty that may arise from a person's complex experiences with these issues. We also recognize that an intellectual response to these objections is only one leg of the journey to faith, one cornerstone in a faith-reconstruction project. We in no way wish to minimize the importance of pastoral counseling, professional therapy (when necessary), prayer, a rhythm of worship, immersion in Scripture, Christian community, and the role of the Holy Spirit.

While we commend the treatment of the issues presented in the forthcoming chapters, our ultimate desire is to point readers to the gospel of Jesus Christ. Our Lord provides holistic healing that begins and substantially progresses in this life and will be complete through his redemptive work in the new creation. We pray that this book will not only serve university and seminary students in the classroom but also

---

skeptics recount interaction with one or more of the issues addressed in this book. https://exskeptic.org/podcast/.

[10] The answers provided in this book fall into the category of "negative apologetics," which seeks to show that objections to Christianity ultimately fail. Negative apologetics also includes showing why non-Christian answers to life's big questions are rationally or existentially insufficient. The information provided here would be complemented by "positive apologetics," which is concerned with showing that Christian truth claims are indeed true, rational, and relevant. In the classroom setting, this book would sit well alongside books that make a positive case for Christianity such as Douglas Groothuis and Andrew I. Shepardson, *The Knowledge of God in the World and the Word: An Introduction to Classical Apologetics* (Zondervan Academic, 2022); William Lane Craig, *Reasonable Faith: Christian Truth and Apologetics*, 3rd ed. (Crossway, 2008); or Douglas Groothuis, *Christian Apologetics: A Comprehensive Case for Biblical Faith* (IVP Academic, 2022).

will equip ministry leaders, pastors, and other motivated learners to competently and charitably engage with this new generation of intellectually inclined seekers, doubters, and deconstructors. By the power of the Holy Spirit, may the faith of many be strengthened, restored, or even newly discovered.

CHAPTER 1

Objection #1: Christianity Is Unnecessary for a Good, Meaningful Life

The American comedy series *The Good Place*, which ran from 2016 until 2020, was a fascinating experiment in prime-time entertainment: an attempt to communicate lofty philosophical concepts through a low-brow, pop culture medium. The main story arc involved the central characters' postmortem attempts to get from the "Bad Place" (eternal torture) to the "Good Place" (eternal paradise) by earning enough points to be classified as a good person. The question that kept viewers enthralled was whether these flawed but lovable men and women would actually make it. [Spoiler alert.] After many ridiculous and sometimes hilarious misadventures during which they grow in their affection for one another, they finally get to the Good Place. To their surprise, an eternity with unlimited access to every conceivable entertainment and sensory pleasure eventually became one of misery, even though they were together.

Why? Because it was entirely devoid of objective meaning, the characters became weary of their pointless existence.

It is interesting that the script writers and philosophical consultants for *The Good Place* zeroed in on the necessity of meaning for human flourishing. Mental health practitioners and researchers who specialize in the emerging field known as the science of happiness have concluded that a meaningful life is one of the essentials of our psychological well-being.[1] Few of us would disagree. However, much debate surrounds related questions about the nature of meaning and how to attain it. Proponents of naturalism, the philosophy that only the material world is real (and therefore, no gods or souls or an afterlife), scoff at the assertion that there is no real meaning to be had outside of the Christian faith and claim that they certainly have meaningful lives with loving relationships, a sense of purpose, and a desire to do good for the sake of others whenever possible. While we can acknowledge that these criteria are part of a good, meaningful life, the deeper question is whether naturalism as a worldview is compatible with authentic meaning, purpose, and goodness. Careful examination will reveal that it is not; unlike Christianity, naturalism cannot offer a sufficient foundation for the intangibles that humanity holds most dear.

Considering the Objection

As will be explained in chapter 11, early twentieth-century physicists and astronomers discovered that our universe is expanding. The fabric of space-time is stretching out in all directions, moving galaxies and galaxy clusters farther and farther away from one another. Meanwhile, thanks

---

[1] "Psychology and the Good Life" was the most popular course in the history of Yale University. It helped increase interest in the field and spawned various online courses for the general public as well as podcasts and websites. For instance, UC Berkeley has an online publication devoted to the science of happiness, *Greater Good Magazine: The Science of a Meaningful Life*.

to the law of entropy, the usable energy supply with which the universe was born is in a relentless decline. In just a few billion years, our sun will have expanded to the point of swallowing up Mercury and Venus, and vaporizing (if not engulfing) Earth as well. Humans will be long gone by that time, since our planet will become uninhabitable long before its utter decimation. Many billions of years later, our sun will complete its life cycle and cease burning, as will every other star. Eventually, all energy anywhere in the universe will be spent and all light will go out. Nothing will remain except a dark, frozen desolation of black holes and corpses of dead stars.[2]

In *The End of Everything (Astrophysically Speaking)*, theoretical cosmologist Katie Mack explains the history of the cosmos and the scientific models of its inevitable demise. In her epilogue, she philosophizes about what this means in terms of human significance: "At some point, in a cosmic sense, it will not have mattered that we ever lived. The universe will, more likely than not, fade into a cold, dark, empty cosmos, and all that we've done will be utterly forgotten."[3] Mack, a scientific materialist (one who claims that the material world is all that exists), is candid about her angst and how she tries to cope with the bleakness of this reality: "I admit it, I still care. I'm trying not to get hung up on it, on the ending, the last page, the end of this great experiment of existence. *It's the journey*, I repeat to myself. It's the journey."[4] Her words poignantly illustrate the quintessentially human desire for ultimate, lasting meaning and reveal her intuition that the end of all things somehow undermines the very concept.

The fact of our own mortality is more than sufficient for sparking meditations on the meaning of life, but recognition of the harsh claim that the *entire human race* is destined to fade into oblivion heightens the

---

[2] The material dissolution of the universe described here is the account that is broadly accepted in secular cosmology. The Christian view is that God may intervene at any time to bring about the end of this cosmic timeline.

[3] Katie Mack, *The End of Everything (Astrophysically Speaking)* (Scribner, 2021), 206.

[4] Mack, 209.

magnitude of our existential predicament. It is curious that other contemporary cosmologists who have written on the subject take a more cheerful attitude toward the end of all things; they encourage fellow materialists to rejoice in the wonders of the astonishing place in which we find ourselves and to simply *invent* our own personal meaning. In his book, *Until the End of Time: Mind, Matter, and Our Search for Meaning in an Evolving Universe*, theoretical physicist and science celebrity Brian Greene details the beginning, evolution, and eventual death of the universe. His scientific narrative is brilliantly written, inspiring cosmic wonder while making notoriously difficult subjects accessible to the non-specialist. Along the way, he makes it clear that he is an entrenched naturalist; he describes his perspective as a "deep-seated reductionist commitment . . . the view that by fully grasping the behavior of the universe's fundamental ingredients we tell a rigorous and self-contained story of reality."[5]

According to Greene, humanity is nothing more than an unplanned, temporary side effect of blind physical processes, and "the universe won't so much as blink" if we are someday obliterated by an asteroid (or any other mortal peril).[6] At the same time, he insists that meaning, moral values, and purpose are legitimate ideas, even though they are merely mental constructs: "Right and wrong, good and evil, destiny and purpose, value and meaning are all profoundly useful concepts, but I am not among those who believe that moral judgments and assignments of significance transcend the human mind. We invent these qualities."[7] "Science," he explains, "is a powerful, exquisite tool for grasping an external reality. But within that rubric . . . everything else is the human species contemplating itself, grasping what it needs to carry on, and telling a story that reverberates into the darkness, a story carved of sound and etched into silence,

---

[5] Brian Greene, *Until the End of Time: Mind, Matter, and Our Search for Meaning in an Evolving Universe* (Vintage, 2021), 118.

[6] Greene, 318.

[7] Greene, 312.

a story that, at its best, stirs the soul."[8] Notice how Greene attempts to soothe any sadness or fear his readers may feel with the balm of scientific wonder and tragic romanticism. We must be brave, create meaning for ourselves, and forge our own significance here and now, for "while we may long for a perdurable legacy, the clarity we gain from exploring the cosmic timeline reveals that this is out of reach."[9]

Theoretical physicist Sean Carroll has expressed similar ideas in his book, *The Big Picture: On the Origins of Life, Meaning, and the Universe Itself.* He is forthright about the impossibility of meaning in a godless universe and our attitude toward our place in the grand scheme of things:

> The longing for life to continue beyond our natural span of years is part of a deeper human impulse: the hope, and expectation, that our lives mean something, that there is some point to it all. . . . It takes courage to face up to the finitude of our lives, and even more courage to admit the limits of purpose in our existence. . . . Ideas like "meaning" and "morality" and "purpose" are nowhere to be found in the Core Theory of quantum fields, the physics underlying our everyday lives. . . . They aren't built into the architecture of the universe; they emerge as ways of talking about our human-scale environment.[10]

Like Greene, Carroll tries to offer his readers existential consolation, and this takes the form of a philosophy he calls *poetic naturalism.* The main idea of this view is that there is more than one way to talk about the world: we can give scientific explanations as well as tell a human story about our lived experience. Subjective versions of meaning, purpose, social responsibility, and creativity are important in the fabrication of our personal life narratives.

---

[8] Greene, 325–26.

[9] Greene, 323.

[10] Sean Carroll, *The Big Picture: On the Origins of Life, Meaning, and the Universe Itself* (Dutton, 2016), 2–3, 388–389.

What Greene and Carroll are suggesting is that we need not embrace nihilism (meaninglessness) in response to the silence and finitude of the universe. Rather, we can and should live in awe of its grandeur, with optimism about finding fulfillment in our lives, and seek to improve the world around us (living for something bigger than ourselves). In a nutshell: a good and meaningful life can be had in spite of how the story will end. Is this truly an intellectually robust and existentially satisfying perspective? To answer this, we must first examine the concept of meaningfulness and how it relates to the idea of a *good* life. Then, we will consider what naturalism truly has to offer and whether it is a livable paradigm.

Philosopher Joshua Seachris uses a construct known as the *meaning triad*—intelligibility, purpose, and significance—to approach the discussion. Intelligibility refers to sense-making and coherence as they relate to the idea of meaningfulness. Simply put, things make sense to us when they fit together appropriately within a unified whole:

> Meaning is about intelligibility within a wider frame. Dissonance results when there is a lack of such intelligibility. It is much the same with life's meaning. We can plausibly view our requests for the meaning of life as attempts to secure the overarching framework or context through which to make sense of our lives in this universe. Our focus is on existentially weighty matters that define and depict the human condition: questions and concerns surrounding origins, purpose, significance, value, suffering, and death and destiny. We want answers to our questions about these matters, and want these answers to fit together in an existentially satisfying way. We want life to make sense, and when it does not, we are haunted by the specter of meaninglessness.[11]

[11] Joshua Seachris, "From the Meaning Triad to Meaning Holism: Unifying Life's Meaning," *Human Affairs* 29, no. 4 (October 2019), 365.

Therefore, one key question is whether our understanding of the "existentially weighty" issues makes sense within our particular worldview—our grand narrative of human existence. The second element of the triad, purpose, pertains to those things around which we structure our lives, the overarching goals toward which we direct our lives. Notice that the concept of purpose presupposes our ability to think, choose, and act with intention. The third part of the triad, significance, is what someone has in mind when they talk about the notion of mattering—something or someone having importance and worth. In some cases, significance can be entirely subjective, but when it comes to existentially weighty matters, significance in an objective sense is usually in view.

We can now evaluate naturalism using the meaning triad rubric. Mack, Greene, and Carroll (the cosmologists previously discussed) acknowledge that their framework for reality excludes meaning in any cosmic, transcendent sense.[12] There is no objective meaning *of* life, so humans must create subjective meaning *in* life to fulfill their characteristic need for a sense of significance, purpose, and value. Despite any sentimental facade one might apply (such as Carroll's "poetic" view), there are at least two serious, perhaps fatal, problems with this project: It is not existentially satisfying, and it requires assumptions about human nature that naturalism itself cannot account for. This means there are features essential to a deeply satisfying degree of meaning that do not fit within the architecture of naturalism. Trying to wedge them in creates a certain incoherence, and intelligibility (in the sense described above) is lost.

Bertrand Russell, the eminent twentieth-century atheist philosopher, described this cosmic conundrum in his famous essay "A Free Man's Worship":

---

[12] I have adopted Seachris's metaphorical use of the term *architecture*, as well as his distinction between terrestrial and transcendent frameworks.

> That Man is the product of causes which had no prevision of the end they were achieving; that his origin, his growth, his hopes and fears, his loves and his beliefs, are but the outcome of accidental collocations of atoms; that no fire, no heroism, no intensity of thought and feeling, can preserve an individual life beyond the grave; that all the labours of the ages, all the devotion, all the inspiration, all the noonday brightness of human genius, are destined to extinction in the vast death of the solar system, and that the whole temple of Man's achievement must inevitably be buried beneath the debris of a universe in ruins—all these things, if not quite beyond dispute, are yet so nearly certain, that no philosophy which rejects them can hope to stand. Only within the scaffolding of these truths, only on the firm foundation of unyielding despair, can the soul's habitation henceforth be safely built.[13]

Notice Russell's point that these tenets of naturalism create a "scaffolding" that excludes the things that essentially shape our lives. He continues by explaining how we, now enlightened about our existential situation and the freedom it affords us, ought to live: by acknowledging that all of humankind is united by our common impending fate: eternal non-existence. We are merely players in a cosmic tragedy, but the show must go on: "Brief and powerless is Man's life; on him and all his race the slow, sure doom falls pitiless and dark. Blind to good and evil, reckless of destruction, omnipotent matter rolls on its relentless way; for Man, condemned today to lose his dearest, tomorrow himself to pass through the gate of darkness, it remains only to cherish, ere yet the blow falls, the lofty thoughts that ennoble his little day."[14]

---

[13] Bertrand Russell, "A Free Man's Worship" in *Selections from the Writings of Bertrand Russell* ed. Louis Greenspan and Stefan Andersson (Routledge, 1999), 32.

[14] Russell, 38.

Although the material world was not designed for us and provides no grounding for concepts like good, evil, courage, justice, and beauty, we still ought to alleviate the suffering of our fellow travelers as best we can and "preserve our respect for truth, for beauty, for the ideal of perfection . . . to live constantly in the vision of the good."[15] Russell knew that a silent, material universe does not bestow such things; but without the restrictions of religion, we can nevertheless assert our human freedom by courageously pursuing the higher goodness, truth, and beauty that we naturally desire.

Russell accepts that his chosen cosmic narrative cannot accommodate the transcendentals (goodness, truth, and beauty) that are necessary for cosmic significance, purpose, and value. Yet, knowing that we cannot live with any semblance of motivation, inspiration, or contentment without them, he exhorts us to boldly and defiantly pursue these "lofty thoughts" as we tread the stage of our brief drama.[16] Greene and Carroll share Russell's materialist philosophy, but they have applied a saccharine veneer for the sake of existential therapy (and public relations).[17] All three believe that life-purpose is something we must create for ourselves, since there is no transcendent purpose for which we were created, no goals beyond the closing curtain. If we are honest with ourselves, this situation can never fully satisfy our more profound desires. Seachris explains that this is one respect in which naturalism lacks intelligibility: "It fails to fit together properly. Why? Because deep human longings, especially along significance, value, and purpose axes, and deep hopes for *ultimate* justice and a *lasting* place for love and felicity are stubborn. These *shalom-esque* longings do not fit (or at

---

[15] Russell, 34.

[16] To illustrate this point, philosophers often quote Macbeth's famous lament, "Tomorrow and tomorrow and tomorrow" (Act V, Scene V), *Macbeth*, Folger Shakespeare Library, https://folger-main-site-assets.s3.amazonaws.com/uploads/2022/11/macbeth_PDF_FolgerShakespeare.pdf.

[17] Atheist existentialist Jean-Paul Sartre found such a strategy distasteful, because it "seeks to eliminate God as painlessly as possible." Jean-Paul Sartre, *Existentialism Is a Humanism* (Yale University Press, 2007), 28.

least do so in thinner form) within a naturalistic universe."[18] A thoroughly materialistic universe cannot get us what we long for. We can certainly cultivate a subjective sense of meaning *in* life, but what we all truly crave is a bestowed meaning *of* life. As Seachris puts it, there is an "ineliminable cosmic element" in our quest for meaning.[19] If naturalism is a true understanding of reality, then we are cosmic orphans muddling along, doing our best to create cheap reproductions of furnishings that are exclusive to the transcendent framework. To the question "Why are we here?" there simply is no answer, because our species is nothing more than an accidental by-product of blind cosmic processes that will eventually swallow us up again. It is up to us to devise our own life purposes, to draw some sense of significance from our relationships and our efforts to make the world a better place during our brief moment in the sun.[20]

Optimistic naturalists suffer from another major problem: a contradiction between their touted idea of *creating* meaning and purpose and what they claim about human nature (what a human *is*). According to naturalism, there is no such thing as an immaterial soul; a human being is merely a physical body animated by a central nervous system, and the "self" or "mind" is really just the brain. Our mental life is the conscious experience of a continual flow of physical brain states. The material world is a closed system and thus there is no "interference" from anything immaterial, like God or a soul. As Greene explains:

---

[18] Seachris, 366.

[19] Seachris, 377.

[20] Friedrich Nietzsche (1844–1900) believed that a godless universe was to be celebrated precisely because it was one in which humankind could cast off the shackles of religion and disregard all systems of morality. His view was that the only worthwhile, rational life objective is the will to power—becoming an übermensch (superman) who boldly creates his own values and imposes them upon others. In the prologue of *Thus Spoke Zarathustra*, he places this philosophy in the mouth of Zarathustra: "The Superman is the meaning of the earth. Let your will say: The Superman *shall be* the meaning of the earth!" Friedrich Nietzsche, *Thus Spoke Zarathustra* (Dover, 1999), 3.

> You and I are nothing but constellations of particles whose behavior is fully governed by physical law. Our choices are the result of our particles coursing one way or another through our brains. Our actions are the result of our particles moving this way or that through our bodies. And all particle motion—whether in a brain, a body, or a baseball—is controlled by physics. . . . Faced with the intransigence of physical law, autonomy withdraws. We are no more than playthings knocked to and fro by the dispassionate rules of the cosmos.[21]

The Big Bang initiated material chain reactions, governed by the laws of nature, that led to conscious brains and every neurochemical event that occurs within them. Our sense of having agency over our thoughts, speech, and behavior is an illusion. As neuroscientist Sam Harris writes, "Free will is an illusion. Our wills are simply not of our own making. Thoughts and intentions emerge from background causes of which we are unaware and over which we exert no conscious control. We do not have the freedom we think we have."[22] Carroll agrees with Harris and believes this is the only view compatible with science: "There is no direct evidence for libertarian freedom [free will], and it violates everything we know about the laws of nature. For libertarian freedom to exist, it would have to be possible for human beings to overcome the laws of physics just by thinking."[23] What Carroll means by "libertarian freedom" is the type of freedom we have in mind when we use the term in plain, everyday language: the ability to truly choose what we do and do not do. This is not the same thing as *feeling* like we are freely choosing; rather, it is an autonomy that transcends material cause and effect. Philosopher of mind J. P. Moreland defines libertarian freedom this way: "I can literally choose to act or refrain from choosing. No circumstances exist that are sufficient to

---

[21] Greene, 147.

[22] Sam Harris, *Free Will* (Free Press, 2012), 5.

[23] Carroll, 381.

determine my choice. . . . I act as an agent who is the ultimate originator of my own actions."[24] Again, if the material cosmos is all there is, causal closure is true, and there is no room for free will. Another way to put this is that our thoughts and behaviors are determined by our brain activity. What goes on in our minds, including the feeling that we are acting with purpose, is a byproduct of processes beyond our control.

Not all naturalists accept this implication of their grand narrative; they reject the idea that all mental events, including our intention to take an action, are inevitable. Some resort to something called *quantum indeterminacy*, which is (to put it as simply as possible) the apparent randomness of subatomic particle activity which theoretically allows uncaused events. The idea is that while we may observe physical determinism at the macro-level, the fact that there seems to be indeterminacy at the micro-level leaves a loophole for free will. It does not. For one thing, it is possible that quantum indeterminacy is illusory, that we currently lack the technology for detecting the mechanism causing the seemingly random quantum events. However, even if we assume that indeterminacy is truly the case, that does not rescue libertarian freedom because (among other, more complicated reasons) there still needs to be an agent *in control* of the action that is intended.[25] Harris sums it up: "Either our wills are determined by prior causes and we are not responsible for them, or they are the product of chance and we are not responsible for them."[26]

---

[24] J. P. Moreland, "Neuroscience and the Metaphysics of Consciousness and the Soul," in *Minding the Brain: Models of the Mind, Information, and Empirical Science*, ed. Angus J. Menuge, Brian R. Krouse, and Robert J. Marks (Discovery Institute Press, 2023), 58.

[25] For an excellent scholarly treatment of the current debate over whether naturalism and libertarian free will can somehow be harmonized in a coherent way, see *The Substance of Consciousness: A Comprehensive Defense of Contemporary Substance Dualism* by Brandon Rickabaugh and J. P. Moreland (Wiley Blackwell, 2024), chap. 9.

[26] Harris, 5.

If free will is an illusion foisted upon us by our brain activity, this falsifies the claim that we can *create* our own meaning in life, *choose* our own life purpose, and *act* according to any moral compass. Philosopher Alex Rosenberg explains this stark reality:

> Our conscious thoughts are very crude indicators of what is going on in our brain. We fool ourselves into treating these conscious markers as thoughts about what we want and about how to achieve it, about plans and purposes. We are even tricked into thinking they somehow bring about behavior. We are mistaken about all of these things. . . . What individuals do, alone or together, over a moment or a month or a lifetime, is really just the product of the process of blind variation and environmental filtration operating on neural circuits in their heads.[27]

In sum, nothing we think or do is truly *chosen*. Consider what this means for human creativity and moral responsibility. All works of art—Homer's epics, Shakespeare's plays, the Sistine Chapel frescoes, the *Lord of the Rings* film trilogy—are merely the inevitable outcome of physics and chemistry, not agents with extraordinary skill and aesthetic sensibilities.

Intuitively, we know that high art is something radically different from serial killing. We praise the artist and condemn the murderer because we assume they have free agency. Yet, if naturalism is true, we cannot live a morally "good life" (however we define it) because goodness cannot be pursued willingly. Harris asks, "If a man's choice to shoot the president is determined by a certain pattern of neural activity, which is in turn the product of prior causes—perhaps an unfortunate coincidence of bad genes, an unhappy childhood, lost sleep, and cosmic-ray bombardment—what can it possibly mean to say that his will is 'free'?"[28]

---

[27] Alex Rosenberg, *The Atheist's Guide to Reality: Enjoying Life Without Illusions* (W. W. Norton, 2011), 210, 255.

[28] Harris, 5–6.

This is another instance of the terrestrial framework lacking a criterion of intelligibility. We are unable to discard our beliefs about the intrinsic value and dignity of human beings and related moral imperatives. When we encounter horrendous suffering or read about moral atrocities, we recoil; our innermost being cries out that things *ought not to be this way*. Aside from the free will problem, if naturalism is true, then even our most powerful moral intuitions are, at most, psychological phenomena produced by a complex symphony of biological and cultural evolutionary processes.[29] If we could rewind the evolutionary clock and start all over, human ideas about good and evil, right and wrong would be different, perhaps dramatically so. Our gut reactions to things like gruesome genocide, child sex trafficking, and animal torture are not a matter of tapping into objective moral truths; there are no *oughts* or *ought nots* woven into the fabric of reality. But, at the end of the day, this is a moot point because of the impossibility of free will within the framework of naturalism.

In his book, *A Significant Life: Human Meaning in a Silent Universe*, Todd May, an atheist philosopher and consultant for *The Good Place*, reflects on the human predicament: "We would have preferred our humanity to be etched into the nature of things as an imprimatur that gives it—and us—significance. Barring that, we would at least have liked a little cosmic support: a God or a telos that assures us of meaningfulness of the years that we spend here. But things are not like that. The universe is silent. We are not anointed, we are not awaited, and we are not welcomed. . . . We are cosmic accidents."[30]

---

[29] Jonathan Haidt has articulated what he calls the Moral Foundations Theory in his book, *The Righteous Mind: Why Good People Are Divided by Politics and Religion* (Vintage Books, 2013). The gist of his idea is that biological evolution produced certain receptor "modules" in response to adaptive challenges and that various cultural dynamics explain why there is diversity in responses to module triggers from one group to another.

[30] Todd May, *A Significant Life: Human Meaning in a Silent Universe* (University of Chicago Press, 2015), 175.

To overcome the sense of meaninglessness this inspires, May endorses the existential therapy of developing a life narrative. He writes, "Since human lives unfold over time, perhaps what gives them meaning is their narrativity. Lives can be conceived as stories, with beginnings, middles, and ends."[31] It is far from clear, however, what kind of deep meaning or genuine fulfillment can result from thinking of our lifespan as a story that we subject to narrative analysis. If there is nothing everlasting about our stories, or the collective stories of humanity, what is their value? From stardust we came, and to stardust we shall return.

Consider the following thought experiment. Imagine that one day we discover an exoplanet that obviously hosted intelligent life for many hundreds of thousands of years but is now a post-apocalyptic wasteland. Footage of the ashy ruins reveals that the creatures apparently obliterated themselves long ago in some sort of radioactive warfare. Other than charred skeletons and the wreckage of weapons and other machinery, there are no other clues from which to piece together their story. We will never know what kind of beings they were—whether they experienced love for their mates and offspring, had moral values anything like ours, or created wonderful works of art. Unbeknownst to anyone else, this extraterrestrial race emerged, persisted for a time, and then passed out of existence. Not even a memory of them continues on. Does it matter that they ever lived? What can be said of the meaning of their lives and any sense of purpose they felt now that they are gone? Now imagine this situation on a cosmic scale. Once the end of *all* things comes to pass, nothing will be any different than if life of any kind had never existed at all. While we are here, we can indeed create elaborate narratives about ourselves, and the human saga may go on for many more millennia; but the problem is, how a story ends makes all the difference. If naturalism is true, we are playing a futile game of charades.

---

[31] May, 63.

Final Thoughts

As we have seen, the optimistic naturalist's claim that one can live a good, meaningful life without God does not stand up to scrutiny. Suggesting that we can simply create our own meaning *in* life despite there being no meaning *of* life ignores the fact that libertarian free will is not a feature of a naturalistic world. Yet, we have the overwhelming sense that we *are* free agents with moral responsibility, beings who can seek goodness, avoid evil, create beautiful things, make scientific discoveries, and intentionally nurture our relationships with others. The human experience simply does not fit within the architecture of naturalism.

Recall Greene's remark about how human beings long for a perdurable (lasting) legacy, which (on naturalism) is out of reach. *Truly* mattering means mattering in a cosmic, eternal sense, as philosophers Stewart Goetz and Seachris explain:

> If naturalism is true, in the end there is nothing but silence concerning the human condition, because the universe is the ultimate reality. The cosmos does not care because it cannot care. We cannot matter from the *sub specie aeternitatis* [eternal] perspective because that perspective is not occupied by a mind or person to whom we could matter. At the cosmic level, there is no one who cares for us, no one who is concerned with us and our deepest joys and sorrows. . . . Despite some real terrestrial significance, there is a salient undercurrent of tragedy to the human condition if naturalism is true.[32]

Naturalism supplies neither a meaning of life nor a feasible account of meaning *in* life. It offers no hope for a world made right, for

---

[32] Stewart Goetz and Joshua Seachris, *What Is This Thing Called the Meaning of Life?* (Routledge, 2020), 86–87.

redemption of humanity's brokenness, or any semblance of cosmic-scale justice for the rampant evil in the world. Sartre is concise on this point; now that man has dispensed with God, "people need to understand that reality alone counts, and that dreams, expectations, and hopes only serve to define a man as a broken dream, aborted hopes, and futile expectations."[33]

The naturalist's claim that humans can live good, meaningful lives depends upon baseless assumptions. By contrast, Christianity says there is an eternal, transcendent God with the attributes and power to satisfy all of these existential longings, who will bring final justice and redeem all brokenness. There are many places in Scripture that tell us about the good, meaningful life the Christian worldview outlines (Gen 1:26–28; 9:1–3; 12:1–3; Isa 43:7; Matt 22:37–40; 28:18–20; Rom 12:1–2; Revelation 21), but consider how our desires for justice, beauty, truth, and a meaningful story culminate in the person and work of Jesus Christ.

> Jesus said again, "Truly I tell you, I am the gate for the sheep. All who came before me are thieves and robbers, but the sheep didn't listen to them. I am the gate. If anyone enters by me, he will be saved and will come in and go out and find pasture. A thief comes only to steal and kill and destroy. I have come so that they may have life and have it in abundance. I am the good shepherd. The good shepherd lays down his life for the sheep." (John 10:7–11)

This means that when we align our lives with God's purposes in Jesus, we are invited to enter into a pasture where we can be safe from the forces that seek to destroy our lives and instead, live our lives to the fullest. All of this is secured by the Ultimate-Meaning-Maker himself, who laid down his life to give us good and meaningful lives. While

[33] Sartre, 38.

naturalism is a dead end, "a firm foundation of unyielding despair," Christianity provides us with a solid foundation on which to build beautiful lives. Christ's atonement for the sins of the world has made a way for us to someday live with him eternally in the perfection of his new creation, experiencing a meaningfulness of a magnitude we cannot even begin to fathom.

CHAPTER 2

Objection #2: God and Human Suffering Are Incompatible

In the introduction to his theological treatise, *The Problem of Pain*, C. S. Lewis recounts how (before his Christian conversion) he would have responded to the question, "Why are you an atheist?" He regarded the vast emptiness of the universe, the brevity and finitude of all life, and the pervasiveness and severity of suffering as evidence against the existence of God. All sentient creatures endure physical pain and inflict pain simply by being born, but humans—because they are rational—also experience psychological miseries and have the ability to purposefully inflict immense suffering:

> In the most complex of all the creatures, Man, yet another quality appears, which we call reason, whereby he is enabled to foresee his own pain which henceforth is preceded with acute mental suffering, and to foresee his own death while keenly desiring permanence. It also enables men by a hundred ingenious contrivances to inflict a great deal more pain than they otherwise could have done

> on one another and on the irrational creatures. This power they have exploited to the full. Their history is largely a record of crime, war, disease, and terror, with just sufficient happiness interposed to give them, while it lasts, an agonised apprehension of losing it, and, when it is lost, the poignant misery of remembering.[1]

Eventually, the universe itself will burn out, and the tragic saga of humanity will have been utterly pointless: "All stories will come to nothing: all life will turn out in the end to have been a transitory and senseless contortion upon the idiotic face of infinite matter."[2] For the pre-Christian Lewis, all of the evil and suffering of the world was indicative of a godless universe, a deity unconcerned with good and evil, or an inherently evil deity.

The problem of evil and suffering (hereafter, the *problem of evil*, since suffering is a kind of evil) is regarded by many, Christians and non-Christians alike, as a formidable challenge to theism. No doubt, deeply painful life events raise difficult existential questions, even in the minds of devout believers. Some have abandoned their faith after a failure to reconcile the idea of a perfectly good, loving, and powerful God with their observation and experience of what seems like senseless, gratuitous suffering. Others maintain a white-knuckled grip on their faith, fighting to focus on biblical truths about the reality of God and his character even as their hearts cry out, "My God, my God, why have you forsaken me?" To be sure, the problem of evil has an existential gravitas that makes it impossible to ignore.

Considering the Objection

The main purpose of this chapter is to deal with arguments from evil against the existence of God; but the emotional dimension, often called

[1] C. S. Lewis, *The Problem of Pain* in *The C.S. Lewis Signature Classics* (HarperCollins, 2017), 552.

[2] Lewis, 552.

the existential problem of evil, must also be addressed. For one thing, it is often the underlying motivation for arguments from evil, but it is also an issue that figures largely into the lives of the faithful. We know that while philosophical and theological responses to evil are necessary to think about, the actual experience of suffering can be excruciating, isolating, and demoralizing. For these reasons, the forthcoming analysis of the different forms of the argument and plausible responses will be followed by a brief discussion of the big "Why?" question that often troubles believers and seekers alike in the midst of terrible circumstances.

Here is a simple statement of what philosophers call the logical form of the argument from evil:

1. If God exists, he is by definition omniscient (all knowing), omnibenevolent (perfectly loving), and omnipotent (supremely powerful).
2. God would know how to prevent evil, desire to prevent evil, and have the power to prevent evil.
3. Yet, evil exists.
4. Therefore, God does not exist.[3]

According to this form of the argument, God's existence and the reality of evil are *logically incompatible* in the same way that a room cannot be dark and light at the same time. Pervasive evil is undeniable, and this fact undermines the rationality of belief in God. The assumption here is that if he existed, he would have created a world entirely devoid of evil, populated by maximally happy creatures.

---

[3] Some nontheists have suggested that the existence of evil is philosophically compatible with a God who is not omnibenevolent or not omnipotent. Douglas Groothuis offers a concise response to this; see *Christian Apologetics*, 2nd ed. (IVP Academic, 2022), 672–73. Ultimately, however, the argument as formulated here begins with the understanding that God, by definition, has these attributes.

Philosopher Alvin Plantinga has responded to the logical form of the argument from evil by pointing out that God may have good reasons for permitting evil, and this possibility eliminates the alleged logical contradiction. What those reasons are is a separate question; the problem is addressed by simply explaining that God's existence is logically compatible with the existence of evil, if God has good reasons for allowing it. The burden of proof falls upon the nontheist, who must identify a true contradiction, but this has not been done.[4] Most nontheists (and theists) who have considered Plantinga's response are persuaded that it is plausible and have thus abandoned the logical version of the argument.

The evidential problem of evil is the focus of the contemporary philosophical debate, and its premises are what average objectors usually have in mind. This version of the problem is concerned with the magnitude and quantity of evil in the world, and some argue that this seemingly gratuitous evil is powerful evidence against theism. In other words, all the egregious evil in the world, which seems utterly senseless, makes it highly *unlikely* that God exists. The evidential argument can be summarized as follows:

1. If God exists, he does not allow any pointless evil.
2. Probably, there is some pointless evil in the world.
3. Therefore, God probably does not exist.[5]

The second premise is the one that should be challenged, but first it is appropriate to consider some of the worst moral atrocities of human history. Reading such accounts in some detail (be forewarned) helps us to better perceive the tremendous weight of some evils and understand why the evidential problem is influential.

---

[4] C. Stephen Evans and R. Zachary Manis, *Philosophy of Religion: Thinking About Faith* 2nd ed. (IVP Academic, 2009), 167–68. See also Douglas Groothuis and Andrew I. Shepardson, *The Knowledge of God in the World and the Word: An Introduction to Classical Apologetics* (Zondervan Academic, 2022), 141–48.

[5] Evans and Manis, *Philosophy of Religion*, 169.

The Horrors of World War II

In *The Rape of Nanking: The Forgotten Holocaust of World War II*, Iris Chang recounts the bloody mass extermination of men, women, and children in the Chinese city of Nanking by invading Japanese soldiers in 1937 and 1938. Death toll estimates range from 260,000 to well over 350,000, but this is only part of the breathtaking horror. Drawing from historical documents and personal interviews of elderly survivors of the massacre, Chang describes the vile manner in which the people of Nanking were mercilessly dehumanized, tortured, and killed:

> Chinese men were used for bayonet practice and in decapitation contests. An estimated 20,000–80,000 Chinese women were raped. Many soldiers went beyond rape to disembowel women, slice off their breasts, nail them alive to walls. Fathers were forced to rape their daughters, and sons their mothers, as other family members watched. Not only did live burials, castration, the carving of organs, and the roasting of people become routine, but more diabolical tortures were practiced, such as hanging people by their tongues on iron hooks or burying people to their waists and watching them get torn apart by German shepherds. So sickening was the spectacle that even the Nazis in the city were horrified, one proclaiming the massacre to be the work of "bestial machinery."[6]

Merely reading about such ruthless, horrific human evil is gut-wrenching; it is difficult to imagine the far more intense experience of the survivors who lived to tell about it. Chang, whose grandparents had escaped the nightmarish barbarity of the invasion and inspired her fervent mission as a historian, died in November 2004 at the age of thirty-six from a self-inflicted gunshot wound.

---

[6] Iris Chang, *The Rape of Nanking: The Forgotten Holocaust of World War II* (Basic Books, 1997), 6.

The events of the Jewish Holocaust of World War II are far more familiar to most of us. Primary school curricula, novels, and films have detailed the terrors: death camps, gas chambers, starvation, medical experimentation on human subjects, and other monstrous methods of torture and execution. In 1945, one of the testimonies given during the Nuremberg war crimes trials was provided by Hermann Graebe, a German engineer who had witnessed Schutzstaffel (SS) soldiers rounding up Jews from a ghetto and forcing them onto trains bound for concentration camps in 1942. He describes the scene:

> The people were driven out of their houses in such haste that small children in bed had been left behind in several instances. In the street women cried out for their children and children for their parents. . . . All through the night these beaten, hounded and wounded people moved along the lighted streets. Women carried their dead children in their arms, children pulled and dragged their dead parents by their arms and legs down the road towards the train.[7]

Later that same year, at Dubno, Graebe watched executions and the disposal of the dead and nearly-dead in mass graves. In his testimony, he described how men, women, children, and infants—some of the 5,000 Jews in the area who were "marked for liquidation"—were transported to the site by truck, then forced to remove all of their clothing before being shot and tossed into one of three large pits:

> People were closely wedged together and lying on top of each other so that only their heads were visible. Nearly all had

---

[7] Hermann Friedrich Graebe, "Affidavits Concerning the Killing of Jews in the Ukraine in 1942 by the Security Police and SD, Including a Detailed Account of Mass Shootings at Dubno and the Liquidation of the Rowno Ghetto," Nuremberg Trials Project, https://nuremberg.law.harvard.edu/documents/1381-affidavits-concerning-the-killing?mode=text.

> blood running over their shoulders from their heads. Some of the people shot were still moving. . . . The people, completely naked, went down some steps which were cut in the clay wall of the pit and clambered over the heads of the people lying there, to the place to which the SS-man directed them. They lay down in front of the dead or injured people; some caressed those who were still alive and spoke to them in a low voice. Then I heard a series of shots. I looked into the pit and saw that the bodies were twitching or the heads lying already motionless on top of the bodies that lay before them. Blood was running from their necks.[8]

The death toll of the Holocaust reached numbers in the millions. In addition to prisoners of war, sick, disabled, homosexual, and Polish people were also targeted by the Nazi war machine.

Evil and Human Agency

We recoil in abhorrence when we read about these gruesome crimes against humanity. Perhaps we sympathize with those who cannot fathom why a perfectly good, all-powerful being would permit such abominable evils and thus conclude that God probably does not exist. Where moral evil is concerned, however, there is a key factor in the equation: Human beings are endowed with free will, and we use this freedom to do both good and evil. God created us with the ability to act freely so that we could be moral agents—the kind of creatures who can freely love and serve him and love our neighbors. There would be no moral value in these actions if we were somehow programmed to do them. At the same time, there would be no moral responsibility for an evil action if it were not freely perpetrated.

---

[8] Graebe, Affidavits.

In granting free will to humanity, God made both abundant goodness and unspeakable evil possible; he did this because the tremendous good of moral freedom outweighs the possibility of moral evil. This response is known as the *free will theodicy*.[9] Instead of a world inhabited by automatons, God desired a world in which creatures can choose to exercise genuine love; but this also means they can choose to do evil. The skeptic may then ask why God did not create a world in which humans always freely choose the morally good. Although this seems to be a logically possible scenario, it fails to truly preserve libertarian free will; in a world created in such a way that humans would never choose evil, God would be the morally responsible agent, since he would be the one who ultimately prevented evil actions through his orchestration of our circumstances. What the humans would have in this hypothetical world is best described as pseudofreedom.[10] Similarly, if opportunities to choose evil were omitted from the world, this would essentially eliminate moral goodness, since there is no real opportunity to choose it over evil. To illustrate this point: Pseudofreedom is what Adam and Eve would have had in the garden of Eden if the tree of knowledge had not been created, and God had not given any other commands that could have been disobeyed.[11]

Nature's Evils

By itself, a free will theodicy seems to only address moral evil. So before exploring other possible responses to the evidential problem, we must examine the seemingly pointless amount of *natural* evil in the world—things like disease, famine, earthquakes, hurricanes, tornadoes, and tsu-

[9] A theodicy is an explanation offered for why God allows evil.

[10] Evans and Manis, *Philosophy of Religion*, 163.

[11] One of the first questions young children tend to ask upon learning about original sin is why God created the tree of knowledge. Hopefully, you are now better equipped to respond.

namis.[12] Two examples should suffice: a horrendous disease and a devastating natural disaster.

The bubonic plague arguably had the largest impact of any infectious disease in recorded history. We now know that the bacterial pathogen involved, *Yersinia pestis*, was rapidly transmitted by fleas on rats and possibly by human lice and contaminated grain. Death by plague was an agonizing and revolting ordeal; the infection traveled through the bloodstream to lymph nodes, and the multiplying bacteria caused something called suppurative buboes—painful swellings in areas such as the armpits, groin, and neck that could grow to be the size of a baseball and turn dark blue or black. Unchecked, the disease spread quickly through a population with a very high mortality rate, and death occurred within about a week.

There have been three known plague pandemics. The first was in the Mediterranean region, beginning in the sixth century under the reign of the Byzantine emperor Justinian and lasting about two centuries. Records are incomplete and debated, but in general, historians believe that upward of five thousand people a day were dying in the city of Constantinople during the worst phase of this pandemic and that the final death toll was in the tens of millions. Corpses accumulated so quickly that many were thrown into mass grave pits, some were packed into towers of the city walls, and others were loaded onto ships that were launched out to sea and set on fire. The second pandemic was the so-called Black Death of fourteenth-century Europe, which wiped out up to 30 percent of the population (about twenty-five million people) within a few years. Outbreaks continued for about four centuries, resulting in the death of two-thirds of the population in Naples and Genoa, and one hundred thousand or more in each of three other major cities: London, Vienna, and Moscow. The third plague pandemic originated in southwest China in the mid-1800s and lasted about a

[12] It should be noted here that moral evils, in some instances, do contribute to the suffering that results from natural evils by failing to either prevent or mitigate effects of natural phenomena.

century, during which it claimed the lives of around twelve million people. It is estimated that, over the course of human history, the bubonic plague has caused over two hundred million excruciating deaths.[13]

Natural cataclysms that leave massive death and destruction in their wake are also cited as evidence of pointless evil. Perhaps you are old enough to remember the Indian Ocean tsunami of 2004. On December 26 at 7:59 a.m., a magnitude 9.1 earthquake occurred miles below the seafloor at a fault line off the coast of Sumatra. Within minutes, the seawater at the northern coast of Sumatra suddenly and drastically receded, leaving a huge expanse of seabed exposed. It was such an odd sight that tourists near the beach walked out to get a better look. They had no clue what would follow just a few moments later—a 167-foot rolling wave of water that would cause over 200,000 fatalities.[14]

Lasting for about ten minutes, the power of the quake that triggered the tsunami was the equivalent of several thousand atomic bombs. Aftershocks continued for around fourteen hours. The infrastructures of residential, vacation, and agricultural areas were decimated, covered in debris laced with rotting corpses. On December 31, a journalist on site described the carnage he witnessed:

> It is almost impossible to escape the stench of decomposing bodies. . . . It has enveloped the city on the northern tip of Sumatra like a sticky slime, carried on the wind to even the few places that survived last Sunday's devastating earthquake and tsunamis. Five hundred soldiers are working from dawn to dusk

---

[13] Kathryn A. Glatter and Paul Finkelman, "History of the Plague: An Ancient Pandemic for the Age of COVID-19," *American Journal of Medicine* 134, no. 2 (February 2021): 176–81, https://www.ncbi.nlm.nih.gov/pmc/articles/PMC7513766/.

[14] "Historical Context," National Oceanic and Atmospheric Administration, last updated February 19, 2025, https://www.noaa.gov/jetstream/tsunamis/historical-context.

> to try to clear the corpses. Around the city work parties clad in rubber gloves and masks are using anything they can to complete their grim task. Most teams have run out of body bags and have no proper equipment to lift the corpses so they are using debris from the street to lever the remains on to black plastic sheeting and trussing them up like parcels ready for posting. No attempt is made to identify them. They are just dumped 30 at a time on trucks and taken off to one of several mass graves that are being dug just outside the city. . . . Buried deep within this debris are almost certainly thousands of bodies that will probably never be found. The occasional limb sticking up through the foetid mud gives the only clue to the natural grave created under the rubble.[15]

Interviewed survivors recounted having small children ripped from their grasp when the seawater slammed into them or seeing family members swept away in the violent currents. Prisoners drowned in their jail cells. In the aftermath, many more died due to the lack of clean water, food, and medical treatment. The remains of several hundred victims were never identified. Across other countries that were less severely inundated by the tsunami's waves, tens of thousands more perished.

These accounts leave us aghast. The terror, physical agony, and grief experienced by the victims and their loved ones is unfathomable; and it is difficult to process the fact that our world is a place where things like plagues and tsunamis inflict extreme suffering and kill indiscriminately. As with moral atrocities, these natural evils lead some to conclude that God probably isn't there; if he were, surely he would have *done something*. We know things ought not to be this way; the sadness and anger we feel about all this terrible suffering goes bone deep.

---

[15] John Aglionby, "Stench of dead bodies is all around. There's no time to identify them—just to take them to mass graves," *Guardian*, December 31, 2004.

Dealing with the Evidential Problem

Let us now circle back to the evidential argument from evil.

1. If God exists, he does not allow any pointless evil.
2. Probably, there is some pointless evil in the world.
3. Therefore, God probably does not exist.[16]

Since most Christians would agree with premise 1, premise 2 is our focus. The objector is claiming that it is more likely than not that there is some pointless evil in the world. By "pointless evil," he or she means evil for which there are no morally sufficient reasons.

The first thing that may be pointed out in response to the evidential argument is that humans do not have a sufficient vantage point from which to determine this probability with any degree of confidence. As J. P. Moreland and William Lane Craig explain:

> As finite persons, we are limited in space and time, in intelligence and insight. But the transcendent and sovereign God sees the end of history from its beginning and providentially orders history so that his purposes are ultimately achieved through human free decisions. In order to achieve his ends God may well have to put up with certain evils along the way. Evils that appear pointless or unnecessary to us within our limited framework may be seen to have been justly permitted from within God's wider framework. . . . We have no idea of the natural and moral evils that might be involved in order for God to arrange the circumstances and free agents in them requisite to some intended purpose, nor can we discern what reasons such a provident God might have in mind for permitting some evil to enter our lives. Certainly many evils seem

[16] Evans and Manis, *Philosophy of Religion*, 169.

> pointless and unnecessary to us—but we are simply not in a position to judge.[17]

Stewart Goetz and Joshua Seachris put it this way: "Indeed, the difference between God's knowledge and our own is so large that it should come as no surprise to us that we do not understand why God allows certain evils. Therefore, in a world where God exists, it is reasonable to assume that we would be in the dark with respect to the explanations of many, if not all, evils."[18] This view is referred to as *skeptical theism*, and its application to the problem of evil is sometimes referred to as the *cognitive limitation defense*.[19] Proponents deny that we could have access to knowledge about how each instance of evil fits within God's higher purpose for every person and the whole of salvation history. After all, how could humanity grasp all of the possible reasons that God would have for allowing evil (in each of evil's historical and future instantiations) given our finitude and God's infinitude. Moreover, Christians trust that God has orchestrated conditions and events such that all evil will be redeemed and good will ultimately prevail. Sometimes he blesses us with beautiful glimpses of this truth, when something painful and seemingly senseless happens to us and later we learn that it was the very thing that protected us from something much worse. Most of the time, we must simply acknowledge the limitations of our knowledge.

Related to the cognitive limitation defense, there is another way to approach the evidential argument from evil: reworking it such that the positive evidence for theism increases the probability that there is no pointless evil in the world. Notice that the first premise of the evidential argument is preserved, but the objects of the second and third premises are switched:

---

[17] J.P. Moreland and William Lane Craig, *Philosophical Foundations for a Christian Worldview*, 2nd ed. (IVP Academic, 2017), 546.

[18] Stewart Goetz and Joshua Seachris, *What Is This Thing Called the Meaning of Life?* (Routledge, 2020), 119.

[19] Evans and Manis, *Philosophy of Religion*, 170.

1. If God exists, he does not allow any pointless evil.
2. Probably, God exists.
3. Therefore, probably, there is no pointless evil in the world.[20]

Once again, the second premise is crucial and requires support. In this case, we have a broad range of philosophical arguments for the existence of God, some of which have premises supported by scientific evidence.[21] The atheistic version of the argument can now be compared with the theistic version, and the question that must be asked is, which one has a more defensible second premise (which one has greater *warrant*); do we have more evidence for the existence of definitively pointless evils, or do we have more evidence for the existence of God? We do not have reasons to believe that we have the epistemic access to judge whether there is any pointless evil, but we do have plenty of good reasons to conclude that God exists.[22] We thus conclude that the theistic argument against pointless evil is considerably more powerful than the evidential argument from evil.

Thus far in this discussion, we have seen that the reality of good and evil is affirmed by the nontheist who uses arguments from evil against theism. Even those who deny morality grounded in the tenets of a religion apparently recognize that the world ought not to be this way, and they express moral outrage when faced with certain grave injustices. When pressed to explain their reaction, they may resort to the claim that what we are experiencing is a fear and aversion to personal suffering produced by blind evolutionary processes that favored superior survival instincts. But deep down, they know that sex trafficking little children, murdering your spouse in cold blood for financial gain, and torturing a homeless dog for sport are definitively evil acts. The problem is, they have no objective justification for condemning any action as evil. The theist could ask: Evil by what measure?

---

[20] Evans and Manis, 171.

[21] See chapters 11 and 12.

[22] Cosmological, design, and moral arguments, for example.

Some nontheists would respond that we "do unto others" because of the important role social cooperation plays in helping *all* of us thrive individually—I scratch your back, you scratch mine, we both benefit. But this account is woefully insufficient. It ignores the fact that, on naturalism, it is entirely possible to inflict suffering on other people for personal gain without reaping any consequences or, for that matter, anyone else finding out about it. Moreover, why be concerned about the welfare of future generations who can do nothing for present society? Why should we take steps to protect the environment and conserve natural resources for people and animals that will not exist for at least another century if *we* can benefit from exploiting nature in the here and now? What does it matter if we abuse or kill domestic animals? After all, they cannot participate in the economy of social cooperation. Not to mention the fact that, within the framework of naturalism, moral sensibilities emerged very recently in the cosmic timeline. If prerational hominid populations that abandoned their sick and disabled, exterminated competing populations for the sake of resources, or raped their females were not doing evil, how would a blind material process like brain evolution make a difference in the objective moral value of a behavior? The ability to make subjective moral judgments of any kind does not produce objective moral values. To say that, for example, rape is objectively evil, one needs an objective evaluator, which naturalism with its denial of God cannot provide.[23] It seems that the nontheist has a worse problem of evil than the theist.[24]

---

[23] See Groothuis and Shepardson, *The Knowledge of God in the World and the Word*, 133–140, 147–148. For a popular level, book-length treatment of the naturalist's habit of borrowing philosophical resources from theism that naturalism cannot provide, see Frank Turek, *Stealing from God* (NavPress, 2015).

[24] It should be noted that some naturalists insist that objective moral values can exist without God. For example, philosopher Erik Wielenberg resorts to a Platonic view in which such values are abstract objects–immaterial brute facts of reality. However, this seems unintelligible, and (among other problems) it does not give an account for why we have a duty to honor those values.

Finally, it is important to acknowledge that philosophical responses to moral and natural evils do very little to comfort someone who is suffering greatly and has done nothing to bring about these circumstances. Often, the problem of evil someone is wrestling with is emotional rather than intellectual. They may feel bitter toward God or like a defenseless and disposable pawn in some inscrutable cosmic game. Perhaps they have abandoned belief in God not because of philosophical reflection on their suffering but because the pain seems utterly senseless, and prayers yield no relief. In these cases, a pastoral rather than philosophical approach is called for; we need to help them experience how Christianity helps us navigate life in this very broken world. When we contemplate the ordeal Christ endured, the unmerited suffering to which he subjected himself for our sakes, it changes our perspective. As Moreland and Craig beautifully explain:

> When God asks us to undergo suffering that seems unmerited, pointless, and unnecessary, meditation on the cross of Christ can help to give us the moral strength and courage needed to bear the cross that we are asked to carry. So, paradoxically, even though the problem of evil is the greatest objection to the existence of God, at the end of the day God is the only solution to the problem of evil. If God does not exist, then we are locked without hope in a world filled with gratuitous and unredeemed suffering. God is the final answer to the problem of evil, for he redeems us from evil and takes us into the everlasting joy of an incommensurable good, fellowship with himself.[25]

When someone is sitting in the proverbial ashes, questioning the goodness or existence of God, the wisest and most compassionate response is to sit with them, listen to them, and weep with them. We should save the philosophizing and theologizing for a later date.

---

[25] Moreland and Craig, *Philosophical Foundations*, 554.

When we suffer, Christ's empathy, his promise that he will never leave nor forsake us, and our hope for the redemption of all things constitute our existential anchor, and it can withstand the worst of storms. We can have confidence that our pain is never pointless, even though it certainly feels that way, perhaps most of the time.

Final Thoughts

Human suffering is universal and arguably the most significant trigger of doubts about the existence of God. The logical problem, which claims that the existence of God is logically incompatible with the evil in the world, is regarded by most philosophers (theists and nontheists alike) as indefensible. This is because there is no logical contradiction inherent to the supposal that God could have morally sufficient reasons for allowing evil. The evidential problem, which underlies the argument for the low probability of God's existence based upon the probability of pointless evil in the world, is the focus of the current debate. As we have seen, there are intellectually rigorous responses. First, there is the free will theodicy, which says that human free will is a good that outweighs the suffering caused by moral evils. Second, there is the cognitive limitation defense, which points out that humans are in no position to discern God's reasons for allowing all the evil in the world, and thus we are not justified in claiming that any evil is, in fact, pointless. Third, the evidential argument can be turned on its head by using the evidence for God's existence to undermine the probability of pointless evil.

It is no small matter that nontheists have a worse problem of evil than theists. Naturalism does not provide adequate grounds on which to claim that any moral action or natural event that results in human suffering is intrinsically evil. According to their narrative, ideas about morality emerged very late in cosmic history, and there is no standard of judgment if there is no paradigm of the good that transcends the material stuff of the world, including human brains. The Golden Rule may help to some extent when it comes to fleshing out an ethical theory. But within the context of naturalism, it fails in important respects, such as explaining why we should not commit evil actions in cases where we have much to personally gain and can get away with it, and when the outcomes of the actions in question will only affect animals or people in future generations.

The emotional aspect of the problem of evil affects us all and often motivates the philosophical arguments. It requires a sensitive and empathetic approach rooted in biblical truths. In Rom 8:28, Paul reminds us that "God causes all things to work together for good to those who love God, to those who are called according to His purpose" (NASB). This verse is so often quoted that there is the danger of regarding any reference to it as cliché or trite, but it is an essential truth about suffering, especially suffering that seems to have no rhyme or reason. On this side of the veil, we see "in a mirror dimly," as Paul puts it (1 Cor 13:12 NASB). But all human suffering will someday be fully redeemed, and we will finally see how it was harnessed for the ultimate good. Meanwhile, we have the presence of God himself through the Holy Spirit to walk with us through suffering. "I will ask the Father, and he will give you another Counselor to be with you forever" (John 14:16). This is key because, while suffering can be isolating, God's very presence is with us in our pain through the Holy Spirit. Suffering awakens and refines us in ways that nothing else can, and sometimes, thanks be to God, we see this in hindsight and are thereby encouraged. As Lewis so memorably puts it, "God whispers to us in our pleasures, speaks in our conscience, but shouts in our pain: it is His megaphone to rouse a deaf world."[26] The Lord Jesus entered into this broken world as a lowly Suffering Servant to rescue us from the enemy's invasion. He's redeeming our pain and is present with us in the Holy Spirit. And this gospel is our ultimate, extraordinary comfort and hope.

---

[26] Lewis, *The Problem of Pain*, 604.

CHAPTER 3

Objection #3: Christians Are Hypocrites

Have you ever been caught in your sin? When I (Ike) was twelve, I was out riding my bike one day and was struck with the strongest youthful curiosity when I looked in the open window of a neighbor's car and saw a pack of cigarettes lying on the seat. Without even thinking much, I reached into the car and stole the pack, interested in breaking it open and trying them myself. However, as I rode away, another neighbor (who was, ironically, smoking on her porch) called out to me and asked what I was doing. I made up a lie and continued on my way. As I got to the bottom of the street, I was overcome with guilt and threw the cigarettes into a bush. I went home and couldn't manage how bad my theft and lying made me feel, and I confessed the whole thing to my dad. He was gracious, comforting, and clear in his instructions. I was to return the cigarettes and apologize to both neighbors. Everyone was gracious, and I never did such a thing again. However, there was another problem inside me. I came from a Christian family, attended a private Christian school, and regularly shared about my Christian faith with unbelieving neighbors. Not only did I sin, I also was a hypocrite. The gracious reader, like my gracious father and neighbors, might chalk up my hypocrisy to age. But the truth is that my hypocrisy persists today. If you're honest with yourself, yours does too.

When Jesus said, "Woe to you, scribes and Pharisees, hypocrites!" (Matt 23:13), he was calling out those who had a "contradiction between what they say and what they do, between the outward appearance and the inward lack of righteousness."[1] While it may be easy to simply identify Jesus's warning as a condemnation of the religious elites of his own day, New Testament scholar Craig Keener contends that Matthew wanted "leaders in his own community to see themselves through the prism of a disobedient religious establishment that opposed their Lord, thereby summoning them to take warning."[2] So whenever there is a contradiction between our words and our actions, we ought to loathe our hypocrisy, for we know that all our sin injures our relationship with God and others. Still, hypocrisy is dangerous in another way. In the United States, spiritual openness is growing, but large numbers of people would say that the hypocrisy of religious people is a key cause for why people doubt Christian beliefs.[3] In our own public speaking and ministry, we have found that hypocrisy is a key reason people give for why they are not Christians. So, are Christians all hopeless hypocrites? In this chapter we will explore why people conclude that Christians are hypocrites, correct cultural myths, and consult the deeper truth of the gospel.

---

[1] Ulrich Wilckens, ὑποκρίνομαι, κτλ, *Theological Dictionary of the New Testament*, ed. Gerhard Kittel, Gerhard Friedrich, and Geoffrey W. Bromiley (Eerdmans, 1972), 8:567.

[2] Craig S. Keener, *The Gospel of Matthew: A Socio-Rhetorical Commentary* (Eerdmans, 2009), 537.

[3] A recent Barna study reports that 42 percent of those with "no faith" say "the hypocrisy of religious people" is a key cause of their doubts about religion. Barna, "Doubt & Faith: Top Reasons People Question Christianity," March 1, 2023, https://www.barna.com/research/doubt-faith.

Considering the Objection

I know that the headline for my past hypocrisy is rather uninteresting: *Local Christian Boy Confesses Petty Theft: Feels Bad and Apologizes.* However, there are much more serious forms of hypocrisy among those who call themselves Christians today. There are three main areas in which the broader culture may notice hypocrisy among Christians: sexual ethics, marriage and divorce, and financial malfeasance. These are all areas where Christians have sometimes and scandalously practiced differently than they preached. Consider first the sex scandals of public Christian leaders.[4] In 2006, former National Association of Evangelicals President Ted Haggard admitted to a same-sex affair with a prostitute and to buying methamphetamine. Ted was also the founder and senior pastor of the 14,000-person New Life Church in Colorado Springs, Colorado, where he taught about the sanctity of marriage, which Christianity defines as a biblical covenant between a man and a woman for life. Though he was forced to resign, he started a new church where he has continued to face allegations of further same-sex and predatory behavior.[5] Another megachurch pastor, Carl Lentz, who led Hillsong Church in New York, admitted to extramarital affairs and was fired from the ministry. His dismissal also was tied to "general narcissistic behavior, manipulating, mistreating people," and "breaches of trust connected to lying, and constantly lying."[6] This kind of sexual hypocrisy is not just found among evangelicals. French journalist Frédéric Martel's 2019 expose, *In the Closet of the Vatican,* reported that upon his election to the papacy, Pope Francis

---

[4] We will consider abuse and misogyny in chapters 4 and 5, respectively.

[5] See Debbie Kelley, "Powerhouse Preacher Ted Haggard Faces New Allegations of Illicit Behavior," *Gazette,* July 23, 2022, https://gazette.com/news/crime/powerhouse-preacher-ted-haggard-faces-new-allegations-of-illicit-behavior/article_e7637edc-0aab-11ed-ac8c-c31007228c88.html.

[6] Ruth Graham, "The Rise and Fall of Carl Lentz, the Celebrity Pastor of Hillsong Church," *The New York Times,* December 5, 2020, https://www.nytimes.com/2020/12/05/us/carl-lentz-hillsong-pastor.html.

apparently was horrified by the commonality of same-sex relationships in the Vatican and called out those who were leading a "double life."[7] Martel alleged that 80 percent of the priests who work at the Vatican are same-sex attracted, but this figure is now seriously doubted.[8] Even so, the sad truth is that the world's largest Christian church, with its traditional biblical view of human sexuality, has at least some deeply hypocritical people working at high levels.

Second, Christians typically preach that marriage is a sacred and life-long commitment between a man and a woman. There is much involved in this theology of marriage including openness to having children, the primary goal of marriage being God's glory instead of human happiness, love as self-sacrificial, and allowance for divorce only in cases of marital unfaithfulness (see Matt 19:1–12). So, you would think that Christians rarely divorce, but that is not the reputation that Christians have in the broader culture. Perhaps you have heard that half of marriages end in divorce and that the divorce rate is just as high among Christians as it is among non-Christians. In fact, the probability of divorce for people with a Christian upbringing is only slightly lower than for those with a non-religious upbringing.[9] As we'll see, the picture is even more complicated than this, but it does lend some credence to the idea that Christians, who say "until death do us part," may not always mean it when life gets messy. This is particularly scandalous to some in the culture who see Christians as the defenders of traditional families. One of the most prominent

---

[7] Frédéric Martel, *In the Closet of the Vatican: Power, Homosexuality, Hypocrisy*, trans. Shaun Whiteside (Bloomsbury, 2019), xviii.

[8] Gerard O'Connell, "New Book, 'In the Closet of the Vatican', Produces a Toxic Cloud of Suspicion," *America*, February 20, 2019, https://www.americamagazine.org/faith/2019/02/20/new-book-closet-vatican-produces-toxic-cloud-suspicion.

[9] Lyman Stone and Brad Wilcox, "The Religious Marriage Paradox: Younger Marriage, Less Divorce," Institute for Family Studies, December 15, 2021, https://ifstudies.org/blog/the-religious-marriage-paradox-younger-marriage-less-divorce. This study used data from women only.

evangelical institutions in the United States is actually called Focus on the Family, and its mission is deeply connected to the traditional and biblical view of marriage and family. So, if Christians are always preaching about marriage and family, then why don't we see more of their marriages staying together?

The truth is that the statistics don't support the common tale that Christians get divorced at the same rate as non-Christians. A 2008 study confirmed that those who call themselves Protestants get divorced at roughly the same rate as all adults (33%), but this divorce rate is much lower for those who call themselves "evangelical Christians" (26%) and "Catholic" (28%).[10] A more recent data analysis by the Institute for Family Studies shows that while the annual divorce rate for those with a non-religious upbringing (5%) is only slightly higher than those with a religious upbringing (4.5%), this actually means quite a bit over time. This means that "the typical marriage of a woman with a religious upbringing is about 10% less likely to end in divorce within the first 15 years of marriage than the typical marriage of a woman with a non-religious upbringing."[11]

Interestingly, the report notes that a key risk in one's likelihood to get divorced is cohabitation with one's partner before marriage.[12] Religious upbringing and identity are important, but approaching marriage and sex God's way is key. The prevailing culture more or less sees the goal of relationships as the happiness of the couple, and sex, it is thought, makes people happy.[13] While we all like to be happy, the biblical pic-

---

[10] Barna, "New Marriage and Divorce Statistics Released," March 21, 2008, https://www.barna.com/research/new-marriage-and-divorce-statistics-released.

[11] Stone and Wilcox, "The Religious Marriage Paradox: Younger Marriage, Less Divorce."

[12] Stone and Wilcox.

[13] This is actually not universally true. For the large majority of women, a committed relationship is a necessary precondition to sex being enjoyed over the long term. See Louise Perry, *The Case Against the Sexual Revolution: A New Guide to Sex in the 21st Century* (Polity, 2022).

ture provides a better aim. When God created the marriage relationship, he commanded the first couple, "Be fruitful, multiply, fill the earth, and subdue it. Rule the fish of the sea, the birds of the sky, and every creature that crawls on the earth" (Gen 1:28). The command is to have children, to work together to take care of God's creation, and to build civilization. Happiness is often a by-product of this union, and so is a deeper peace: "Both the man and his wife were naked, yet felt no shame" (Gen 2:25). Strictly speaking, though, happiness is not the goal of marriage, and sex is never disconnected from marriage in the Christian worldview.

Again, if the goal of a romantic relationship is happiness, and sex makes you happy, then, of course, any romantic relationship will include premarital sex. But the biblical picture of sex is of something that exists only inside of marriage. This is what is meant in the Bible when it says, "This is why a man leaves his father and mother and bonds with his wife, and they become one flesh" (Gen 2:24). Sex makes two people into a unity, and this is partially what marriage is about. The sad thing about our current cultural moment is that cohabitation has been drastically on the rise in recent generations. "In the 1960s, about 5% of newlyweds cohabited before marriage. In the 2010s, it was more than 70%."[14] So we shouldn't be surprised when we see higher likelihoods for divorce among cohabiting couples since they are missing out on the goal of and means toward a godly marriage by ignoring the way in which marriage was designed from the beginning.

None of this is to cast judgment on those who have had sex outside of marriage, those who have lived together, or those who have been divorced. But when sex and marriage are approached God's way, the data suggest that divorce is much less likely.[15] We shouldn't be judgmental, but still, Christians are wrong when they champion the Bible's teaching on

[14] Stone and Wilcox.

[15] In particular, some of those who have left a spouse have done so to escape abuse or because of unfaithfulness, two reasons the Bible condones.

marriage but live out of step with God's standards on sex. Yet God can forgive our sins. Moreover, as we've already shown, we're all in the same boat with respect to hypocrisy. We are all sinners needing grace from God, and the biblical view is that we ought to offer that same grace to one another. "Therefore, every one of you who judges is without excuse. For when you judge another, you condemn yourself, since you, the judge, do the same things" (Rom 2:1).

Third, Christian leaders have come under considerable scrutiny in the twentieth and twenty-first centuries because of financial scandals in their churches and ministries. Christians teach that money given to religious ministries is a sacred offering. In fact, one of the most famous stories of Jesus's ministry is when he overturns the money changers' tables in the Jewish temple. Quoting the prophets Isaiah and Jeremiah, Jesus "said to them, 'It is written, my house will be called a house of prayer, but you are making it a den of thieves!'" (Matt 21:13). However, evangelical pastors are sometimes seen as swindlers and confidence men in the popular imagination, and this is not without cause. The televangelist Jim Bakker was sentenced to prison in 1989 on twenty-three counts of fraud and one of conspiracy after he solicited millions in donations for, among other things, a failed Christian theme park.[16] More recently, a court in Singapore found megachurch pastor Kong Hee guilty of "misappropriating $35.9 million in church funds to promote his wife's singing career in the U.S. and Asia," money that had been donated to their City Harvest Church for ministry investments.[17] If that weren't enough, many in the broader culture simply have disdain for the ways in which some

---

[16] Art Harris, "Jim Bakker Gets 45-Year Sentence," *Washington Post*, October 24, 1989, https://www.washingtonpost.com/archive/politics/1989/10/25/jim-bakker-gets-45-year-sentence/e1edd0c8-3739-4dab-a40d-da204a4b81ae.

[17] Jake Maxwell Watts, "Singapore Court Finds Pastor Guilty of $35 Million Fraud," *Wall Street Journal*, October 21, 2015, https://www.wsj.com/articles/singapore-court-finds-megachurch-pastor-guilty-of-embezzling-more-than-35-million-1445412217.

pastors and ministry leaders solicit donations from the faithful in tithes and offerings, sometimes tied to promises of wealth and prosperity.[18]

One should not conflate the financial scandals of some religious leaders with the behavior of religious adherents. As Rebecca McLaughlin argues, "In North America, regular service attenders donate 3.5 times the money given by their nonreligious counterparts per year and volunteer more than twice as much."[19] Still, the Bible has nothing good to say to Christian leaders who are guilty of sins involving money and greed. We have already discussed Jesus's cleansing of the temple money changers who were using religious devotion to gain unjust wealth. But throughout his ministry, we see his strict condemnation of religious leaders guilty of financial sin. When Jesus taught that one cannot "serve both God and money" (Luke 16:13), the religious leaders rejected him. "The Pharisees, who were lovers of money, were listening to all these things and scoffing at him. And he told them, 'You are the ones who justify yourselves in the sight of others, but God knows your hearts. For what is highly admired by people is revolting in God's sight'" (Luke 16:14–15). Jesus casts righteous judgment on leaders who say one thing but do another regarding money. He hates this kind of sin and hypocrisy, but he also welcomes the repenting hypocrite. We see this in the story of Zacchaeus, a Jewish tax collector employed by the Romans. Zacchaeus collected more taxes than what were owed, thereby betraying his own people through his financial

[18] The so-called "prosperity gospel" falsely claims that if you are generous with your money to Christian causes, then God will reciprocally bless you financially. For a response, see Craig L. Blomberg, *Neither Poverty Nor Riches: A Biblical Theology of Possessions*, New Studies in Biblical Theology, vol. 7 (IVP Academic, 1999), 25. "Such theologies at times actually garner significant followings and offer great hope in contexts of impoverishment, precisely because people's circumstances are so drastic. But ultimately their failures either create great guilt complexes in the followers of such movements or engender great disillusionment with Christianity in general."

[19] Rebecca McLaughlin, *Confronting Christianity: 12 Hard Questions for the World's Largest Religion* (Crossway, 2019), 61.

malfeasance. Upon meeting Jesus, Zacchaeus declares, "Look, I'll give half of my possessions to the poor, Lord. And if I have extorted anything from anyone, I'll pay back four times as much."

"Today salvation has come to this house," Jesus told him, "because he too is a son of Abraham. For the Son of Man has come to seek and to save the lost" (Luke 19:8–10).

When you see Jesus, you see someone who hates financial hypocrisy. This simply underscores the fact that when you have moral disgust at financial hypocrisy and corruption, you are much closer to Jesus than you might think. In that case, while struggling to reconcile the failures of Christians with an identification with Christ, you must persevere in seeking Jesus. When you do, you will see that despite church leaders' failures, you will see Jesus's deep love for the Christian church, his hatred for all sin (even yours), and his sure desire and ability "to seek and to save the lost."

We must acknowledge that Christians are hypocrites in the most natural and biblical sense of the term: Their lives show a "contradiction between what they say and what they do, between the outward appearance and the inward lack of righteousness."[20] Scripture is clear that all of humanity is guilty of this. "All have turned away; all alike have become worthless. There is no one who does what is good, not even one. Their throat is an open grave; they deceive with their tongues. Vipers' venom is under their lips" (Rom 3:12–13). We say one thing, but we practice deceit as we turn away from doing the right thing. The Bible explains that all humanity has the law of God written on our hearts (Rom 2:14–15), but we all fail to obey. James warns, "If anyone is a hearer of the word and not a doer, he is like someone looking at his own face in a mirror. For he looks at himself, goes away, and immediately forgets what kind of person he was" (1:23–24). Our natural condition is to neglect to do the

[20] Wilckens, ὑποκρίνομαι, κτλ, *Theological Dictionary of the New Testament*, 8:567.

good that we know we ought to do. It's even worse than this because even when we hear the Word of God, the natural human response is to reject it: "They say to the seers, 'Do not see,' and to the prophets, 'Do not prophesy the truth to us. Tell us flattering things. Prophesy illusions. Get out of the way! Leave the pathway. Rid us of the Holy One of Israel'" (Isa 30:10–11).

And Jesus is even more critical of religious leaders who practice hypocrisy, knowing that the sin of leaders will often lead their followers astray, as well. "Woe to you, scribes and Pharisees, hypocrites! You clean the outside of the cup and dish, but inside they are full of greed and self-indulgence. Blind Pharisee! First clean the inside of the cup, so that the outside of it may also become clean" (Matt 23:25–26). These leaders made themselves look like they were good followers of the Jewish religious law, but they justified their own sin in their hearts.

Here is the key distinction: Of course people are hypocrites, but the problem becomes intractable when anyone approves of their hypocrisy. Paul is particularly helpful on this score. When describing what Christians proclaim to be the basic human problem, sin, Paul confesses, "So I discover this law: When I want to do what is good, evil is present with me" (Rom 7:21). He says he wants to obey God's commands, but he cannot escape his own temptation to sin. In fact, he describes his hypocrisy as "waging war against the law of my mind and taking me prisoner to the law of sin in the parts of my body" (7:23). Paul, a hero of the faith and key leader of the early church, sees that hypocrisy is at the root of humanity's basic problem. He's confessing his own hypocrisy concerning sin, but this is what Jesus came to cure. He laments, "What a wretched man I am! Who will rescue me from this body of death? Thanks be to God through Jesus Christ our Lord!" (7:24–25). He's not saying that he was fully delivered, but that Jesus had definitively secured his deliverance and was in the process of fully delivering him through Jesus's finished work on the cross. We know this because Paul continued to admit in his writing, "Who is weak, and I do not feel weak? Who is led into sin, and I do not inwardly burn?" (2 Cor 11:29 NIV). His struggle is not over, but he is trusting in God to save him from his sin. So should we consider the nature of Christian hypocrisy.

Christians are indeed hypocrites who simply claim to have found the cure in Jesus Christ.[21] Now surely some who would make the accusation that Christians are hypocrites would know of Christians who denied their hypocrisy, who claimed to be living holy lives, but who were missing the mark. We know that these people exist, and perhaps they are more visible, as pride shouts louder than humility. However, an attitude of self-justification and denial of sin is contrary to the way of life laid out in the Bible. Moreover, the simple fact is that high-profile cases aside, most Christian leaders serve the church without scandal, but instead with quiet faithfulness and humble awareness of their own sinful tendencies. Thus, the existence of hypocritical leaders should not deter earnest seekers from considering the Christian message.

Moreover, hypocrisy, even Christian hypocrisy, is actually related to the truth of the Christian worldview. In particular, outrage at hypocrisy only makes sense in a world in which God exists as the absolute moral authority. That is, if God does not exist, then one cannot meaningfully declare that one ought not to practice hypocrisy. After all, in a world without God, hypocrisy could simply be one style of living or one kind of cultural ethical expression among many about which it would be unfashionable to cast judgment. "To each his own," you might say. "You do you." If hypocrisy is your thing, then all the better for you. Yet we do not behave this way, for hypocrisy grieves us all. Whenever we complain about another's hypocrisy, we are, as C. S. Lewis says, "not merely saying that the other man's behaviour does not happen to please him," but we

[21] None of this entails that a Christian leader caught in sexual or financial sin should continue to lead.

are "appealing to some kind of standard of behaviour . . . or Law or Rule of fair play or decent behaviour or morality."[22] To avoid making ourselves the moral standard and to avoid special pleading, we must admit that the only grounding for the proposition *one ought not to be a hypocrite* is something that can rightly sit above all cultures, individuals, and throughout history as the standard-bearer. This *something* must be a personal mind, as impersonal forces cannot make judgments. And this mind must be itself pure, as no standard-bearer would be a proper judge unless that standard-bearer were righteous itself. At this point, we're talking less about an *it* and more about a person, and this is partially what Christians have in mind when they utter the word *God*. Consider this argument formally:

1. If God did not exist, then hypocrisy could be acceptable, all things being equal.
2. However, hypocrisy is not acceptable, all things being equal.
3. Therefore, God exists.

This is a *modus tollens*, a particular form of a logical syllogism, and if the premises are true and in the proper argument form, then the conclusion follows necessarily.[23] So hypocrisy discredits Christians, but its existence doesn't discredit the Christian worldview. The existence of hypocrisy actually confirms the Christian worldview by showing that God exists as the objective evaluator who rightly judges that hypocrisy is wrong. Christianity teaches that humanity is accountable to God for all of our moral failures, but there is more to the story.

---

[22] C. S. Lewis, *Mere Christianity*, The C. S. Lewis Signature Classics (HarperCollins, 2017), 15.

[23] Some readers will recognize that this argument's basic form follows the axiological argument as defended by J. P. Moreland and William Lane Craig in their *Philosophical Foundations for a Christian Worldview*, 2nd ed. (IVP Academic, 2017), chap. 26. For how C. S. Lewis formulates his moral argument, see Andrew I. Shepardson, *Who's Afraid of the Unmoved Mover: Postmodernism and Natural Theology* (Pickwick, 2019), 27–34.

Final Thoughts

The cost of following Jesus is everything that you have, especially your hypocritical sin. As Jesus says, "If anyone wants to follow after me, let him deny himself, take up his cross, and follow me" (Mark 8:34). The language of one's "cross" would have made the reader or hearer think about the Roman cross, a tool of torture and execution. So Jesus is implying that to follow him, one must literally be willing to suffer and die. But it is more than that. It means that one must live as if one has died to their old way of life, with its hypocrisy (sexual, financial, and otherwise), to truly follow him. So Jesus continues, "For whoever wants to save his life will lose it, but whoever loses his life because of me and the gospel will save it" (v. 35). Craig Blomberg notes that Jesus is teaching us that "there is a clear prioritizing of spiritual above material security in this context."[24] There is no amount of money or sex or success that can bring you close to God. Only laying down your life to receive the new life that Jesus offers can save you.

We have already shown that the Christian perspective on reality entails that we are all hypocrites in various ways. And it is directly into this world of ugly hypocrisy that Jesus comes. He should have been welcomed by the religious leaders who said they were looking for the Messiah; but with their actions, they simply rejected him. The Roman governor Pilate said he thought Jesus was innocent, but then he handed Jesus over to be flogged and crucified. His friends said they would be willing to suffer and die with him; but with their actions, most of them abandoned him when he went to the cross. Jesus understands hypocrisy because he became a victim of others' hypocrisy to defeat the root cause of hypocrisy, sin, on the cross. And for the victims of hypocrisy as well as for the repenting hypocrites, his words are hope and life. You may be the victim of someone else's hypocrisy, of having your life and future turned

---

[24] Blomberg, *Neither Poverty nor Riches*, 137.

upside down by someone you trusted who said the right things but lived completely differently. To you, Jesus would say, "Blessed are the poor in spirit, for the kingdom of heaven is theirs" (Matt 5:3). Jesus says that if you sense your own brokenness and vulnerability, you are actually in a unique place to receive everything that God's kingdom has to offer. This means that Jesus is offering you peace, healing, forgiveness, and hope for the future. Now think about your own hypocrisy and the ways in which you wish you were different. You wish that your desires would change. You want to live rightly. To you, Jesus says, "Blessed are those who hunger and thirst for righteousness, for they will be filled" (v. 6).

CHAPTER 4

Objection #4: Christian Ministries Are Abusive

Revelations of abuse in Christian ministries have grieved Christians and drawn the ire of Christianity's detractors. Many claim that Christianity, in its theology and power structures, is inherently abusive and that Christian ministries are uniquely notorious for misusing their power to harm their members. Consequently, Christian public witness and the personal faith of many have suffered as knowledge of and experience with abuse has increased. For example, news of the sexual abuse of young people by Catholic priests has led 37 percent of US Catholics to "question whether they would remain in the [Catholic] church."[1] In a study of women who were victims of clergy-perpetrated sexual abuse, 75.6 percent of victims reported that their "experience with the church after the abuse negatively affected [their] spiritual life," and 59.3 percent

[1] Jeffrey M. Jones, "Many U. S. Catholics Question Their Membership Amid Scandal," *Gallup* (March 13, 2019), https://news.gallup.com/poll/247571/catholics-question-membership-amid-scandal.aspx.

said their "experience with the church after the abuse negatively affected [their] relationship with God."[2]

Any honest assessment of this issue must readily acknowledge the shortcomings of self-proclaimed Christians who have failed to uphold the essence of Christian ethics in various ways. This is important for two reasons. First, Scripture recognizes that sometimes groups of people can miss the mark of God's moral perfection collectively. This seems to be part of what is happening with Jesus's indictment of the scribes and Pharisees in Matt 23:13–36. They were guilty of hypocrisy, restricting people's ability to worship God, spiritual blindness, neglecting spiritual virtues of all sorts, and even killing prophets. In contrast, Jesus said the people of God are responsible for discerning systemic sin and calling for repentance and reform. The second reason for the public acknowledgment of moral failures in Christian ministries is to protect the trustworthiness of those who abide by biblical standards. Followers of Christ must renounce "secret and shameful things" (2 Cor 4:2), confessing faith in Jesus and speaking the truth about him so that "as grace extends through more and more people, it may cause thanksgiving to increase to the glory of God" (4:15). Repentance of all sin (including abuse in Christian ministries) is deeply tied to our public witness.

With that said, it is also critical to explain how any and all forms of abuse are at odds with biblical Christianity. This chapter will examine the key accusation of detractors: that Christianity is an instantiation of an inherently abusive patriarchy. We will investigate the nature of this claim and explain how it arises from a misunderstanding of Christian theology. Moreover, we will show that Christianity uniquely possesses the resources to judge abuse and provide healing and hope to victims.

---

[2] David Kenneth Pooler and Liza Barros-Lane, "A National Study of Adult Women Sexually Abused by Clergy: Insights for Social Workers," *Social Work* 67, no. 2 (April 2022): 128.

Considering the Objection

Popular blogger Virginia Duan tells the story of a friend who "had so many thoughts about the evangelical god being an idol made in the image of abusive, power[-]hungry men—narcissistic, self-obsessed—and you know what? She's not wrong."[3] Joanne Carlson Brown and Carole R. Bohn note that feminists may differ on the question, "Is it possible to be a feminist and retain some attachment to the Christian tradition?" For some feminists, Christianity "is so entrenched in and undergirded by patriarchy" that attempting to change the Christian tradition in light of feminist critiques would actually make the Christian religion disappear.[4] Mary Daly argues:

> The qualities that Christianity idealizes, especially for women, are also those of a victim: sacrificial love, passive acceptance of suffering, humility, meekness, etc. Since these are the qualities idealized in Jesus "who died for our sins," his functioning as a model reinforces the scapegoat syndrome for women. Given the victimized situation of the female in sexist society, these "virtues" are hardly the qualities that women should be encouraged to have. Moreover, since women cannot be "good" enough to measure up to this ideal, and since all are by sexual definition alien from the male savior, this is an impossible model. Thus doomed to failure even in emulating the Victim, women are plunged more deeply into victimization.[5]

---

[3] Virginia Duan, "Leaving Christianity Is Like Leaving an Abusive Relationship," *Scary Mommy*, August 27, 2021, https://www.scarymommy.com/christianity-like-leaving-abusive-relationship.

[4] Joanne Carlson Brown and Carole R. Bohn, "Introduction," in *Christianity, Patriarchy, and Abuse: A Feminist Critique*, eds. Joanne Carlson Brown and Carole R. Bohn (Pilgrim, 1989), xiii.

[5] Mary Daly, *Beyond God the Father: Toward a Philosophy of Women's Liberation* (Beacon, 1973), 77.

The idea is that traditional understandings of Christology, sin, and salvation reinforce women's place in the victimizing patriarchy. For other feminists, a reexamination of how traditional understandings of "grace, the cross, and sacrifice apply to the situation of women today" are needed, recognizing that the traditional understandings of these doctrines have been used to subjugate women.[6] Feminists such as these might argue that perhaps Christianity has some valid purpose today, but we must critically reexamine traditional theologies to root out the patriarchy from Christian communities. While we don't deny the fact that Christian leaders and theologians have used religious power and misused Christian theology in sinful ways, perhaps even especially toward women, what ought to be examined is to what extent the real message of Christianity and the Bible are inherently entwined with ways of looking at the world that devalue and ultimately subjugate women.

First, Christianity rightly emphasizes and idealizes the virtues of sacrificial love, humility, and meekness for all humans, but does not call for the "passive acceptance of suffering." Sacrificial love is a virtue because it is first embodied in God himself, who sacrifices himself for the sake of our forgiveness and liberation. "This is how we have come to know love: He laid down his life for us. We should also lay down our lives for our brothers and sisters" (1 John 3:16). The virtue of sacrificial love is what Jesus models for us and for our salvific benefit (for benefits in this present age and in the age to come), not something that God merely demands we do for his sake. The results are not simply spiritual, but deeply tied to the physical well-being of others: "If anyone has this world's goods and sees a fellow believer in need but withholds compassion from him—how

---

[6] Karen L. Bloomquist, "Sexual Violence: Patriarchy's Offense and Defense," in *Christianity, Patriarchy, and Abuse*, 68. She is hopeful, "Although we cannot assume that Jesus totally transcended the patriarchal society of his day, he is depicted by the Gospel writers as having resisted assuming a certain kind of divine power or control over others. . . . His identity was seemingly not dependent on exercising control over others."

does God's love reside in him? Little children, let us not love in word or speech, but in action and in truth" (1 John 3:17–18).[7] Sacrificial love does not reduce a woman to the status of slave or victim, but it lifts women up by providing for their well-being and empowering them to be equal agents of God's generous love in the world. A key locus for this kind of sacrificial love is in Christian marriage, where men and women are not to jockey for position, but where husbands and wives obey the command to "submit to one another out of reverence for Christ" (Eph 5:21 NIV).[8]

Christianity commends humility, as well, and it is difficult to see why humility would be a tool of the patriarchy unless one were to equivocate on the use of the term *humility* to connote *humiliation*. Indeed, injustices toward women in patriarchal cultures have removed their agency, limited their prospects, and reduced them to far less than equal participants in church, home, and society. That indeed, is humiliation. However, humility is different, and if the critique of Christianity is regarding the virtue of humility, then it is misplaced because humility is essential to God's ethic regarding equality and relational healing. Humility is first modeled by Jesus, the incarnate Son of God who gave up his divine prerogatives to serve humanity (Phil 2:8), and our imitation of Christ on this score is God's vehicle for human redemption. Just consider what happens when all the men and women in a Christian community "in humility consider others as more important than yourselves. Everyone should look not to his own interests, but rather to the interests of others" (2:3b-4). This assumes

[7] The word for "love" here is the well-known *agape*, used in John to talk about God's very essence and purpose, which is "made visible in the sending and self-sacrifice of the Son. . . . God's primary purpose for the world is his compassionate and forgiving love which asserts itself despite the world's inimical rejection of it." See W. Günther and H.-G. Link, "Love," in *New International Dictionary of the New Testament Theology*, ed. Colin Brown (Zondervan, 1976), 2:546.

[8] Of course, there is more to marriage than mutual submission, but marriage requires nothing less. See Rebecca Merrill Groothuis, *Good News for Women: A Biblical Picture of Gender Equality* (Baker, 1997), chap. 7.

that different people (e.g. men and women, young and old, dominant and minority cultures, and of course, each individual) have different interests. Humility is the great equalizer, God's solution to each person's sinful tendency to look out only for the self or for one's own group.

Meekness is also misunderstood in this regard as a tool of the patriarchy. While meekness connotes, in Western cultures, mildness or submissiveness, the biblical beatitude, "Blessed are the meek, for they will inherit the earth" (Matt 5:5 NIV), is a challenge primarily to Zealots. These were Jewish religious warriors who thought that violent power (to overthrow the Romans) was the necessary ingredient in inaugurating the kingdom of God. Jesus is saying that the truly powerful are the ones who do not use their power to violently gain personal satisfaction, but who are wholly dependent on God.[9] Meekness is a virtue that Jesus predicates of himself.

> All things have been entrusted to me by my Father. No one knows the Son except the Father, and no one knows the Father except the Son and anyone to whom the Son desires to reveal him. Come to me, all of you who are weary and burdened, and I will give you rest. Take my yoke upon you and learn from me, because I am lowly and humble in heart, and you will find rest for your souls. For my yoke is easy and my burden is light. (Matt 11:27–30)

Consider what Jesus is claiming here. He has a divine relationship with God the Father, the Lord of heaven and earth. "All things" have been entrusted to him, which implies complete power and control. And he is the unique revelator of God's knowledge. But he uses all of this power and position to reveal God's comfort and rest.[10] This does so much more

---

[9] See Craig S. Keener, *The Gospel of Matthew: A Socio-Rhetorical Commentary* (Eerdmans, 2009), 104–7.

[10] F. Hauck and S. Schulz, "πραυς, πραυτης," in *Theological Dictionary of the New Testament*, eds. Gerhard Kittel and Gerhard Friedrich (Eerdmans, 1977), 6:649.

than simply liberate one from a kind of patriarchy because it actually undermines the politics of power and control whereby people are reduced to their gender, ethnicity, or place of power in society. It looks to God as the source of liberation through the inauguration of his kingdom, where there is lasting peace and rest. The biblical virtue of meekness is not reducing a woman to the role of submissive victim. Instead, it elevates her (and indeed, all who practice the virtue) to a privileged place of being a disciple of Jesus and receiving his gentle, restful, and loving leadership.

Mary Daly also accuses Christianity of commending the "passive acceptance of suffering."[11] It is true that Christianity does not commend the politics of control and coercion to ensure that each receives his or her due. For example, Jesus commands his followers, "But I tell you, don't resist an evildoer. On the contrary, if anyone slaps you on your right cheek, turn the other to him also" (Matt 5:39). And about the Messiah, it is said, "He was oppressed and afflicted, yet he did not open his mouth. Like a lamb led to the slaughter and like a sheep silent before her shearers, he did not open his mouth" (Isa 53:7). However, this does not mean that Christian suffering is passive or unresistant to evil. The command to turn the other cheek must be read in terms of the political zealotry of first-century Palestine. As Craig Keener argues, "It does not mean that an abused wife must remain in the home in the face of abuse . . . rather, Jesus' teaching does mean that we depend on God rather than on human weapons, although God may sovereignly raise up human weapons to fight the oppressors."[12] Christians are to depend on God for justice, resisting evil by refusing to live according to the "eye for an eye and tooth for a tooth" politics of control. That said, the government has a legitimate role in fighting against abuse, and Christians should fully endorse and cooperate with good governments that seek to punish abusers (see Rom 13:1–7).

---

[11] Daly, *Beyond God the Father*, 77.

[12] Keener, *Matthew*, 131.

Second, we must acknowledge that the sinful use of power with respect to sex and abuse has sometimes made its way into the power structures of the church. This is the argument of Caryn A. Reeder in her book *The Samaritan Woman's Story: Reconsidering John 4 After #ChurchToo*.[13] She argues that sometimes, in Christian ministries, masculinity is misdefined to be about power and uncontrollable sexuality, purity has been commended with respect to its promise of bountiful sex within marriage, femininity has too often been couched within sexuality and chastity, and women have been reduced to potential stumbling blocks for men. These misdefinitions are misleading at best and false and evil at worst. They do not represent life in the kingdom of God. When Christian subcultures commend these things, they do indeed adulterate Christianity's credibility. But even these things are accidental (that is, not essential) to Christian faith. Christianity has a radical message of equality for men and women, sexual purity empowered by the Holy Spirit, and self-sacrificial honoring of one another as children of God rather than as potential stumbling blocks. While Christians ought to repent for their misrepresentations of the gospel, the very public witness to the truth, rationality, and existential viability of the Christian faith depends on Christianity's radical ethical message.

Third, the outrage at issues of inequality and subjugation are much more at home in a Christian worldview than they are in a world without God. Consider the claim that abusive power is wrong. If God does not exist, and the doctrine of humanity made in the image of God is false, then abusive power may simply be an adaptive feature of the evolutionary process. In fact, there is a considerable and growing body of psychological literature that takes up the evolutionary factors that cause abuse and violence, including the idea that since intimate partner violence is often correlated with male-partner worries about female-partner

---

[13] Caryn A. Reeder, *The Samaritan Woman's Story: Reconsidering John 4 After #ChurchToo* (IVP Academic, 2022).

infidelity, a man may abuse his female partner to ensure that any children she may be carrying are indeed his own.[14] Creatures in the animal kingdom seem to exhibit no restraint in using their strength to kill and eat, copulate, or dominate other animals through fear. The law of nature seems to be that strength is rewarded with a chance to pass on one's genes through reproduction. If a creature is weaker, then all the worse for that creature's chances at survival. So it would be for human abusers and their victims. No one seeks to punish the male animal that copulates with a female by force. There is no moral blame for one creature that wounds another. Thus, there is no room for outrage toward abuse in a world without God.

However, the existence of God and the doctrine that all people are made in God's image change the conversation. Tom Holland makes this case in his book *Dominion*. Jesus's inclusion of women as his disciples and Paul's contention that "there is no Jew or Greek, slave or free, male and female; since you are all one in Christ Jesus" (Gal 3:28) show a radical vision of equality and dignity for each human being. Regarding even liberal feminism, Holland argues, "Any condemnation of Christianity as patriarchal and repressive is derived from a framework of values that was itself utterly Christian."[15] Christians who object to the abusive sexualization of women, the abuses of purity culture, and the inequality inherent in some patriarchal expressions of Christian ministry rightly embody the

---

[14] See for example, Aaron T. Goetz, Todd K. Shackelford, Valerie G. Starratt, and William F. McKibbin, "Intimate Partner Violence," in *Evolutionary Forensic Psychology: Darwinian Foundations of Crime and Law*, eds. Joshua D. Duntley and Todd K. Shackelford (Oxford University Press, 2008). See also Bernadette Wren, John Launer, Graham Music, Michael J. Reiss, and Anne Swanepoel, "Can an Evolutionary Perspective Shed Light on Maternal Abuse of Children?" in *Clinical Child Psychology and Psychiatry* 26, no. 1 (November 24, 2020): 283–94, https://doi.org/10.1177/1359104520974418.

[15] Tom Holland, *Dominion: How the Christian Revolution Remade the World* (Basic Books, 2019), 532.

Christian ethic modeled by Jesus.[16] Their public witness against abuse and for the truth is a kind of lived proclamation of the good news that God is remaking the world in Jesus.[17]

Final Thoughts

All of this points to the truth that Jesus himself suffered the worst kinds of abuse to bring an end to our sinfully abusive cultures and propensities. Throughout his life, entrenched powers mocked Jesus and attempted to control him and his message. He narrowly escaped multiple attempts to physically abuse him and kill him. Eventually, he offered himself to become abused in the most public way possible. He was beaten, flogged, cut with thorns, and crucified. Even in the middle of this torturous abuse, soldiers, onlookers, religious leaders, and the criminals he was crucified alongside offered constant verbal abuse. But Jesus saw this as a way to completely undermine the cultures of sinful abuse that humans so easily create. In the middle of all this ugliness, Jesus said, "Father, forgive them, because they do not know what they are doing" (Luke 23:34). Through his death, he offers something this world cannot offer: forgiveness and the ability to heal the most ugly, internal places in the human person that cause sinful abuse. His death at the hands of Roman abusers was actually God's way of bringing an end to the power of violence, subjugation, abuse, and the politics of control. This is why the Bible says that Jesus's death is how God "disarmed the rulers and authorities and disgraced them publicly; he triumphed over them in him" (Col 2:15).

---

[16] For an explication of how the sexualization of women has actually been the accidental result of liberal feminism, see Louise Perry, *The Case Against the Sexual Revolution: A New Guide to Sex in the 21st Century* (Polity, 2022).

[17] For the eschatological understanding of Christianity's theology of power to redeem sinful social structures, see Stephen Sykes, *Power and Christian Theology* (Continuum, 2006), esp. chap. 4.

CHAPTER 5

Objection #5: Christianity Is Misogynistic

"Christianity is patriarchy!" So goes the common wisdom of contemporary culture. The basic contention is that because of its teachings on gender, Christianity is deeply tied to systems that repress women and have done so for centuries. This claim must be taken very seriously. If Christianity is misogynistic, this undercuts the claim that in Christ, God has definitively revealed himself to all humankind with a message equally dignifying to women and men. For some, the idea that Christianity subjugates women is the roadblock that keeps them from considering its other truth claims, including the gospel.

In the previous chapter, we considered some deep concerns around abuse that threatens the well-being of women. In this chapter, we will build on this foundation to consider why some perceive Christianity as misogynistic, separate historical myth from fact, and then explore the gospel's revolutionary message regarding male and female equality. As we shall see, while it is true that many Christians have been horribly misogynistic, the Christian faith, in its core theology and in its most important historical representations, strongly affirms women's equal value in every sphere of life.

Considering the Objection

For many women, the perception that Christianity is misogynistic begins with personal experiences. When my (Ike's) wife had her first performance review in a Christian not-for-profit institution, her boss remarked, "I think that most of the women who work here would be better off just being stay-at-home mothers. But not you; you're gifted." While he probably meant this as a compliment, it reflected an inherently sexist premise about the capabilities of women in general. Although accusations of sexism get thrown around all too easily, countless women can attest to similar experiences within the Christian sphere. This goes to show that Christians are sometimes guilty of misogynistic comments and attitudes of which they may or may not be aware. For example, there is an incipient sexism in some well-intentioned behaviors of male leaders seeking to protect the people they lead. Those who have been around evangelical circles as long as we have may be familiar with the so-called Billy Graham Rule, which prohibits men from meeting alone with women who are not family members.[1] Ironically, while this principle is meant to protect women and men from sexual temptation or merely the perception of impropriety, it functionally objectifies women, treating them

---

[1] Twentieth-century evangelist Billy Graham explained in his autobiography that, at a meeting of evangelists, they made some commitments to ensure the integrity of their ministries: "We all knew of evangelists who had fallen into immorality while separated from their families by travel. We pledged among ourselves to avoid any situation that would have even the appearance of compromise or suspicion. From that day on, I did not travel, meet or eat alone with a woman other than my wife. We determined that the apostle Paul's mandate to the young pastor Timothy would be ours as well: 'Flee . . . youthful lusts' (2 Timothy 1:22, KJV)." See *Just as I Am: The Autobiography of Billy Graham* (HarperOne, 1997), 128.

not as cherished sisters in Christ but as potential stumbling blocks for male leaders. With that said, Christians certainly ought to be charitable toward those who practice such things rather than automatically assuming that a sinful attitude is at play. In my role in various levels of church leadership, I (Ike) will meet alone with a woman, but never behind a closed door, solely for the protection of the woman's reputation and my own. I always suggest that the worry about reputation is unfair, and that I am committed to shepherding, mentoring, or partnering in ministry with the woman to the fullest extent. Such candid explanations are helpful, because well-meant exercises of caution and care may inadvertently make women feel devalued.

Sexism, like virtually all other sins, has persisted throughout the history of Christianity. As Caryn A. Reeder explains, "Beginning in the second century, church leaders expressed concern for the safety of unmarried women dedicated to service in the church if men saw and desired them. Reports of harassment, exploitation, and rape . . . appear in sources from the Middle East and across Europe, up to and beyond the Reformation."[2]

Sexism exists in the modern church, as well; the #ChurchToo scandal has revealed that many women have been the victims of sexism, harassment, and abuse in Christian religious communities in the modern West.[3] Consider Bible teacher Beth Moore's story: "About a year ago I had an opportunity to meet a theologian I'd long respected. I'd read

---

[2] Caryn A. Reeder, *The Samaritan Woman's Story: Reconsidering John 4 After #ChurchToo* (IVP, 2022), 12. Reeder cites Tertullian, *On the Veiling of Virgins* 14.2; John Chrysostom, *Homilies on 1 Timothy 8*; and John Calvin, *Genesis*, trans. John King, 2 vols. (Banner of Truth Trust, 1965), 2:218.

[3] While not endorsing their accounts of the particular causes and solutions, Beth Allison Barr and Emily Joy Allison have at least accurately portrayed significant pervasive elements of sexism in some Christian subcultures in their respective works. See Beth Allison Barr, *The Making of Biblical Womanhood: How the Subjugation of Women Became Gospel Truth* (Brazos, 2021); and Emily Joy Allison, *#ChurchToo: How Purity Culture Upholds Abuse and How to Find Healing* (Broadleaf Books, 2021).

virtually every book he'd written. I'd looked so forward to getting to share a meal with him and talk theology. The instant I met him, he looked me up and down, smiled approvingly and said, 'You are better looking than ________________.' He didn't leave it blank. He filled it in with the name of another woman Bible teacher."[4]

This behavior is repugnant and sinful, but it may not be that we can simply chalk up this kind of behavior to a single theologian's sinfulness. In fact, it seems to be the case that some Christian circles have a deeply ingrained problem with sexism. In their study on Catholic communities in Poland, researchers Małgorzata Mikołajczak and Janina Pietrzak found that those cultures were more likely to embody "benevolent sexism," their term for behaviors and attitudes in which women who attempt to break out of traditional gender roles are regarded with suspicion and hostility, and those women who embrace the role of mother and "delicate, moral caretaker" are praised as the ideal.[5] While the researchers found no correlation between Polish Catholics and a hostile sexism that claims that women are inferior to men, women in these Polish Catholic communities are nevertheless pressured to conform to those social norms. That is, women who do not accept a more traditional role in home and family are victims of "benevolent sexism" in these contexts.

Second, some who perceive Christianity as misogynistic highlight the fact that some biblical characters exemplify sexism, put innocent women at risk, or even sexually abuse women. This would not be noteworthy were the perpetrators clearly the antagonists of these biblical stories. But sometimes one reads of men who are otherwise heroic, yet guilty of devaluing or misusing women in various ways. In Genesis 12, Abram, escaping a famine by traveling from Canaan to Egypt, puts his wife, Sarai,

---

[4] Beth Moore, "A Letter to My Brothers," *Living Proof Ministries Blog*, May 3, 2018, accessed Jan. 23, 2024, https://blog.lproof.org/2018/05/a-letter-to-my-brothers.html.

[5] Małgorzata Mikołajczak and Janina Pietrzak, "Ambivalent Sexism and Religion: Connected Through Values," in *Sex Roles* 70 (May 28, 2014): 87–399.

at considerable risk by conspiring with her about her identity: "Look, I know what a beautiful woman you are. When the Egyptians see you, they will say, 'This is his wife.' They will kill me but let you live. Please say you're my sister so it will go well for me because of you, and my life will be spared on your account" (vv. 11b–13). While it's technically true that Sarai is Abram's half-sister (see Gen. 20:12), the issue isn't as much with lying as with putting Sarai at considerable risk. The Pharaoh of Egypt brought Sarai into his harem, and Abram accumulated wealth because of his association with her. While the text doesn't make clear whether the Pharoah ever consummated his relationship with Sarai, Abram's plot could have exposed his wife to sexual abuse.[6] Other examples would be Abram's grandson Jacob, who withheld his love from his first wife Leah and preferred his second wife Rachel, and David who, under royal summons, brought Bathsheba into the palace to have sex with her. His kingly authority effectively eliminated any significant consent or choice on her part. If biblical "heroes" behave thusly, then one could see why some might accuse Christianity of being sexist.

In fact, the Bible reports much worse from those who are never represented as devout worshippers of God. Yet people like Abram, Jacob, and David are typically revered as heroes in the faith, not clear negative examples of those who oppose God. Even so, here is where we must think critically about what it means for a story to appear in the Bible. For Abram, his lying is portrayed as foolish and dangerous (see Gen 12:17–20). For Jacob, his favoring of his wife Rachel at the expense of his wife Leah is often answered with God showing favor to Leah (see Gen 29:31–35; 30:17, 19–21). Jacob's family, too, is seen as bearing the negative repercussions of his favoritism, with his sons' hatred of Joseph

[6] There is much more happening in this passage of course, especially since it is primarily about God's faithfulness to his promise to give Abram and Sarai a son, implying that she was spared the worst of potential outcomes. See John Goldingay, *Genesis*, Baker Commentary on the Old Testament: Pentateuch (Baker Academic, 2020), 194–201.

and anxiety at potentially losing Joseph's brother Benjamin (both sons of Rachel) to Egyptian bondage. David's sin with Bathsheba is condemned by the prophet Nathan, and David repents and bears the consequences of his sin (see 2 Sam 12:1–25). The biblical picture does not turn these men's behavior into hero-stories, quite the opposite. As Rebecca McLaughlin wisely notes, "Throughout the Old Testament, we see sin resulting in appalling treatment of women by men—and vice versa. We see murder and rape and exploitation. But this is a diagnosis, not a prescription. The Bible does not endorse what it reports."[7]

In fact, one of the larger themes of the Bible is that God chooses the children of Israel, and indeed all his people, despite their faithlessness and sin. The story of Joseph is clear on this. Joseph was sold into slavery by his brothers, suffering the consequences of Jacob's favoritism. But God used his enslavement to place Joseph in the Egyptian bureaucracy so that he could build up large food stores in Egypt that would feed people (including Jacob's whole family) from all over the ancient world during a famine. As a vindicated Joseph declared when forgiving his brothers, "You planned evil against me; God planned it for good to bring about the present result—the survival of many people" (Gen 50:20). As Paul wrote to Timothy, "If we are faithless, he remains faithful, for he cannot deny himself" (2 Tim 2:13).

Third, some views within the church regarding gender are targets for claims of sexism. All Christians hold that men and women are ontologically (that is, with respect to their being or existence) equal and that men and women have unique roles within a marriage. At the least, men cannot be mothers and women cannot be fathers. However, Christians differ in their positions on some of the particulars; some hold that the husband and the wife share authority equally and should practice fully mutual submission, while some hold that the husband has a unique

[7] Rebecca McLaughlin, *Confronting Christianity: 12 Hard Questions for the World's Largest Religion* (Crossway, 2019), 134.

place of leadership authority. Where ministry is concerned, some Christians believe that women and men can serve in any role to which they are called by God, and some believe that only men are divinely called to certain leadership and teaching roles.[8] The Christian insistence that men and women are not fully interchangeable along with the fact that many Christians believe that men are uniquely appointed to lead in various ways puts Christianity at odds with the dominant belief in the modern West: that regardless of biological sex, one can be and do whatever one wants.

Indeed, many in our culture simply see Christianity as an instantiation of a patriarchy that has suppressed women for millennia. Think about stereotypical gender roles that say men should be strong and dominant while women should be meek and subservient. Most see Christianity as especially guilty in defining and reinforcing such stereotypes, teaching that the first woman was created to be a "helper" to her husband (see Gen 2:20), wives need to submit to their husbands (see Eph 5:22), and women should not teach or have authority over men (see 1 Tim 2:12).[9] While it was previously noted that Christians do not agree on simplistic

---

[8] The former group in both cases refer to themselves as egalitarians and the latter group as complementarians. Our intention is not to settle this debate here, but to simply point to its complexity. For a defense of egalitarianism, see Ronald W. Pierce, Cynthia Long Westfall, and Christa L. McKirland, eds., *Discovering Biblical Equality: Biblical, Theological, Cultural, and Practical Perspectives*, 3rd ed. (IVP Academic, 2021). For a defense of complementarianism, see John Piper and Wayne Grudem, eds., *Recovering Biblical Manhood and Womanhood* (Crossway, 2021). For a treatment of both sides with respect to church leadership, see James R. Beck, ed., *Two Views on Women in Ministry* (Zondervan Academic, 2005).

[9] Egalitarians seek to faithfully interpret these passages in light of historical, grammatical, and cultural insights that affirm mutual submission between husband and wife (see Eph 5:21) and the fact that many women are referred to as leaders in the Bible in various ways. While complementarians affirm that men are uniquely appointed to lead in the church and the home, they affirm that women are of equal value to men and have important roles in home and church that men cannot fulfill.

bumper-sticker readings of these passages (e.g. "Women stay silent!" or "Only men can lead!"), and many Christians indeed affirm that women can lead in church and home, it remains the case that the general public perception of Christianity suffers on this issue. Contending against what she considers to be socially constructed gender roles, feminist theologian Yolanda Dreyer writes, "Christianity has contributed to the restriction of women rather than helping them to develop. Women are taught to sacrifice themselves for the sake of others and, in doing so, they disappear into the background."[10] This becomes worse if we attempt to get back to what the Bible says about the relationship between men and women. African scholars T. T. Rugwiji and M. A. Masoga argue that the Bible, particularly the Old Testament, betrays inherently sexist attitudes that have been maintained in the modern church. Despite the examples of women in the Bible who fight for independence (women such as the Hebrew midwives in Exodus 1; Rahab in Joshua 2; Deborah in Judges 4–5; and Esther), the Bible more loudly commends Mary as a hero of faith for women. "Mary is portrayed as being 'submissive' and 'deprived' of her individual rights in order to posit her as being the mother of the 'Messiah of the world.'"[11] The idea here is that the modern church simply perpetuates these biblical sexist attitudes and, indeed, oppresses women in its leadership structures and theologies of gender.

There are important reasons to conclude that Christian doctrine is not inherently sexist. The Christian worldview regards women both as equal to men in value and as uniquely wonderful creations of God in their own right. In Genesis 1, humankind is created in the image of

---

[10] Yolanda Dreyer, "Women's Spirituality and Feminist Theology: A Hermeneutic of Suspicion Applied to 'Patriarchal Marriage,'" *HTS Teologiese Studies/Theological Studies* 67, no. 3 (2011): 2, https://doi.org/10.4102/hts.v67i3.1104.

[11] T. T. Rugwiji and M. A. Masoga, "The Quest for Gender Equality in the Bible: Indigenous Knowledge Perspectives on the Church's Position Towards Women and Leadership in Africa," *Gender and Behaviour* 15, no. 2 (2017): 9061.

God, and it is both men and women who reflect the divine image: "So God created man in his own image; he created him in the image of God; he created them male and female" (Gen 1:27). The phrase *image of God* means that humanity represents God's authority and something of what God himself is like in character and ability.[12] Some might contend that the reason for the creation of the woman in Genesis is that the man needed a "helper." But this is due not to the woman's subordinate status, but to the fact that the man was created first and working (that is, in need of help) in the garden of Eden. As Rebecca Merrill Groothuis argues, "The observation that the woman was created to help the man in no way leads to the conclusion that she was created *only* to help the man. . . . There is no reason to assume that once she was created, help was not given and received mutually between the man and the woman."[13] Men and women are to serve one another as equals, and we see this especially in how Christians are taught to relate to one another in the New Testament. For example, wives are told to submit to their husbands in Eph 5:22, but this verse only makes sense in terms of the broader context of "submitting to one another in the fear of Christ" in verse 21. Further, husbands are told to "love your wives, just as Christ loved the church and gave himself for her" in verse 25, but this teaching only makes sense in terms of (1) Christ's sacrificial servanthood and (2) the Bible's general command to imitate Christ's sacrificial servanthood. This is precisely the general command we see in Phil 2:5–8: "Adopt the same attitude as that of Christ Jesus, who, existing in the form of God, did not consider equality with God as something to be exploited. Instead he emptied himself by assuming the form of a servant, taking on the likeness of humanity. And when he had

---

[12] For example, humans are persons who have the powers of rationality and relationality and the ability to make meaningful choices.

[13] Rebecca Merrill Groothuis, *Good News for Women: A Biblical Picture of Gender Equality* (Baker, 1997), 132.

come as a man, he humbled himself by becoming obedient to the point of death—even to death on a cross."

Whatever the Bible teaches about the relationship between men and women, it is definitively within the anthropological context of equality and mutuality and the Christological context of sacrifice and service.

If this were not enough to paint the biblical picture of God's view of women, we need only to look to the example of Jesus. Throughout his ministry, we see Jesus honoring, protecting, and esteeming women in ways that surely scandalized his contemporaries. Jesus blamed men, not women, for the sin of lust (Matt 5:28), and he made divorce, which placed uneven hardship on women, harder (Matt 5:31–32; 19:1–12). He welcomed and healed women who would have been outcasts in his culture, particularly prostitutes, Gentiles, and a woman who had been bleeding for twelve years. Jesus had female disciples to whom he offered theological instruction, and while not treating women as if they were identical to men, he equally celebrated their faith and contributions to his ministry.[14] When he encountered the Samaritan woman at the well, he scandalously flouted cultural and religious norms by addressing her, and her life was transformed by his attention and revelation. She boldly spread the word about Jesus to her town and many believed that he was the Messiah when they heard her testimony.[15]

Across the West, we see a fourth way in which Christianity is a target of accusations of sexism in the abortion debate (which we will address

---

[14] On the above and the question of why women were not members of Jesus's first apostles, see "Jesus' View of Women" in Douglas R. Groothuis, *On Jesus*, Wadsworth Philosophers Series (Wadsworth/Thomson, 2003).

[15] See John 4:1–42. A common reading of this story is that the woman was in sin for having been attached to so many different men. However, Caryn A. Reeder challenges this notion by suggesting that we know too little about this woman's story and quite much about the poor treatment of women in the ancient world to paint the Samaritan woman in a wholly negative light. See Reeder, *The Samaritan Woman's Story*, chaps. 5–6.

more significantly in chapter 6). The typical way in which this is stated is through claiming that any legal restrictions placed on a woman's access to abortion are an attempt to control and exploit women's bodies and sexuality.[16] US Rep. Alexandria Ocasio-Cortez argues that religious people are the culprit: "Abortion bans aren't just about controlling women's bodies. They're about controlling women's sexuality. Owning women. From limiting birth control to banning comprehensive sex ed, US religious fundamentalists are working hard to outlaw sex that falls outside their theology."[17] The implication is that US pro-life Christians are the unique agents of modern misogyny in their attempts to place restrictions on abortion.

Christian cultures, while surely missing the mark many times, have been overwhelmingly beneficial to women throughout history, especially when compared to many non-Christian cultures.[18] The idea that a woman's body is her own, not the property of her husband or father, is a unique contribution of Christian theology to Western civilization.[19]

---

[16] Consider the advocacy organization Amnesty International which, on its website's section titled "My Body My Rights," claims that restricting access to abortion is part and parcel of a much greater sexism. Amnesty lists the harrowing stat that "1/10 girls worldwide aged under 18 have been forced to have sex or perform sexual acts" next to the very different stat that "40% of women of childbearing age live in countries where abortion is banned, restricted or not accessible," both being part of the same "global scandal." That is, rape and sexual abuse are seen to be equivalent to the inability to access abortion. Amnesty International, "My Body My Rights," https://www.amnesty.org/en/get-involved/my-body-my-rights.

[17] Zack Budryk, "Ocasio-Cortez: Abortion Bans Are About 'Owning Women,'" *The Hill,* May 16, 2019, https://thehill.com/homenews/state-watch/443981-ocasio-cortez-abortion-bans-are-about-owning-women/.

[18] None of this is to say that non-Christian cultures have always and everywhere been bad for women. Our focus is on rebutting the charge that Christianity is sexist.

[19] See Tom Holland, *Dominion: How the Christian Revolution Remade the World* (Basic Books, 2019), 530.

In the earliest churches, women thrived because Christians adopted large numbers of girls, often abandoned to die as infants simply because they were not boys. Women had more children and lived longer because Christians didn't perform dangerous surgical and chemical abortions, which often sterilized otherwise healthy women. These same values, scandalous in the ancient world, lie behind the modern pro-life movement. The goal is not to control women's bodies, but to equally value each human being formed in the mother's womb (and each mother herself) as made in God's image.

As Rodney Stark argues about the early church, "Within the Christian subculture women enjoyed far higher status than did women in the Greco-Roman world at large."[20] Medieval women such as Julian of Norwich, Catherine of Genoa, Teresa of Ávila, Catherine of Siena, and many others made significant theological contributions to Christian thought; Christian convictions helped many Christian women to see their bodies as a means to approach the humanity of God in Christ.[21] Christian convictions were at the core of the earliest women's and civil rights movements. Consider escaped slave Sojourner Truth's "Ain't I a Woman" speech from 1851: "That little man in black there, he says women can't have as much rights as men, 'cause Christ wasn't a woman! Where did your Christ come from? Where did your Christ come from? From God and a woman! Man had nothing to do with Him."[22]

---

[20] Rodney Stark, *The Rise of Christianity: A Sociologist Reconsiders History* (Princeton University Press, 1996), 95.

[21] See Mark A. Noll, David Komline, and Han-Luen Kantzer Komline, *Turning Points: Decisive Moments in the History of Christianity*, 4th ed. (Baker Academic, 2022), 299–300.

[22] Sojourner Truth, "Ain't I a Woman," *National Park Service*, https://www.nps.gov/wori/learn/historyculture/sojourner-truth.htm. There is some dispute about the exact text of the speech. See https://www.thesojournertruthproject.com/compare-the-speeches.

Final Thoughts

Lamentably, many Christians have been and are misogynistic in their attitudes and actions. But as we have seen, this is unbiblical because Christian theology is deeply affirming of women. Christianity provides unique explanations of and answers for the deeply human sin of sexism. The Bible tells us of this problem in its earliest chapters. In Genesis 3, we see a picture of the first man and woman giving in to their own pride and committing sin together for the first time. In these earliest moments, the brokenness and alienation between the sexes begins. The man blames the woman (and in a way, God), "The woman you gave to be with me—she gave me some fruit from the tree, and I ate" (v. 12). By blaming Eve, Adam shirks his responsibility and casts her in the more negative light. To the woman, God explains what sin will do to her relationship with the man: "Your desire will be for your husband, yet he will rule over you" (v. 16b). The word *desire* here equates to something like a desire to dominate her husband, but instead of her dominating him, he will use his strength to rule over her.[23] We see this pattern of sinful brokenness throughout history: Women seek to control men in various ways, but men too often use their power to dominate women. Like everything else, gender relations were affected by the curse upon creation. The wonderful news is that the gospel provides a holistic remedy.

At the incarnation, God the Son submitted himself to gestation within a woman, Mary, and she submitted her will to God's: "Be it unto me according to thy word" (Luke 1:38 KJV). Jesus came of age under the protection of his mother and then used his ministry to teach, elevate, and honor women. At his crucifixion, we see Jesus making provision for the care of his mother. Upon his resurrection, he entrusted the proclaiming of the gospel first to a woman. Jesus inaugurated a countercultural way

---

[23] I owe this observation to Richard Hess. For a helpful discussion of this passage, see John Goldingay, *Genesis*, 83.

of life in which the goal is not to be first, to be in charge, or to dominate others, but to humble oneself and to serve. To those who are proud and domineering, Jesus says, "The first will be last." To those who have been abused and who have suffered, he says, "The last will be first" (Matt 20:16). The way of this world, wherein men seek to rule and women fight back, is passing into a world where the reality, even now through Jesus's kingdom, is that "there is no Jew or Greek, slave or free, male and female; since you are all one in Christ Jesus" (Gal 3:28). For all those who have suffered misogyny and domination and every manner of sexual brokenness, there will be ultimate resolution and redemption: "He will wipe away every tear from their eyes. Death will be no more; grief, crying, and pain will be no more, because the previous things have passed away" (Rev 21:4).

CHAPTER 6

Objection #6: Christians Want to Control Women's Bodies

When I (Melissa) was about ten years old, one of my family members borrowed a copy of Margaret Atwood's novel *The Handmaid's Tale* from the county library. I clearly remember being captivated by the strange cover art—two figures walking beside a tall brick wall, wearing long red robes and white caps with angular protrusions. Already an avid reader, I was intrigued and asked what the book was about. I was given an age-appropriate response: It was about women who were kept as prisoners and forced to have babies. How awful! I had no interest in reading such a disturbing book. At the time, I still did not know how women came to be pregnant, but I had gathered that giving birth was a terribly painful ordeal that I wanted nothing to do with, ever. The idea that a woman could be *forced* into a life of child-bearing slavery was utterly horrific to me.

Although I probably heard *The Handmaid's Tale* mentioned a few times over the ensuing thirty-some years, it captured my attention again in 2017, when the television adaptation made its debut. The red robes and white caps worn by the show's characters were soon appearing at political demonstrations and women's marches as a way of protesting legislation that would place restrictions on abortion. Was Atwood's book actually about abortion prohibition? I wondered. I picked up a copy of the book to see for myself and discovered that it was not. In fact, it was about the state-sanctioned rape of fertile women in a dystopian world where environmental toxins had caused mass sterility. I wondered why these pro-choice activists had adopted the garb of the handmaids to promote abortion rights and why some carried picket signs with slogans like "No Forced Breeding." After all, no one had suggested legalized sex slavery. Yet, this is how the narrative was spun for dramatic effect, reinforcing the perception that pro-lifers (most of whom are Christians) believe that women should not have control over their own bodies. As we shall see, this is a misleading caricature, and it completely dodges the foundational pro-life assertion that the preborn are innocent human beings with an inalienable right to life.

Considering the Objection

The pro-life position is not held exclusively by Christians, but because it is intrinsic to orthodox Christianity,[1] it is often targeted by critics of the faith. The core issue behind the objection is bodily autonomy, which includes the right to make our own decisions about medical procedures. In the case of elective abortion, however, there are unique ethical

---

[1] A defense of this assertion is outside the scope of this chapter. Two excellent resources for those interested in such a defense are "What Does the Bible Have to Say About Abortion?" The Museum of Abortion, June 9, 2021, https://abortionhistorymuseum.com/2021/06/09/what-does-bible-say-about-abortion/, and "What the Early Church Believed: Abortion" Catholic Answers, https://www.catholic.com/tract/abortion.

complications that must be navigated.[2] We will begin with the central question—the nature of the preborn—and then examine related issues that inevitably arise in the bodily autonomy conversation.

What Is Meant by "the Preborn"?

The question of when a new human life begins is not difficult to answer from a scientific perspective. In a global survey published in 2021, biologists from 1,058 academic institutions were asked this question, and 96 percent responded that fertilization marks the beginning of a new human life.[3] Prenatal development is an amazing and complex biological saga, but here are some of the highlights that will help contextualize the forthcoming discussion. Within twenty-four hours of fertilization, a single-celled zygote with a complete set of chromosomes is formed, and this is the first developmental stage of a new human being. As one prestigious and widely-used embryology textbook puts it, "Human development begins at fertilization when a sperm fuses with an oocyte to form a single cell, the zygote. This highly specialized, totipotent cell (capable of giving rise to any cell type) marks the beginning of each of us as a distinct individual."[4] The zygote possesses the unique genetic and epigenetic information that will determine its sex and other physical characteristics. Because it is very large, relatively speaking, it can be seen with the naked eye, and

---

[2] Elective abortions are those that are chosen and not deemed medically necessary. Therapeutic abortions are legal in all fifty states; abortion restrictions never apply to the removal of ectopic or other life-threatening pregnancies, the emergency early delivery of a preterm baby to save the life of the mother, or post-miscarriage D&C procedures.

[3] See Steven Andrew Jacobs, "The Scientific Consensus on When a Human's Life Begins" *Issues in Law and Medicine*, 36, no. 2 (Fall 2021): 221–33, https://issuesinlawandmedicine.com/wp-content/uploads/2023/09/Jacobs_36n2.pdf.

[4] Keith L. Moore, T.V.N. Persaud, and Mark G. Torchia, *The Developing Human: Clinically Oriented Embryology*, 11th ed. (Elsevier, 2018), 11.

has the built-in biological potentiality for reaching maturity (barring a lethal genetic mutation). By the time it reaches the mother's womb for implantation—about a week later—it has developed into an embryo made up of well over one hundred cells.

At six weeks' gestation, the embryonic human has a heartbeat. And by the end of the eighth gestational week, the bones, organ systems, hands, feet, and eyes are noticeable. Only two weeks later, the now-so-called fetal human is unmistakably human; he or she has fully formed arms, legs, fingers, and toes. Within another couple of weeks the digestive and urinary systems are functioning, and by the end of the sixteenth week, the fetal human is responding to sensory stimuli, thumb-sucking, smiling, and sometimes kicking strongly enough to be noticed by the mother.[5] The age of gestational viability, when the baby could survive outside of the womb (with intensive medical care) if born prematurely, is only seven weeks later, at the end of the twenty-third week of pregnancy. Under normal circumstances, however, development continues in-utero, and the baby is born during the fortieth week.

The bottom line here is that it is scientifically well established that the preborn are individual, whole human beings from the beginning of their development at the zygotic stage. Yet, while in utero, they do have characteristics that differ from a newborn human. If any argument for the moral permissibility of abortion is to succeed, it must show that at least one of these prevents the unborn human from having the same inalienable rights as the newborn human. To sum it up in a simple question: Is the principle of human equality—i.e., equal dignity, equal rights—inapplicable to a preborn human because of his or her temporary physical attributes? It will be helpful to consider what those are as we pursue the answer to this question. In his book, *Understanding Abortion: From Mixed Feelings to Rational Thought*, University of Rhode Island professor

[5] With my (Melissa's) first pregnancy, I noticed this fluttery "quickening" during the sixteenth week. It was about the eighteenth week with my second.

(emeritus) Stephen D. Schwarz presents a useful acronym for the biological distinctives of the preborn—SLED:

S: Size
L: Level of development
E: Environment
D: Degree of dependency

For the child is:
Smaller;
Less developed;
in a different Environment;
and more Dependent.[6]

These are the only differences between a preborn human and a newborn human, and they are all, Schwarz argues, morally irrelevant to the question of essential humanity. To understand why none of these can be used as a reason why the preborn human being does not qualify for equal human rights, including the right to life, we only need to consider the following.

Size: The intrinsic value of a human being is not proportional to their size. A baby that is four minutes old has the same value as a four-year-old or a forty-year-old, even though they all differ drastically in physical size. The preborn human is merely smaller than the born.

Level of development: The issue here is very similar. The toddler is more developed than the newborn, and the teenager is more developed than the toddler. Thus, intrinsic value cannot be relative to how developed the human is.

---

[6] Stephen D. Schwarz, *Understanding Abortion: From Mixed Feelings to Rational Thought* (Lexington Books, 2012), 51–52.

> Environment: The environment a child inhabits is related to the needs he or she has at his or her stage of development. For example, a baby that is born several weeks early and thus lives in an incubator until it is safe to live outside of it is no less valuable than the baby that is born full-term and does not need an incubator. "The pre-born child," writes Schwarz, "is in the incubator of his mother's womb . . . the necessary environment he needs while still small and fragile, what he needs for protection, nourishment, and growth. . . . The difference . . . is one of needs, not of reality or worth and dignity."[7]
>
> Degree of dependency: We are all dependent on other human beings to one degree or another, and this changes dramatically over the course of our lives. A newborn relies on its caregivers for all of its survival needs, but as a healthy teenager they are far more independent. This does not mean that the newborn is a less valuable human being. In the same way, the preborn's dependency cannot dictate its value. Also consider the fact that many of us, should we live to old age, will become increasingly dependent upon caregivers; but of course this will not diminish our humanity.

If one of these differences is used as moral justification for killing an unwanted preborn human, then there is arguably no reason why that difference cannot also be used to justify killing an unwanted newborn. If none of these differences can be a criterion for denying the humanness of a born human being, then none of them are sufficient for denying the humanness of the preborn, and humanness grants us all equal human rights. Note that humanness is an all-or-nothing kind of thing; it is not something that can be had to one degree or another. An entity is either human or it is not.

---

[7] Schwarz, 52.

So, here we reiterate the question, What is meant by "the preborn"? It is a distinct, living, whole, and innocent human being. *Humans* are deliberately killed during abortion procedures.[8] Thus, in an attempt to defend abortion as morally permissible, some reframe their position by arguing for a distinction between humanness and personhood. The idea is that the right to life only belongs to persons, and personhood requires certain properties that some human beings (including the preborn) do not have. One common example is conscious self-awareness; another is the ability to form relationships with others. Ultimately, this approach fails in essentially the same way as the argument against humanness fails—we can point to examples of born humans who lack some criterion cited as necessary to personhood. Pro-life scholarship includes a wide range of compelling arguments for fetal personhood; but even if it could be shown that every single one of them fails to demonstrate personhood with complete certainty, the scientific consensus on the humanness of the preborn stands. This means that the permissibility of elective abortion would still require indisputable proof that fetal humans are not human enough to qualify for the most basic human right: the right to life. Besides, whether any criteria could ever draw a convincing distinction between human beings who have personhood and human beings who do not (highly doubtful), the corresponding assumption that killing the latter class of humans is ethically permissible is entirely unjustified.[9]

For abortion to be ethically permissible, there must be no doubt whatsoever about the inhumanness (or sub-humanness) of the preborn;

---

[8] This is not merely a rhetorical spin on the issue; as Scott Klusendorf and others have documented, many abortion advocates have publicly and explicitly stated that abortions kill human beings. See Scott Klusendorf, *The Case for Life: Equipping Christians to Engage the Culture*, 2nd ed. (Crossway, 2023), 14–15.

[9] For extensive discussion on the personhood angle, see Christopher Kaczor, *The Ethics of Abortion: Women's Rights, Human Life, and the Question of Justice* (Routledge, 2010). Scott Klusendorf's *The Case for Life* is a good introductory level treatment.

but we have a multitude of reasons to conclude that they are members of the human family.

The Bodily Autonomy Objection

Virtually everyone would agree that no one has the moral authority to intentionally destroy an innocent human life. The average person on the street who thinks of themselves as "pro-choice" typically denies that the preborn are human beings until some arbitrarily chosen stage of gestation. Others, as aforementioned, try to play the personhood card. However, abortion rights advocates who acknowledge the humanness and the personhood of the preborn nevertheless maintain that this category of human life is the exception. Why? Because in their view, the woman's right to bodily autonomy supersedes the human rights of the preborn. They argue that it is therefore unethical to prevent a woman from obtaining an elective abortion. Various arguments involving hypothetical scenarios have been devised in the attempt to support this assertion. One example is the violinist analogy developed by Judith Jarvis Thomson in her famous 1971 essay, "A Defense of Abortion." Thomson argues that a woman who desires an elective abortion simply does not want the preborn human using her body for life support, and exercising one's right to bodily autonomy by withdrawing that support is not the same thing as the intentional killing of a human being. She offers the following thought experiment:

> You wake up in the morning and find yourself back to back in bed with an unconscious violinist. A famous unconscious violinist. He has been found to have a fatal kidney ailment, and the Society of Music Lovers has canvassed all the available medical records and found that you alone have the right blood type to help. They have therefore kidnapped you, and last night the violinist's circulatory system was plugged into yours, so that your

> kidneys can be used to extract poisons from his blood as well as your own. The director of the hospital now tells you, "Look, we're sorry the Society of Music Lovers did this to you—we would never have permitted it if we had known. But still, they did it, and the violinist is now plugged into you. To unplug you would be to kill him. But never mind, it's only for nine months. By then he will have recovered from his ailment, and can safely be unplugged from you."[10]

Thomson grants that people have a right to life and (for the sake of argument) that the preborn are people, but "having a right to life does not guarantee having either a right to be given the use of or a right to be allowed continued use of another person's body—even if one needs it for life itself."[11] Thus, she contends, unhooking yourself from the violinist, even though you know he will die as a result, is your right and not unethical.

Thomson's analogy does not succeed because the parallels she tries to draw do not work. First, unless a woman is raped (a matter that will be discussed later), her pregnancy is the natural result of intentional sexual activity. This is not even remotely akin to being hooked up to a very sick stranger while you are unconscious. Even if pregnancy was not desired, it remains the case that consensual sexual intercourse resulted in conception and thus the preborn human's dependency upon the woman's body. Her reproductive system and that of her sexual partner functioned according to their design, and a new life was created as a natural result. Second, an abortion would be the premeditated, active killing of the viable preborn human, whereas the violinist would die of his disease if you disconnected from him and another form of life-support could not be found in time. Thus, this is a false analogy. Removing life support from a human is

---

[10] Judith Jarvis Thomson, "A Defense of Abortion," *Philosophy & Public Affairs* 1, no. 1 (1971): 47–66.

[11] Thomson, 47–66.

different from actively killing a human. Think of it this way. In the violinist situation, you could: (A) choose to continue helping, (B) choose not to help, or (C) kill him and eliminate the question. However, in the case of pregnancy, there is no option B, to simply choose not to help; the mother either allows the continuation of life or seeks a procedure that intentionally terminates that life.

Another dissimilarity between the two scenarios is that the pregnant woman has a moral obligation to the human being she helped create, an obligation that might not apply to someone artificially attached to her without her consent, whom she did not create. It is widely recognized that parents have moral duties toward their children that they do not have toward others. Some in the pro-choice camp argue that the preborn, unlike born children, are parasitic, like the violinist. This also is a false analogy; as Scott Klusendorf puts it, "A parasite is an alien being who should not be present. The mother's child was conceived with her own flesh and blood and is where he naturally belongs at that stage in his development."[12]

The violinist analogy is part of a loose category known as Good Samaritan arguments, which are all used in defense of a woman's right to bodily autonomy in the case of pregnancy. Other examples use organ donor and blood donor scenarios to argue that we are never obligated to donate an organ or some of our blood even if someone will die if we refuse. The above critique applies to these Good Samaritan arguments as well. In the case of the preborn, there is a healthy person in their appropriate biological environment who will live unless someone intentionally takes specific measures to kill them. Being underdeveloped and thus vulnerable is not equivalent to being terminally ill.

Where human rights (including bodily autonomy) are concerned, the pro-life position is more inclusive because it recognizes the rights of

---

[12] Klusendorf, *The Case for Life*, 247.

preborn humans. It contends that the preborn possess intrinsic human rights by virtue of being members of the human race, period.

What About Pregnancy in Cases of Rape?

Pro-life advocates fully recognize that the reality of rape presents an extraordinary difficulty. Even some who are unapologetically pro-life in all other cases related to elective abortion believe that an exception could be made for rape survivors. The pregnant woman did not consent to the sexual act, and she is now confronted with a compounded crisis. Pregnancy is a major physical and psychological experience for all women; but for a woman who has been raped, there is massive trauma directly associated with her pregnancy. A horrendous injustice has been perpetrated against her, body and soul, and she now has a physical reminder growing in her womb. If she does not have an elective abortion, she must endure a pregnancy that was forced upon her and will undoubtedly be a constant reminder of the rape. Those of the pro-choice persuasion argue that it is neither just nor compassionate to deny this woman the opportunity to mitigate the severity of her psychological injury by ending the "ongoing assault" to her body.

Rape is an atrocity, and a survivor deserves the most abundant, extravagant love and care it is possible to give. At the same time, the humanitarian conviction of the pro-life position, that the preborn are innocent human beings with equal intrinsic value, is not eliminated by the circumstances of their conception. This core truth brings necessary clarity to the conversation. There are two human beings involved, and an elective abortion would kill one of them. This would amount to executing someone for the crime of another, and that is antithetical to justice. The difficulty of what the woman is facing is unfathomable, and thus an appropriate articulation of why Christians believe that even rape does not justify abortion is absolutely crucial: Killing the preborn human only exacerbates the horror and injustice, not only by taking an innocent life but also in terms of the psychological, spiritual, and biological damage inflicted upon the mother. Moreover, many have never considered the enormous redemptive power a pregnant rape survivor has the power to wield; Christian philosopher Christopher Kaczor beautifully articulates this:

> Unfortunately, nothing, including having an abortion, can undo a rape. However, to bear a child conceived in these most difficult of circumstances is to perform an act that is in complete contradiction of what takes place in a rape. In rape, a man assaults an innocent human being; in nurturing life, a woman protects an innocent human being. . . . In rape, a man imposes himself to the great detriment of another; in nurturing life, a woman makes a gift of herself to the great benefit of another. While, unfortunately, rape once perpetrated can never be undone, the rationalizations, maxims, and motives of rape are never so completely rejected as when someone chooses life in the most difficult circumstances, circumstances that make such a choice heroic.[13]

The true Christian concern is for the greatest possible flourishing of both woman and child, not for the child alone. Opposing the killing of the preborn is in no way at odds with the best interests of the woman. While many would dispute this, it is nonetheless important to state it for the sake of making the Christian pro-life position abundantly clear.

It is worth mentioning here that while Christian traditions differ in their position on contraceptive measures, even the Roman Catholic church (perhaps the most restrictive in this regard) allows non-abortifacient emergency contraception for rape survivors.[14] The ethical statement of the Catholic Medical Association reads:

---

[13] Christopher Kaczor, *The Ethics of Abortion: Women's Rights, Human Life, and the Question of Justice* (Routledge, 2011), 184.

[14] Abortifacient contraceptives are those that can terminate a very early pregnancy. Intrauterine devices (IUDs) and birth control pills are included in this category.

> A female who has been raped should be able to defend herself against a potential conception from the sexual assault. If, after appropriate testing, there is no evidence that conception has occurred already, she may be treated with medications that would prevent ovulation, sperm capacitation, or fertilization. It is not permissible, however, to initiate or to recommend treatments that have as their purpose or direct effect the removal, destruction, or interference with the implantation of a fertilized ovum.[15]

The point being, no pro-life advocate would suggest that a physician caring for a rape survivor should not take every safe medical route possible to prevent fertilization.

Bodily autonomy rights always have limits—no one has the right to do things with their body for the purpose of intentionally harming or killing another innocent human being. As pro-life philosopher John Ferrer explains, "We recognize that all human rights are bound, on every side, by the rightful domains of other human beings. My right to swing my arm ends at your face, right? Bodily autonomy has *never* meant freedom from all unwanted responsibilities. . . . Since pro-choice "autonomy" entails the privilege to kill, by fiat, another innocent human being, destroying all latent rights/rights-claims they may have, that isn't liberty, it's tyranny."[16]

To be sure, pregnancy is a wholly singular situation involving the relationship of one person's body to another person's body, but there are still no good reasons to conclude that the mother's bodily rights entitle her to take the life of her preborn child.

---

[15] Catholic Medical Association, "Statement on Emergency Contraception in Cases of Rape," September 14, 2015, https://www.cathmed.org/assets/files/CMA_Statement_on_EC_After_Rape_(NCBC_edited_version)_PDF.pdf.

[16] Personal correspondence, quoted with permission. John Ferrer, PhD, is a Fellow at Equal Rights Institute (https://equalrightsinstitute.com) and the founder and curator of the virtual Abortion History Museum (https://abortionhistorymuseum.com).

Are Christians Merely Pro-Birth?

The claim that Christians within the pro-life movement are merely pro-birth, not truly pro-life, is a common talking point, and it is not made exclusively by pro-choice partisans. Generally speaking, the accusation is that many Christians are inconsistent; they are passionate and proactive about preventing abortion but not about protecting the lives and health of people in general. In other words, someone who *truly* cares about the sanctity and dignity of life would be "whole life pro-life." They would be equally concerned about things like hunger, affordable healthcare, homelessness, human trafficking, and a myriad of other issues. Consider the following statement made by a senior fellow of Democrats for Life of America (and Catholic) Robert G. Christian about the so-called whole life movement:

> The whole life movement is not a rival of the pro-life movement. Instead, it seeks to purify the pro-life movement of its inconsistencies. A pro-life movement that ignores infant mortality rates, starvation, or the degradation of the environment simply does not deserve the label 'pro-life.' It becomes a mere euphemism for supporting laws that restrict access to abortion. It becomes detached from the understanding of human dignity and worth that should animate the movement. Only a whole life approach can make the pro-life movement authentically pro-life.[17]

At a surface level, such statements sound good and reasonable, but the implicit assumptions and misguided ideas behind them create confusion. Clarification is crucial.

We should first acknowledge that an ethical position indeed loses some of its credibility in the eyes of the beholder when it is applied

---

[17] Robert G. Christian, "What Is the Whole Life Movement?" *Millennial Journal*, February 3, 2016.

inconsistently. The Christian position is indeed "womb to tomb" when it comes to the sacredness and dignity of all human life; and *as the global church*, we must collectively reflect this conviction. However (and this is a crucial point), the ethical consistency of the church does not mean that a movement under the umbrella of the church or in which the church heavily participates cannot have a narrower focus, such as fighting to save the preborn from premeditated killing, rescuing people trapped in sex trafficking, working to feed the hungry, building affordable housing, or digging water wells in developing nations. Efficacy is maximized when there is a clear focus and concentration of resources within individual organizations. God calls different people to different areas, and he equips them accordingly. First Cor 12:12–27, the "members of the body" passage, is highly relevant here. Holistic health and functionality of the body means recognizing the specialized virtues of each and every part. Caring deeply about human life in the broad sense does not entail spreading our personal time, effort, and charitable donations equally among every Christian cause related to the value of human life. For one thing, that is impossible for anyone. For another, such dilution would actually undermine every mission in question. As Klusendorf puts it, "While our Christian ethic is broad and inclusive, it doesn't follow that the operational objectives of the pro-life movement must be broad and inclusive as well. Expanding those objectives will bankrupt the pro-life movement. As the old military adage goes, 'He who attacks everywhere attacks nowhere.'"[18] We need missions with laser-focused objectives, most especially where millions of lives hang in the balance.

A related source of confusion stems from the co-opting of the "pro-life" label. This is done by some Christians (such as the activist quoted above), but it is also done by nonbelievers, especially those who make the "pro-birth not pro-life" claim. When language is used imprecisely, we end up talking past each other, which is counterproductive and unnecessarily

[18] Klusendorf, *The Case for Life*, 47–48.

divisive. "Pro-life" should be reserved specifically for making reference to a particular view on elective abortion and organizations devoted to promoting that view. This would make it synonymous with "anti-abortion." Other terms can be used to describe the broader ethical framework that encompasses all issues related to human survival and flourishing. Making this distinction adamantly and frequently would bring a great deal of clarity to the conversation in both the church and the public square.

A related matter that must be considered is the relative urgency and ethical weightiness of the various issues surrounding the sanctity and dignity of life. For instance, curtailing the government-sanctioned, premeditated killing of innocent, vulnerable human beings outweighs improving the quality of life for those struggling with poverty, which far outweighs the implementation of wise environmental protection policies. They are not morally equivalent. When we are in the position of having to choose between two or more specific courses of action and there are moral issues (such as human value) involved, we must choose to address the most urgent. Abortion is, quite literally, a life-and-death situation, and nothing surpasses a life-and-death situation. Imagine you have two young children in your care, ages two and four. You take them to a park and sit down with them to play in the sandbox. You become preoccupied with unmolding a bucket of wet sand, and the two-year-old wanders several yards away. You turn your head just in time to see her fall into a koi pond, and you know she cannot swim. Just as you spring up to run to her rescue, the four-year-old begins panicking and screaming about having sand in her eyes. No one else is around, so what do you do? Triage takes no more than a split second: you run to save the toddler from drowning. Do you care about the four-year-old's pain and distress? Of course you do, but the imminent danger of death is far worse. It would be absurd for someone to accuse you of not being truly pro-life because of your actions.

Finally, the "pro-birth" claim is sometimes intended as the accusation that Christians do not care about the plight of low-income parents, especially single mothers. This is demonstrably false in a variety of ways. For example, contrary to popular belief, pro-life crisis pregnancy assistance centers, largely supported by churches and individual pro-life Christians, do far more than counsel women about alternatives to abortion. Consider Heartbeat International, an organization that was started in 1971 by an obstetrician and a refugee from Nazi Germany. Today it has a network of over 3,500 pregnancy assistance centers, maternity homes, and non-profit adoption agencies around the world. These affiliates provide prenatal care and other pregnancy-related assistance; but they also work to provide infant care supplies, clothing, transitional housing, free or affordable daycare, employment guidance, parenting classes, and a host of other services for women and their children. They even offer abortion recovery programs.[19] Aside from pro-life organizations, a host of other Christian charities around the world work tirelessly to provide assistance to single mothers. Statistics have shown, time and time again, that Christians give far more to charity, and they foster or adopt children at a higher rate than secular people.[20] Should we be doing more? The answer to that question is always yes. The point, however, is that the global church has always sought to alleviate the suffering of the poor and otherwise downtrodden.

Final Thoughts

In sum, the claim that Christians want to control women's bodies is a severe distortion of the pro-life position. It ignores the central question of the abortion issue: what the preborn *are*. Scientifically speaking, the preborn are distinct, living human beings from single-celled zygote onward; so if their right to life is to be challenged, it must be on the basis of some

---

[19] Heartbeat International, Life Trends: 2024 Report, https://www.heartbeatinternational.org/images/pdf/Life Trends Report Digital 2024 (web).pdf.

[20] For statistical information on charitable giving by Christian conservatives versus progressives, libertarians, and non-Christians, see Arthur Brooks, *Who Really Cares? The Surprising Truth About Compassionate Conservatism* (Basic Books, 2006).

physical criteria. As we have seen, this does not work. Any chosen property of the preborn, such as relative size or level of dependency, could also be used to rule out the equal value of some born human beings.

The pro-life position is the most inclusive because it says that preborn human beings have equal worth and dignity and thus the same rights as the rest of us. It is undeniable that crisis pregnancies resulting from rape present horrendously difficult circumstances, but the pro-life position is that killing an innocent preborn human because they were conceived in rape ignores the fact that they are just as valuable as their mother. Bodily autonomy rights always have limits, the most important being those that prevent the harm or death of an innocent human being.

Christianity is not merely "pro-birth," and pro-life activism is by no means limited to abortion prevention. Crisis pregnancy organizations, which are largely funded by the church, offer many support services to women both before and after their babies are born, such as medical care, material assistance, and education. Some are even equipped to offer residential programs and recovery services to women living in the aftermath of an abortion. The biblical view is that all lives are sacred and deserving of protection, thus we have an ethical obligation to help those in need with compassion, mercy, and love. Matthew 25 is apropos; it reveals how, upon his return, Christ the King will separate true believers from those who falsely claimed to be:

> "For I was hungry and you gave me something to eat; I was thirsty and you gave me something to drink; I was a stranger and you took me in; I was naked and you clothed me; I was sick and you took care of me; I was in prison and you visited me." Then the righteous will answer him, "Lord, when did we see you hungry and feed you, or thirsty and give you something to drink? When did we see you a stranger and take you in, or without clothes and clothe you? When did we see you sick, or in prison, and visit you?" And the King will answer them, "Truly I tell you,

> whatever you did for one of the least of these brothers and sisters of mine, you did for me." (vv. 35–40)

At the core of the Christian worldview is a deep love and affirmation of all humans as made in the image of God and a mission to care for the most vulnerable. Indeed, let us strive to show generosity toward pro-life rescue missions and compassion and support to women facing crisis pregnancies. Through such actions, we can promote the preservation of life, proclaim the gospel of Christ's forgiveness and redemption, and bear witness to the abundant life he freely offers.

CHAPTER 7

Objection #7: Christianity's Intolerance Has Spawned Violent Crusades and Inquisitions

Throughout much of my academic career, I (Ike) have also worked in the technology sector. This has been valuable in a number of ways, including providing opportunities to start conversations about faith with many who have no tie to a local church or any religious faith of their own. Once, when I joined a Monday morning team meeting at a venture-backed startup, my then-boss asked the team, "What did you do this weekend?" I was excited to share because at that time, I was devouring historian Tom Holland's *Dominion: How the Christian Revolution Remade the World*. Holland is a secular historian who writes about how Christianity reshaped Western societies with values like human equality, freedom of conscience, and the importance of protecting the weakest among us.[1] I shared with the team that I had started reading a book about how, throughout history, Christianity had given birth to some of the best things in Western civilization. My boss sarcastically engaged, "Oh, like the Crusades?" Seeing this as a moment to bring more light than heat, I said, "That's a great question. The Crusades are actually . . ." My boss cut me off, "That's enough. Probably not a good idea to talk about that." I was planning to explain how the Crusades were far more complicated than most people think.

The claim that Christianity's intolerance has been the cause of great evil in the world must be taken seriously. Centuries of violent Crusades and Inquisitions loom large in our culture's imagination. While there is rampant historical myth surrounding these episodes, they cannot be dismissed wholesale as rogue groups of self-proclaimed Christians behaving badly. Heinous crimes against humanity have been committed in the name of Christ, but on what scale, by whom, and under what political and cultural circumstances? More important, did these actions reflect the teachings of Jesus, his apostles, and the objectives of the original New Testament church? As is always the case with such notorious instances of human depravity, the history is incredibly complicated and thus prone to oversimplification, gross exaggeration, and misinterpretation.

In this chapter, we will examine the Crusades and Inquisitions within their historical context, in an effort to separate fact from common propaganda. What we shall find is that these were indeed terribly lamentable episodes, but far more complex than most summarizations reveal. Many who acted under the sign of the cross failed to live up to the tenets of the faith, which do not condone the intolerance and related violence that characterized those volatile centuries of holy wars, torturous examinations, and executions. In truth, Christianity teaches tolerance, freedom of religion, peacemaking, and the intrinsic worth of every human being;

---

[1] See Tom Holland, *Dominion: How the Christian Revolution Remade the World* (Basic Books, 2019).

and these values have shaped our intuitions about how we ought to treat those with whom we disagree.

Considering the Objection

Historically, the word *tolerance* has been associated with ideas like freedom of speech and the free exercise of religion. To show tolerance in the classical sense is to respect people who have different convictions and to refrain from coercion tactics, especially violence. This principle is integral to the Christian worldview and has, when rightly practiced, greatly benefited Western civilization.[2] In recent decades, however, "tolerance" has morphed into the idea that we must avoid openly judging the truthfulness or rationality of all other belief systems, because to express disagreement in any manner would be to make adherents of those systems feel disrespected or even oppressed. The irony here is that this view is self-defeating; it is inherently intolerant toward one group: those who believe we should be free to properly (logically and respectfully) critique other truth claims.[3] Another problem is that the "to each his own

---

[2] For a helpful comment on this notion of tolerance, see Garrett J. DeWeese and J. P. Moreland, *Philosophy Made Slightly Less Difficult: A Beginner's Guide to Life's Big Questions* (IVP Academic, 2005), 86–87.

[3] Consider the following argument:

1. The modern version of tolerance (MVT) is that one ought not conclude that any perspective is false in service of being kind and accommodating to all perspectives.
2. Christianity claims that Christian beliefs are uniquely true (CBUT).
   2a. CBUT entails not-MVT because Christianity concludes that Christianity is uniquely true and that any perspective that denies central elements of Christianity (such as Islam, Hinduism, and Buddhism's rejection of Trinitarian monotheism, for example) is false (not-MVT) on that score.
3. Therefore, if MVT, then not-CBUT.
4. However, MVT validates all perspectives (1) including CBUT (2).
5. Therefore, if MVT, both CBUT (4) and not-CBUT (3).

truth" attitude, when carried out consistently, has terrible consequences; it prohibits the open disagreement with worldviews that include ideas like racial supremacy and the acceptability of genocide. By contrast, the classical—and Christian—understanding of tolerance says that while we should not use coercive force to change someone's mind, we certainly have a moral obligation to strongly and unequivocally condemn things like racism and defend anyone vulnerable to the outworking of its nefarious purposes. This means we actually have a duty to fight against the modern version of tolerance.

Many in the broader culture are unaware of how deeply problematic the modern version of tolerance is, and one of the ramifications of this has been a tendency to regard Christianity as inherently intolerant because of its claim of exclusivism (Jesus as the only way to salvation), its teaching on sexuality, or because of a shallow understanding of historical episodes such as the Crusades and Inquisitions—or, all of these reasons. The accusation will never go away, since objective truth claims related to morality and religion in general are a prime target. Thus, for the sake of truth, Christians must willingly suffer this rejection for the sake of Jesus while remaining committed to joyful and humble (classical) tolerance of those with whom we disagree (Jas 1:2–4). We are strangers in a strange land, to use Moses's phrase (Exod 2:22).

Christianity also teaches that humankind is a fallen, sinful race that fails to conform to godly standards over and over again, and will continue to do so until Christ returns and ends this broken, earthly order of things. Those who profess Christianity still sin, sometimes spectacularly. It should come as no surprise that throughout the church's history, some Christians have targeted other people or people groups due to a lack of tolerance (in the classical sense). Still, there is much work that can and should be done to clarify and correct, and the pursuit of truth is never a

---

6. However, (5) denies the law of noncontradiction.
7. Therefore, not-MVT.

vain endeavor. Let us consider, then, two of the more infamous historical episodes commonly cited as paradigmatic of Christianity's violent intolerance: the Crusades and the Inquisitions.

The Crusades

During the reign of Constantine (AD 272–337), the first Roman emperor to convert, Christianity was finally legalized.[4] This was a monumental turning point for the early church, which had suffered cultural opposition and even the martyrdom of some of its central figures since the apostolic age. As one popular historian writes, "Christianity moved swiftly from the seclusion of the catacombs to the prestige of palaces."[5] Once it became enmeshed with statecraft, Christianity attracted a great number of people—particularly those with political ambition—but many of these "converts" retained elements of pagan belief and practice.[6] This set the stage for the misappropriation of the Christian faith, and this began in some quarters within a matter of decades. While Constantine had advocated for religious toleration of pagans, those who followed him in imperial leadership in the fourth and fifth centuries abandoned this ideal. They persecuted pagan priests, burned their temples, and destroyed their idols.[7]

To be sure, plenty of other historical examples of religious intolerance and related violence wrongly carried out under the banner of Christianity could be described, but the Crusades of the high Middle Ages are arguably the most notorious and most often misconstrued. The tale that is typically told is that Christian intolerance reached a boiling point by

---

[4] The Edict of Milan (AD 313).

[5] Bruce Shelley, *Church History in Plain Language*, 5th ed. (Zondervan Academic, 2021), 115.

[6] Shelley, 123.

[7] See John Dickson, *Bullies and Saints: An Honest Look at the Good and Evil in Christian History* (Zondervan, 2021), chaps. 6 and 11.

the eleventh century, with popes and princes stirring up so much hatred toward Muslims and Jews that a series of holy wars ensued. First, the Crusaders set out to reclaim Jerusalem for Christianity, torturing, killing, and pillaging all along the way. Upon their arrival in the holy city, an indiscriminate massacre was carried out against the resident Muslims and Jews, and Jerusalem was retaken. Bloodthirsty Crusaders, hyped on religious zeal, executed similar campaigns for well over a century. And interfaith relationships have suffered ever since. "The verdict seems unanimous," writes medieval history scholar Paul Crawford: "From presidential speeches to role-playing games, the crusades are depicted as a deplorably violent episode in which thuggish Westerners trundled off, unprovoked, to murder and pillage peace-loving, sophisticated Muslims, laying down patterns of outrageous oppression that would be repeated throughout subsequent history."[8] So much for a religion of loving your neighbors and turning the other cheek, say Christianity's critics. Is this characterization even close to the truth?

Human history is incredibly messy. Conflicts like the Crusades were understood in many different ways even while they were occurring. They have been recounted and reinterpreted many times over the ensuing centuries, and there is even an entire subdiscipline of historiography (the study of how histories are written) devoted to the Crusades. Attaining a perfectly accurate account is an impossible goal, to be sure. But we have more than sufficient evidence to judge summaries like the one above as serious distortions and to confidently conclude that the Crusades resulted from a convoluted combination of political and ecclesial dynamics, economic concerns, moral corruption, enemy conquests, and the supreme religious significance of the Holy Lands for Christians, Muslims, and Jews alike. A properly detailed historical analysis is well beyond the scope of this chapter, but a general outline of events paired with the insight of

---

[8] Paul F. Crawford, "Four Myths About the Crusades," *The Intercollegiate Review* (Spring 2011), 13.

esteemed historians specializing in the medieval period will help us put the Crusades in better perspective.

The first Crusade began in 1096, but the key events leading up to it can be traced to Muhammad, a political leader and the founding prophet of Islam. When he was forty years old, Muhammad began sequestering himself in a cave for extended periods of spiritual meditation. On one of these occasions (he claimed), he was visited by the angel Gabriel, who began revealing the laws of God (eventually collected in the Quran). Muhammad gained a following and organized a military force for the purpose of waging war (jihad) against Arab towns and then the trading city of Mecca.[9] The new religion was both a faith and a form of governance, which powerfully motivated jihad; if a soldier died during battle, he was considered a martyr and (according to Islam) would be rewarded with a sensual paradise for eternity. Expansionism was a cornerstone of the Muslim worldview; as historian and Crusades expert Thomas Madden explains:

> Traditional Islamic thought divided the world into two spheres, the Dar al-Islam (Abode of Islam) and the Dar al-Harb (Abode of War). The Dar al-Islam consisted of those lands directly ruled by Muslims and subject to Islamic law. The Dar al-Harb, which included the Christian world, was the place in which Muslims were enjoined to wage jihad against unbelievers, capturing their lands and subjecting their peoples. In this way it was believed that the Dar al-Harb would shrink and the Dar al-Islam would correspondingly increase until it covered the entire world.[10]

Thus, within just eight years of Muhammad's death in 632, an emerging Muslim empire had taken over all of North Africa and Cyprus, and most

---

[9] Thomas F. Madden, *The Concise History of the Crusades* 3rd ed. (Rowman & Littlefield, 2013), 2.

[10] Madden, 3.

of the Middle East and Spain.[11] In 636, Muslim troops entered Palestine, and a lengthy siege began, eventually ending with the surrender of the Christians and Jews who lived in Jerusalem.[12] Within a century, Persia, Egypt, and Syria had all been taken and subjected to Muslim rule.[13] By the eighth century, half to two-thirds of Christendom had been conquered.

Despite the aggressive spread of the Muslim Empire, Christian pilgrims continued to travel to the Holy Lands to worship, and mass pilgrimages took place in the ninth and tenth centuries. Muslim leaders were, generally speaking, tolerant of both Christian and Jewish pilgrims, who were regarded as worshippers of the same God (yet theologically misguided) and permitted to live in relative freedom and peace—as long as the expansion of the Muslim Empire was in no way hindered, that is.[14] As Crawford explains, during this same period, from the mid-ninth century to the mid-tenth century, "Benedictine monks were driven out of ancient monasteries, the Papal States were overrun, and Muslim pirate bases were established along the coast of northern Italy and southern France, from which attacks on the deep inland were launched."[15] Counterattacks were organized by the Byzantine Empire, with a measure of success in terms of regaining territories.

In the eleventh century, major persecution of Christians began. The Church of the Holy Sepulchre in Jerusalem was destroyed in 1009, and then Jerusalem was violently seized—from the occupying Muslims—by a fanatical Turkish branch of Islam that was on the rise. These Seljuk Turks made enormous military progress in the east. And in 1095, about forty years after the Great Schism had separated Western and Eastern Christianity, the Eastern (Byzantine) emperor pleaded with Pope Urban II for help.

---

[11] See Rodney Stark, *God's Battalions: The Case for the Crusades* (HarperOne, 2009), 12.

[12] See Stark, 18.

[13] See Madden, *The Concise History of the Crusades*, 3.

[14] See Madden, 3.

[15] Crawford, "Four Myths About the Crusades," 14.

Although the pope did not have authority over military troops, he had massive political influence. That year, at the Council of Clermont, he set the wheels in motion to defend Constantinople (the capital established by Constantine) and try to retake possession of the Holy Lands. Fighters joining the cause were promised forgiveness of sins and other spiritual benefits.

Thus, the First Crusade was launched in 1096. "From a distance," writes Madden, "the crusades do look like great armies organized and directed by the church against enemies of Christ, yet from within the ranks it was a very different picture. . . . A crusade army was, in effect, a loosely organized mob of soldiers, clergy, servants, and followers heading in roughly the same direction for roughly the same purposes."[16] About 40,000 men marched eastward, well aware of the treacherous nature of the journey and the great financial sacrifice. Some were experienced mercenaries, and some desired to plunder enemy territory; but most of the noblemen who took up the call were God-fearing and passionate about defending the church. As Madden explains, "A crusade army was a curious mix of rich and poor, saints and sinners, motivated by every kind of pious and selfish desire, yet it could not have come into being without the pious idealism that led men to risk all to liberate the lands of Christ."[17] Unsurprisingly, small factions with their own agendas sprang up during the church-sanctioned movement, and some committed war crimes of the worst imaginable sort. In Germany, for example, many Jews, including women and children, were slaughtered for their financial resources or in religious retaliation. These rogue Crusaders believed that since Jews had been responsible for the crucifixion of Christ, these multi-city massacres were justified. It should be noted that some local bishops did everything they could to protect the Jews, but many still perished.[18]

---

[16] Madden, *The Concise History of the Crusades*, 10.

[17] Madden, 13.

[18] Madden, 18.

After defeating the Turkish forces in the heavily fortified city of Nicaea (host of the Council of Nicaea in 325) in 1097, the focus of the Crusade moved to Antioch, which was won in June 1098. It was another year of political intrigue and minor battles before a few thousand Crusaders finally reached Jerusalem, where many Muslim and Jewish people were killed. But it was not the total massacre that some accounts suggest:

> By the standards of the time, adhered to by both Christians and Muslims, the crusaders would have been justified in putting the entire population of Jerusalem to the sword. Despite later highly exaggerated reports, however, that is not what happened. A great many of the inhabitants, both Muslims and Jews, were killed in the initial fray. The best modern estimates put the number of dead between three and five thousand people. Yet many others were allowed to purchase their freedom or were simply expelled from the city. Later stories of the streets of Jerusalem coursing with knee-high rivers of blood were never meant to be taken seriously. Medieval people knew such a thing to be an impossibility. Modern people, unfortunately, often do not.[19]

The Holy City was won and a Latin kingdom of Jerusalem established, but it was not to last. Six more major Crusades were launched, but none as successful as the first. Jerusalem was eventually retaken by Muslim forces in 1291, and the era of the Crusades ended with the fall of the city of Acre that same year.

The Crusades were a mixture of defensive fighting, political maneuvering, and misplaced religious enthusiasm. Many people suffered and died by the Crusaders' swords, and what we would regard today as egregious war crimes were certainly committed. Were horrendous acts carried out in the name of Christ during the Crusades? Undoubtedly. Yet, the

---

[19] Madden, 32.

far more important question is whether those acts were consistent with Christian doctrine, and the answer to that is that they were most assuredly not. The moral history of the church during the era of the Crusades is out of sync with the timeless moral logic of Christianity. We must remember that political Christianity is, at best, only partially Christian.

The Inquisition

During his papacy, Pope John Paul II formed commissions to study historical episodes that have stained the reputation of the Catholic church. In 1978, the first year of his reign, he launched an open-ended investigation into the infamous Galileo affair. He did the same for the Inquisition in 1994. In his Apostolic Letter for the Year of Jubilee in 2000, *Tertio Millennio Adveniente*, John Paul II expressed deep sorrow and repentance on behalf of the Catholic church for past mistakes, including "intolerance and even the use of violence in the service of truth."[20] He went on to say that the church has an

> obligation to express profound regret for the weaknesses of so many of her sons and daughters who sullied her face, preventing her from fully mirroring the image of her crucified Lord, the supreme witness of patient love and of humble meekness. From these painful moments of the past a lesson can be drawn for the future, leading all Christians to adhere fully to the sublime principle stated by the [Second Vatican] Council: "The truth cannot impose itself except by virtue of its own truth, as it wins over the mind with both gentleness and power."[21]

---

[20] Pope John Paul II, *Tertio Millennio Adveniente* (2000), https://www.vatican.va/content/john-paul-ii/en/apost_letters/1994/documents/hf_jp-ii_apl_19941110_tertio-millennio-adveniente.html.

[21] Pope John Paul II.

A special Mass, a Day of Pardon, was held on March 12 of that year. It included extended public prayers of confession for sins of intolerance, including the use of coercive violence.[22]

Although these events were publicized, not much seems to have been done to enlighten the general public about the findings of the Commission, which had spent years investigating the Inquisition. As with the Crusades, the history is incredibly complex and has been grossly distorted, some claiming that millions were tortured and executed for heresy. While one chapter cannot offer a comprehensive historical treatment, it can at least present a fair summary of the church-sanctioned attempts to eliminate heresy. Preliminary clarification is necessary: "heresy" does not mean unbelief or having a different religion; it is the rejection of a particular tenet of Christianity and teaching another idea in its place. "The Inquisition" refers to an institution within the church that carried out a diverse series of coercive proceedings intended to ensure doctrinal purity.

The year 1184 is typically cited as the year the Inquisition was formalized, because this is when Pope Lucius III decreed that bishops should be proactive in identifying and curtailing heresy in their respective dioceses.[23] In the early thirteenth century, under Pope Gregory IX and then Pope Innocent IV, the activities of the Inquisition were centralized. Papal inquisitors, mainly Dominicans (members of a French order founded in 1216), were sent to European regions where heresy was gaining influence.[24] Although the maximum punishment for heresy was death, the

---

[22] For further detail, see the Vatican document "Day of Pardon (12 March 2000)," https://www.vatican.va/jubilee_2000/jubilevents/events_day_pardon_en.htm.

[23] The Ad abolendam bull was issued by the pope at the Synod of Verona on November 4, 1184.

[24] The Cathars of France were a primary target. See Robin Vose, "A Brief History of the Inquisition," Hesburgh Libraries of Notre Dame, Department of Rare Books and Special Collections, University of Notre Dame, 2010.

medieval inquests were rarely anything other than simple persuasion; even when torture was authorized by the pope as a method of examination, it was rarely employed.[25] As medieval history scholar Robin Vose explains, the objectives of the inquests "were mainly to prevent the overzealous prosecution of heretics by individual bishops and to enforce procedures that were meant to be penitential rather than strictly punitive."[26] Dickson elaborates:

> The process in a typical town went as follows: inquisitors gave a public sermon on heresy and true doctrine; they announced a thirty-day "period of grace" during which people could confess their wanderings or inform on known heretics; the formal inquiry itself involved interviewing witnesses and defendants; finally, inquisitors gave a public announcement of restoration or ongoing guilt. Those who were restored had to perform some penance, whether set prayers, a pilgrimage, temporary confinement in prison, or the wearing of a special cross for a period of time (sometimes for life). Those who resolutely refused to stop advocating heresy were declared guilty and handed over to state authorities for sentencing.[27]

The state had a vested interest in the elimination of heresy, as they believed it to be a danger to social order. Their threat of execution by burning at the stake was in itself a powerful deterrent.

The Spanish Inquisition, which began in the fifteenth century, is the most notorious episode of the church's involvement in official investigations of heresy. Until this point medieval Spain was by and large a land of religious syncretism, which flourished in the absence of definitive statements about heresy. Theological ignorance among Christians

---

[25] Dickson, *Bullies and Saints*, 221.

[26] Vose, "A Brief History of the Inquisition."

[27] Vose.

was rampant, and superstition and even witchcraft tainted both belief and devotional activities. "Religious practice among Christians was a free mixture of community traditions, superstitious folklore and imprecise dogmatic beliefs. . . . It was a situation that church leaders before the fifteenth century did very little to remedy," writes historian Henry Kamen.[28] As in many other Mediterranean regions, Christians, Jews, and Muslims lived alongside one another, and many Christians believed that salvation was just as attainable through the other Abrahamic faiths.[29] Still, fourteenth-century Spain was a place plagued by anti-Semitic attitudes, discrimination, and even hostilities, such as the massacres perpetrated by fanatical mobs in 1391, destruction of Jewish towns, and coerced baptism (which produced a multitude of *conversos*—new Jewish Christians).[30] It should be noted that royal authorities attempted to protect the Jews and condemned forced conversions, but many Jews saw the prudence of converting. As Christians, they could enjoy all the social and legal advantages that were denied to Jews, such as unrestricted land ownership, attainment of noble status, and intermarriage with the aristocracy.[31]

The following century brought a steady increase of anti-Semitic prejudice and hostility. In some Christian regions, anti-Semitism had been brewing for quite some time, partly because of the circulation of gruesome stories about Jewish atrocities committed against Christian infants and children.[32] Interfaith relations deteriorated further when some *conversos* who took advantage of the civil benefits of their Christian status continued to practice Judaism. Historian of religion Gretchen Starr-LeBeau explains why this exacerbated political and social tension:

---

[28] Henry Kamen, *The Spanish Inquisition: A Historical Revision* 4th ed. (Yale University Press, 2014), 7.

[29] Kamen, 8.

[30] Kamen, 15.

[31] See Gretchen Starr-LeBeau, *Seven Myths of the Spanish Inquisition* (Hackett, 2023), 28.

[32] Kamen, *The Spanish Inquisition* 26.

> European governments operated on the premise that Christians would naturally support their God-anointed king or queen. What if the conversos were not genuinely sincere Christians? Could they be trusted? Would they betray a kingdom to its enemies? Envy and jealousy might also have played a role . . . as those conversos who were economically successful benefited financially from their new status as Christians. Was their "conversion," then, simply an economic ploy?[33]

Growing suspicion became a significant catalyst for the 1478 formation of the Spanish Inquisition, which was requested by King Ferdinand V (he and his wife Isabella had political and economic motivations) and permitted by the pope. A few years later, the king appointed Tomás de Torquemada as First Grand Inquisitor of Spain, and this launched two decades of Jewish expulsions (by a 1492 edict) and judicial tribunals in which *conversos* were interrogated. Some (a small fraction, the most recalcitrant) were subjected to torture and even execution.[34] Such severe measures were not unique to the Inquisition; both were integral components of European tribunals.

By the early decades of the sixteenth century, thousands of *conversos* had been reconciled to the church (a process which often involved cash payment). *Conversos*, secret Muslims, and Protestants made up the largest numbers of those who were investigated. Some were convicted, but the vast majority of cases did not result in execution; the cumulative death toll by the end of the second decade of the sixteenth century probably did not exceed two thousand.[35] The Spanish Inquisition remained active in one form or another until its formal end in 1834. Based on extant records, it is estimated that approximately three thousand were executed

---

[33] Starr-LeBeau, *Seven Myths*, 28.

[34] See Dickson, *Bullies and Saints*, 224.

[35] See Kamen, *The Spanish Inquisition*, 68.

during its last three centuries.[36] With the exception of Torquemada's horrific campaign, the Spanish Inquisition was, at the time, known for its comparatively lenient policies and humane treatment of prisoners.[37]

Although it is important to correct the historical myth surrounding the Inquisitions, we should by no means minimize how egregious it is that *anyone at all* suffered or died for their religious beliefs or practices with the consent of the church. There is simply no justification for such evil. Christians should feel deep sorrow for any hatred or violence committed in Jesus's name. The Bible has harsh words of judgment for people who resort to such measures.[38] Consider Psalm 11, which tells us that God's people can take refuge in him in times of uncertainty and destruction, but that God judges people who use illicit violence: "The Lord examines the righteous, but he hates the wicked and those who love violence" (v. 5). Unjust violence is opposed to the ways of God. Likewise, any hatred that Christians have had toward those who are not Christians betrays the spirit of Jesus's call to love our neighbors as ourselves (Mark 12:31) and to avoid judging others (Matt 7:1–5; Rom 14:10).[39]

In light of the sins of hatred and violence committed in Jesus's name at any point in history, Christians everywhere should walk through this life in full acknowledgment that we are all sinners; and we know that the same fallen nature that existed in those by whose order or hands people were coerced, hurt, or killed in the past exists in us too. Scripture speaks generally of all humankind, "Their feet are swift to shed blood; ruin and wretchedness are in their paths, and the path of peace they have not known" (Rom 3:15–17). In light of this reality, we should live in a

---

[36] See Dickson, *Bullies and Saints*, 224–25, 227–28.

[37] See Dickson, 226–27.

[38] This does not mean that there are not legitimate uses of violence under proper authority. See Gen 9:6 and Rom 13:1–7.

[39] Jesus's command not to judge others' sins is different from our ability to make moral judgments. In the former case, judging others' sins actually commits the sin of pride; but in the latter case, we are simply making moral evaluations.

spirit of repentance about our tendency to sin against our fellow human beings, knowing that only through Christ is there grace, hope, and assurance of ultimate healing.

Final Thoughts

Christianity teaches that humanity is the crown of God's creation. As God's image-bearers, we have supreme value and significance among all creatures. Yet since Adam and Eve's loss of innocence in the garden of Eden, sin has tainted all of creation, including our own souls. The French philosopher and mathematician Blaise Pascal believed that only Christianity can account for this two-sidedness in humanity: "Man's greatness and wretchedness are so evident that the true religion must necessarily teach us that there is in man some great principle of greatness and some great principle of wretchedness."[40] Pascal is making a careful claim here. He's saying that whatever conclusion one comes to about the nature of religious or spiritual reality, one's decision must be able to account for the fact that humans are a grand contradiction of beauty and brokenness, goodness and evil, love and hatefulness, truthfulness and deceit. Our deep intuition is that things ought not to be this way, and Christianity reveals why they are.

Far from being a religion of intolerance, Christianity offers a more satisfactory version of tolerance through its notions of religious freedom, the role of the state, and its theology of peacemaking. First, the biblical notion that human beings have equal worth and dignity by virtue of being made in God's image assumes that people have the right to freedom of conscience with respect to their views on religion and spirituality. The early church father Tertullian argued as much when Christians were facing religious intolerance in the Roman Empire: "See that you do not end up fostering irreligion by taking away freedom of religion

---

[40] Blaise Pascal, *Pensées* (Penguin, 1966), 149, 430.

and forbid free choice with respect to divine matters, so that I am not allowed to worship what I wish, but am forced to worship what I do not wish. Not even a human being would like to be honored unwillingly."[41] Moreover, Scripture suggests that the role of the state is not to enforce religious orthodoxy or to coerce people to believe certain things, but to protect them from just such evildoers who would seek to use illicit force. In Romans, Paul writes, "For rulers are not a terror to good conduct, but to bad. Do you want to be unafraid of the one in authority? Do what is good, and you will have its approval. For it is God's servant for your good. But if you do wrong, be afraid, because it does not carry the sword for no reason. For it is God's servant, an avenger that brings wrath on the one who does wrong" (13:3–4).

True Christian faith does not lead to religious violence, but to radical peacemaking. Jesus says, "Blessed are the peacemakers, for they will be called sons of God" (Matt 5:9). James agrees that it is not violence and coercion that serve God's purposes, but "the fruit of righteousness is sown in peace by those who cultivate peace" (3:18). Any failures to live according to the centrality of freedom of conscience, the proper role of the state, and the call to peacemaking should not count against Christianity, but against the Christians who have failed to live out the call of Christ.

[41] See Tertullian, *Apology*, trans. S. Thelwall, rev. and ed. Kevin Knight (Christian Literature, 1885), chap. 24, https://www.newadvent.org/fathers/0301.htm.

CHAPTER 8

Objection #8: Christianity Is Colonialist

I (Ike) remember reading as a child Dr. Martin Luther King's "I Have a Dream" speech and feeling exhilarated by his biblical call for justice, his Christian vision for human equality, and his assurance that one day, all of humanity, regardless of color, religion, or race, would live together in freedom and unity.[1] However, as much as I was exhilarated, I also possessed some childish naivete about both the significance of the speech and the problem that it was seeking to address. My family is of European descent, and growing up I knew very few people from other backgrounds. However, as I got older, talking about history with my father became one of my favorite pastimes. He told me about the Civil War and heroes of his like Frederick Douglass and John Brown. I soon learned that the story of

[1] See Martin Luther King, "'I Have a Dream' Speech by Dr. Martin Luther King, Jr., March on Washington for Jobs and Freedom, August 28, 1963," Marshall University, OneMarshallU, https://www.marshall.edu/onemarshallu/i-have-a-dream.

the United States, and indeed humanity, was filled with both moral heroes and those who hated, enslaved, and killed others based on their ethnicity.

For me, learning about the sins of racism and slavery was slow and safe. But for many, the depravity of the human heart toward other humans for things like their names, their skin color, their religion, their country of origin, or their race is a brutal and daily reality. Sadly, the depravity of the human heart extends even to those who call themselves Christians, and church history has many tales of so-called Christians claiming superiority for themselves and oppressing those who look different or who come from a different culture. For these reasons, some have simply come to the conclusion that Christianity is racist or colonialist. Some would say that Christianity is the white man's religion that seeks to dominate or change any person or culture who fails to fit into its white culture. For example, Elijah Muhammad, the former leader of the Nation of Islam, claimed that Christianity was "a religion organized and backed by the devils for the purpose of making slaves of black mankind."[2]

However, this does not accurately represent the way of Jesus that we read about in the Bible or important lessons about how that way of life has been embodied in Christian history. Instead, while Christian history is indeed filled with stunningly evil examples of racism and other kinds of ethnic hatred and injustice, biblical Christian religion shows a concern for justice, ethnic equality, and care for the lowest in society that many Christians have splendidly observed. In this chapter, we consider the objection that Christianity leads to racism, colonialism, and slavery. We will explore some of the worst ways in which Christians have indeed been guilty of these things, but we will also point to core elements of Christian theology and practice that show that Christianity is a religion of ethnic equality and care for the downtrodden. Charlatans abound, and those who call themselves "Christian" have surely committed evils on the most

---

[2] Elijah Muhammad, *Message to the Blackman in America* (Secretarius Memps, 1973), 18.

egregious scale. Yet the influential core of the world Christian movement, its theology, and its Lord, speak a better word. The chapter will close with thoughts on how Jesus's life and redemptive work point us to the glorious message of his grace and love for all peoples.

Considering the Objection

In no way should this chapter be read as an attempt to minimize the sins of racism that are so obviously a part of the Christian church's past and present. However, what this chapter intends to demonstrate is that the biblical message of ethnic equality and justice was and is heeded by many in the global Christian church. That said, we must be clear-eyed about the many ways in which that message has not been heeded. We will explore "Christian" racism, colonialism, and slavery in turn. First, let's consider the accusation that Christianity is racist. Before exploring this accusation in depth, it is important to clarify what we mean by *race*. Most people use this term as a term intending to indicate some real difference between peoples based on their ethnicity or skin color (e.g. the African race or white people). While we don't deny that skin comes in many shades, *race* is a term invented relatively recently in the West, though prejudice based on physical attributes goes potentially far back into antiquity.[3] In the sixteenth and seventeenth centuries, European scientists interested in the science of classification invented the concept of race to categorize humans by the broad geographical places of origin where they were first encountered: "European, Asiatic, American, and African."[4] However, these scientists went beyond classification by

[3] For a study on the proto-racist attitudes held by some in antiquity, see Benjamin Isaac, *The Invention of Racism in Classical Antiquity* (Princeton University Press, 2004).

[4] Neil Shenvi and Pat Sawyer, *Critical Dilemma: The Rise of Critical Theories and Social Justice Ideology—Implications for the Church and Society* (Harvest House, 2023), 213.

physical attributes to include mental and cultural features as well. As Neil Shenvi and Pat Sawyer report, "Unsurprisingly, the categories developed by European scientists placed Europeans at the top of the racial hierarchy and justified the enslavement of Africans, who were regarded as inherently inferior, both mentally and culturally."[5] Charles Darwin posited as much when discussing the differences in mental and moral capacity between Europeans ("the highest races") and those whom he broadly referred to as "the lowest savages." "Nor is the difference slight in moral disposition between a barbarian, such as the man described by the old navigator Byron, who dashed his child on the rocks for dropping a basket of sea-urchins, and a Howard or Clarkson; and in intellect, between a savage who uses hardly any abstract terms, and a Newton or Shakspeare [*sic*]."[6] Darwin suggests that while there is not a fundamental (that is, in kind) difference between the races, there are serious differences in degree such that Europeans are mentally and morally superior.

This "scientific" scheme of classification by race was supported by the "doctrine of discovery," wherein a previously inhabited land was considered "undiscovered until a European Christian nation 'discovered' it."[7] This doctrine, along with a sense of racial superiority, gave license for European colonization, which will be discussed later; but it carried with it the assumption that European culture and civilization were of primary value in the emerging geopolitics of the age of discovery.[8] Despite the

---

[5] Shenvi and Sawyer, 213–14.

[6] Charles Darwin, *The Descent of Man, and Selection in Relation to Sex* (Project Gutenberg, 2000), chap. 3, retrieved November 9, 2024.

[7] Brandon Washington, *A Burning House: Redeeming American Evangelicalism by Examining Its History, Mission, and Message* (Zondervan Reflective, 2023), 77.

[8] There is no need to reject the common phrase "age of discovery" and its cognates, so common in Western history books because *for the Europeans*, they were indeed seeing places that were new *to them* as Europeans. What we reject is the connotation that the lands were undiscovered by anyone before being visited by Europeans.

fact that these lands had peoples and cultures before European arrival, the idea of discovery rendered these people in a lesser state in the minds of Europeans, as if the people's pre-European reality were irrelevant. For example, the interest in the translation and dissemination of Buddhist texts by Western intellectuals came at the expense of appreciating the uniqueness of the Buddhism practiced by peoples throughout Asia. The result was an "idealized Buddhism" based on texts rather than the complex and culturally unique Buddhisms practiced by the actual religious adherents of Asian lands.[9] Racial superiority went much further than the misappropriation of indigenous religions as Europeans often simply thought that the peoples they encountered were backward and corrupt. Dutch traders in Indonesia, for example, often looked down on the local Indonesian populations they interacted with and the Chinese labor they imported to work the land. Said one tobacco planter, "[The] Chinese are bold arch-swindlers and the Javanese are lazy and hot tempered."[10] These feelings of superiority by Europeans based on the cultural and ethnic factors are at the heart of the claim that Christianity is racist.

The charge of racism is perhaps most poignant when considering the relationship between Europeans and Africans. European Christians have often been guilty of feelings of racial superiority toward Africans, which led to slavery and other abuses of human rights. While we will look more closely at slavery later, the racism required to justify chattel slavery included theological and philosophical underpinnings. Blackness itself was often seen as a sign of God's curse on someone as the fulfillment of Noah's curse on his son Ham, who saw Noah's naked body when Noah was drunk in his tent. While it is not clear what Ham did to his

---

[9] Harold A. Netland, *Christianity and Religious Diversity: Clarifying Christian Commitments in a Globalizing Age* (Baker Academic, 2019), 83.

[10] Budiman Minasny, "The Dark History of Slavery and Racism in Indonesia During the Dutch Colonial Period," *The Conversation*, July 2, 2020, https://theconversation.com/the-dark-history-of-slavery-and-racism-in-indonesia-during-the-dutch-colonial-period-141457.

father (some options include sexually assaulting his father, assaulting his mother, or simply seeing his father in an inappropriate fashion), Noah pronounces a curse on Ham's son Canaan: "Canaan is cursed. He will be the lowest of slaves to his brothers" (Gen. 9:25).[11] While this passage does nothing to indicate that *blackness* is what was cursed, historically, many Christians, Jews, and Muslims have interpreted black skin as the physical manifestation of the curse of Ham. American Presbyterian minister James A. Sloan declared as much in 1857: "The Great Lawgiver saw fit, in his good pleasure, not to destroy Ham with immediate death, but to set a mark of degradation on him. . . . All Ham's posterity are either black or dark colored, and thus bear upon their countenance the mark of inferiority which God put upon the progenitor. . . . Black, restrained, despised, bowed down are the words used to express the condition and place of Ham's children."[12]

Even when freed from slavery, Africans were not able to outrun the culture of inferiority that existed in Christianity. For example, Richard Allen, a Methodist preacher who had bought his freedom from slavery, faced so much racial prejudice in post-Revolutionary Philadelphia that he started the African Methodist Episcopal Church simply to have the ability to worship and serve God freely.[13]

The history of racism is long and terrible, but these examples serve to show that there ought to be no sweeping under the rug the fact that Christians have been guilty of racism. What is fascinating about these examples is how poorly they reflect actual biblical teaching and key examples from Christian history on the value and interaction of different

---

[11] For helpful options on interpreting this passage, see John Goldingay, *Genesis*, Baker Commentary on the Old Testament: Pentateuch (Baker Academic, 2020), 155–56.

[12] David M. Goldenberg, *The Curse of Ham: Race and Slavery in Early Judaism, Christianity, and Islam* (Princeton University Press, 2003), 176.

[13] See Esau McCaulley, *Reading While Black: African American Biblical Interpretation as an Exercise in Hope* (IVP Academic, 2020), 75.

cultures and ethnicities. Starting with Jesus, who was not a white man but a Middle Eastern Jew,[14] you see concern for those who were ethnic outsiders. This is clear in his deliverance from demonization of the Syrophoenician woman's daughter (Mark 7:24–29), his dignifying of the Samaritan woman at the well (John 4:1–26), and his healing of the Roman centurion's servant (Luke 7:1–10). In these examples, Jesus addresses Gentiles, commends their faith, attends to their theological concerns, and provides spiritual and physical healing at their requests. Even when Jesus suggests that his calling is only to the Jews, such as in the deliverance of the Syrophoenician woman's daughter ("Let the children be fed first, because it isn't right to take the children's bread and throw it to the dogs" [Mark 7:27]), his honoring of the woman's request for deliverance is a foreshadowing of the fact that Jesus's ministry would culminate in his Great Commission to make disciples of all nations (Matt 28:18–20). This commission would have been scandalous to Jesus's predominantly Jewish audience, but Jesus was showing that his church was to be a home for all peoples who would follow him.[15]

The earliest Christian church took Jesus's example to heart, but they also experienced the human tendency to divide over culture. The Gentile Luke reports in Acts 6 that in the early days of the church, when the number of disciples was increasing, a dispute arose between the Jerusalem church's Hellenistic and Hebraic Jews regarding the daily distribution of food to the two groups' population of widows. It seems that however food was being distributed, it led to the favoring of Hebraic Jews over the Hellenistic Jews. New Testament scholar Craig Keener explains that Jews from the Diaspora all over the ancient world

---

[14] See James Martin, "Jesus Was Not White. Here's Why We Should Stop Pretending He Was," *America: The Jesuit Review*, June 26, 2020, https://www.americamagazine.org/faith/2020/06/26/jesus-was-not-white-heres-why-we-should-stop-pretending-he-was.

[15] See Craig L. Blomberg, *Jesus and the Gospels: An Introduction and Survey*, 3rd ed. (B&H Academic, 2022), 213.

would often come back to Jerusalem as they got older to be buried in Israel, which was a sign of virtue. "Thus an apparently disproportionate number of foreign Jewish widows . . . lived in Jerusalem."[16] Given this disproportionality and the socioeconomic problems caring for widows from different backgrounds entailed, perhaps it is no wonder that a young group of Jesus's followers would favor their native Hebraic population over the foreign population. However, to allow this to continue would not be in keeping with the way of Jesus, which was marked by generosity and justice (see for example Jesus's warning in Matt. 23:23–24). So, the leaders of the church asked the church to appoint seven men in good standing to oversee the fair distribution of food. "So they chose Stephen, a man full of faith and the Holy Spirit, and Philip, Prochorus, Nicanor, Timon, Parmenas, and Nicolaus, a convert from Antioch" (Acts 6:5). The names here are telling as all of them are Greek. This means that to solve the problem of ethnic favoritism, the church chose "first-or second-generation Jewish immigrants to Palestine—hence members of the offended minority. One is even a proselyte—a former Gentile who had converted to Judaism."[17] The earliest Christians, while not free of all temptation to sin, understood that the way of Jesus means that you practice "the royal law prescribed in the Scripture, Love your neighbor as yourself," but if the church failed and showed "favoritism, you commit sin and are convicted by the law as transgressors" (Jas 2:8–9).

This means the Christianity that formed from the earliest communities of Jesus's followers had an ethic of equality that put them at odds with the politics of ethnicity (and sex) of the Roman world around them. Theologian Esau McCauley notes that when Paul says in Galatians 3, "For those of you who were baptized into Christ have been clothed with

---

[16] Craig S. Keener, *The IVP Bible Background Commentary: New Testament* (IVP Academic, 2014), 338.

[17] Keener, 338.

Christ. There is no Jew or Greek, slave or free, male and female; since you are all one in Christ Jesus" (vv. 27–28), he is making a political statement that is both this-worldly and otherworldly (both political and theological) at the same time. He is saying that being a Roman citizen does not put someone in a better place to receive heaven's blessings. He is saying that being one of the Caesars does not make one closer to divinity. He is saying that "being a Jew does not make you more of an heir to the promises in Christ than being a Gentile."[18] Paul's teaching would have been a radical redefinition of the nature of one's background, especially for the question of Jewish identity in the Galatian church. Our ethnicities are not erased through Jesus, but neither do our ethnicities make us candidates for unfair or preferential treatment given the magnitude of God's grace. This biblical ethic of equality is precisely what was behind Dr. Martin Luther King's protests of Jim Crow laws. "King said that the current practices throughout the North and the South were a manifestation of the kingdom of darkness and that the kingdom of the beloved son called for a different way."[19]

Sitting behind all this concern for equality and justice lies a simple distinction that is vital to understanding Christianity's relationship to favoritism. Surely, Christianity as an empirical (that is, how it may be observed in the world at various times) religion has had racists in its midst. Yet strictly speaking, Christianity is not a white religion or a black religion or even a Jewish religion. Biblically speaking, Christianity is the fulfillment of God's plan through Abraham and the children of Israel that "all the peoples on earth will be blessed through you" (Gen 12:3). This is a simple distinction, and perhaps it seems artless next to the empirical racism embodied often among Christians. But to reject the central Christian claims about God's plan to redeem for himself a people from among all of the peoples of the earth, to reject God's invitation that

[18] McCauley, *Reading While Black*, 114.
[19] McCauley, 62.

"whosoever will, let him take the water of life freely" (Rev 22:17 KJV), to reject the persecuted and ethnically Jewish Savior of Jew and Gentile alike is shortsighted when faced with the simple truth that Christianity is a religion for all humankind that rejects ethnic favoritism and any doctrine of racial superiority.

It is not merely the feelings or expressions of racial superiority that are at the heart of the concern that Christianity leads to racism, colonialism, and slavery. Instead, we must also contend with the actions of "Christians" who colonized or enslaved peoples on the grounds of doctrines of racial or ethnic superiority. Let us next address the history around Christianity, colonialism, and missionaries. When people accuse Christianity of being colonialist, they typically mean that Christian missionaries, in league with some form of political power, represent Christianity as a religiopolitical force that is coercive in its attempts to win converts. Such was Gandhi's experience of Christianity in India: "Unfortunately, Christianity in India has been inextricably mixed up for the last one hundred and fifty years with British rule. It appears to us as synonymous with materialistic civilization and imperialistic exploitation by the stronger white races of the weaker races of the world."[20] There has surely been such an ugly history to reckon with in Christianity. For example, Portugal's conquest of lands in fifteenth-century Africa was supported by Pope Nicholas V in order for Portugal to benefit from Africa's resources and for Africa to become civilized and Christianized.[21] One recent African response to the West's history of mixing colonialism and missionary activity is Kenyan President Jomo Kenyatta's critique of Christians' interfering with "female circumcision,"

---

[20] Mahatma Gandhi, *Gandhi on Christianity*, ed. Robert Ellsberg (Orbis, 1991), 44.

[21] See Washington, *A Burning House*, 64–65. This eventually led to a slave trade where captured and enslaved Africans were "tithed" to Catholic churches that were established on the continent.

claiming that Christian attempts to stop the practice are attempts to erase Kikuyu culture.[22]

Starting in 1600, with license from the English Queen Elizabeth I, Britain gradually subdued more than 70 percent of the Indian subcontinent through its East India Company and later through direct colonial control. Despite the fact that the Christian church had been established in India for centuries prior through the so-called Thomas Christians and through Roman Catholic missions, "The nineteenth century witnessed a large influx of Western missionaries to India, so the missionary presence in India coincided with the period of British colonial rule."[23] While the history is complex and even included colonial authorities attempting to thwart missionary activity, the impression left on most Indians was that Christianity was inexorably linked to British power and control.[24] In its colonial administration of the Philippines, the United States carried a sense of a God-given mission. Consider Sen. Albert Beveridge's speech from 1900:

> The Philippines are ours forever, "territory belonging to the United States," as the Constitution calls them. And just beyond the Philippines are China's illimitable markets. We will not retreat from either. We will not repudiate our duty in the archipelago. We will not abandon our opportunity in the Orient. We will not renounce our part in the mission of our race, trustee, under God, of the civilization of the world. And we will move forward to our work, not howling out regrets like slaves whipped to their burdens but with gratitude for a task worthy of our strength and

---

[22] Jomo Kenyatta, *Facing Mount Kenya: The Tribal Life of the Gikuyu* (Secker and Warburg,1938; Random House, 1965), 128. Citation is to the 1965 edition. "Female circumcision," more accurately known as female genital mutilation, is the nonmedical removal of the clitoris and often leads to other injuries, chronic pain, and long-term medical complications.

[23] Netland, *Christianity and Religious Diversity*, 106.

[24] Netland, 107.

> thanksgiving to Almighty God that He has marked us as His chosen people, henceforth to lead in the regeneration of the world.[25]

Beveridge's sense of mission included a duty to God and country to fulfill a racial, economic, and moral mission that conflates the tasks of reaching China's markets with "the regeneration of the world." Another example is the Canadian Residential School system, an alliance between the Canadian government and various Christian churches, which affected over 150,000 children of Canada's First Nations. According to Canada's Truth and Reconciliation Commission, in a period of over one hundred years, Canada "separated children from their parents, sending them to residential schools. This was done not to educate them, but primarily to break their link to their culture and identity."[26] Thousands of children died from disease, and thousands more were subject to various forms of abuse in the schools.

These examples of the conflation of colonial power and religious influence are the truth behind the accusation that Christianity leads to an abusive colonialism. Yet these examples stand out, not just for the feelings of grief they rightly induce, but for how alien they are to the most important examples in Christian thought and history, which have sought to care for the lowly and oppressed and to use any worldly power, not for self-aggrandizement, but for the benefit of others. In the early Christian church, prior to the legalization of Christianity in the Roman Empire, Christians used what little power and resources they had to serve others, especially those who were suffering the most. For example, during

---

[25] Albert J. Beveridge, "U.S. Senator Albert J. Beveridge speaks on the Philippine Question, U.S. Senate, Washington, D.C., January 9, 1900," USC US-China Institute, https://china.usc.edu/node/20547.

[26] The Truth and Reconciliation Commission of Canada, *Honouring the Truth, Reconciling for the Future: Summary of the Final Report of the Truth and Reconciliation Commission of Canada* (Truth and Reconciliation Commission of Canada, 2015), 2, https://irsi.ubc.ca/sites/default/files/inline-files/Executive_Summary_English_Web.pdf.

a plague epidemic in AD 260, Bishop Dionysius of Alexandria commended the work of faithful Christians who were caring for the sick, even at their own peril: "The best of our brothers lost their lives in this manner, a number of presbyters, deacons, and laymen winning high commendation so that death in this form, the result of great piety and strong faith, seems in every way the equal of martyrdom."[27] It is notable that leaders of the church are commended in this way. In fact, this type of behavior scandalized the pagan Emperor Julian who hated "the impious Galileans" for supporting "not only their poor, but ours as well, everyone can see that our people lack aid from us."[28] About this culture of tangible care for the weakest in society, the historian Michael Green notes that the early Christians "made the grace of God credible by a society of love and mutual care which astonished the pagans and was recognized as something entirely new."[29] Of course, having more mainstream power changes things by attracting people who would misuse Christianity for their own gain or wield power without care for the weakest in society as some of the previous examples show. But the simple truth of the Christian ethic in such teachings as "I am my brother's keeper," "Do unto others as you would have them do onto you,"and "It is more blessed to give than to receive" made the Christian church a force for good in the world.[30]

Even when Christians misused their power for colonial gains that resulted in theft, murder, and slavery, it was Christians who used the resources of the true Christian message to call for prophetic correction and repentance. The Catholic priest Bartolomé de Las Casas, upon seeing the condition of oppressed peoples in the New World, indicted the Spanish colonial government (and its alliance with the pope) for the

---

[27] Rodney Stark, *The Rise of Christianity: A Sociologist Reconsiders History* (Princeton University Press, 1996), 82.

[28] Stark, 84.

[29] Michael Green, *Evangelism in the Early Church*, rev. ed. (Eerdmans, 2003), 171.

[30] Stark, *The Rise of Christianity*, 84.

injustice of its colonial control. "It is most evil, tyrannical, libelous of the sweet name of Christ, and the cause of infinite new blasphemies against the true God and the Christian religion."[31] Las Casas knew the true Christian message and used his authority as a priest to correct the colonial powers. Other Christians have used their voice and power to lobby for global reform of the human tendency to colonize and to politically control weaker peoples. It was the Lebanese Christian Charles Malik who led the effort to draft the UN Universal Declaration of Human Rights, which includes, among other things, rights to free speech, religion, life and liberty; a rejection of slavery; equal protection under the law; due process; the rights to asylum, property, and peaceful assembly; and special care for mothers and children. It was Malik's belief that all humans are made in the image of God that led to statements in the Declaration such as "All human beings are born free and equal in dignity and rights. They are endowed with reason and conscience and should act towards one another in a spirit of brotherhood."[32] While the sins of colonialism are inexcusable, the Christian faith has the intellectual resources to reject the misuse of power for colonial gain; and there is no justification of colonialism that can stand up to the life and message of Jesus Christ.

Even in Christian missionary work, despite terrible missteps in the past, the best of Christian missionaries have long sought to avoid a softer colonial control of indigenous churches in lands to which missionaries have been sent. For example, Henry Venn, the head of the Church of England's Church Missionary Society in the early twentieth century, sought to turn over control of churches to local leadership as soon as possible. "He believed if the missionaries respected the habits of the people they converted, the churches they established would come to be seen as

---

[31] Bartolomé de Las Casas, "Thirty Very Juridical Propositions," in Washington, *A Burning House*, 78.

[32] Universal Declaration of Human Rights, United Nations, https://www.un.org/en/about-us/universal-declaration-of-human-rights.

part of the way of life of each community, rather than as the Europeans' church."[33] The goal was not to use religion to manipulate and control local populations, but to offer the gospel and to "move on."[34] One of the fastest growing missionary sending organizations in the twentieth century, the Foursquare Church, founded by missionary and preacher Aimee Semple McPherson, eventually codified this policy of empowering indigenous leadership and local churches to govern and lead themselves:

> It [missions] requires releasing the church in self-expression and self-government. . . . Its style of worship, fellowship, teaching, caring, and outreach must be appropriate to the culture in which it is ministering. Such contextualizing of ministry releases the church to serve its society more effectively and fruitfully. Further, the church must be structured in such a way as to release contextualized ministry. Form must follow and free function.[35]

Christian missionary practice is not inherently colonialist. When it is modeled after biblical principles, it leads not to central Western control, but to empowered local leadership. The preceding are just a few counterexamples to some awful trends in Christian practice that we do not deny, but that we reject as not in keeping with true Christian thought and practice. Christians have provided and do provide better and more beautiful examples of godly missionary practice that rebuke our tendency to sin and affirm God's love for all peoples in Jesus.

This leads us to the darkest part of the accusation that Christianity leads to racism, colonialism, and slavery: the fact that Christians have often been guilty of practicing and justifying the enslavement of other humans.

---

[33] The Truth and Reconciliation Commission of Canada, *Honouring the Truth*, 31.

[34] Truth and Reconciliation Commission of Canada, 31.

[35] John L. Amstutz, *Disciples of All Nations: Continuous Mission Until He Comes* (Los Angeles: Foursquare Media, 2009), 37, https://foursquaremissionspress.org/wp-content/uploads/2017/06/Disciples-of-All-Nations.pdf.

A common view is that of Hector Avalos, who argues, "The Bible endorses horrific ideas and practices. One of these horrific practices is slavery, one of the most tragic and vicious institutions ever devised by humanity. For about 1900 of the last 2000 years of Christian history, it was self-described Christians who kept slavery, in some form or another, a viable institution."[36] The key passage that people like Avalos point to is Leviticus 25, which prohibits the enslavement of fellow Israelites but seems to allow for the enslavement of Gentiles.

> Your male and female slaves are to be from the nations around you; you may purchase male and female slaves. You may also purchase them from the aliens residing with you, or from their families living among you—those born in your land. These may become your property. You may leave them to your sons after you to inherit as property; you can make them slaves for life. But concerning your brothers, the Israelites, you must not rule over one another harshly. (Lev 25:44–46)

This seems fairly categorical at face value: the Hebrews were allowed to buy and sell and inherit other human beings in the ancient world. Perhaps the New Testament fails to make this question any less difficult since Jesus did not directly address the keeping of humans in a state of slavery, and Paul seems to affirm the practice, "Slaves, obey your human masters with fear and trembling, in the sincerity of your heart, as you would Christ" (Eph 6:5; see also Col 3:22). These teachings lead to the conventional wisdom, and indeed moralistic accusation, that Christianity is *in favor* of the practice of slavery. Richard Dawkins assumes as much in describing the changing moral Zeitgeist in the modern West: "Slavery, which was taken for granted in the Bible and throughout most of history, was abolished in civilized countries in the nineteenth century. . . .

---

[36] Hector Avalos, *Slavery, Abolitionism, and the Ethics of Biblical Scholarship* (Sheffield Phoenix, 2013), 4.

In society, there exists a somewhat mysterious consensus, which changes over the decades."[37] He argues that things like slavery are affirmed by historical religions because religion is merely a product of culture, not of divine revelation, so of course, religions like Christianity will simply mirror the moral norms of their times. Christians today may reject slavery; but if they do so, it is because they are simply the products of their changing cultures, not because of some divinely inspired religious texts.

The justifying reasons for the practice of slavery among those in history who called themselves Christians are manifold. Historian Noel Rae explains that among those who took part in the transatlantic slave trade, "Christian slaveholders . . . had two favorite texts, one from the beginning of the Old Testament and the other from the end of the New Testament."[38] The first of these, says Rae, is Gen 9:18–27. This is the "Curse of Ham" passage that we examined previously, which was used to suggest that "Ham was made black, and his descendants were made Africans."[39] The second favorite passage that Rae notes was used to justify slavery is Eph 6:5–7. Beyond a biblical basis for slavery, many Christians saw slavery as a way to fulfill the Great Commission. The Puritan preacher Cotton Mather, in 1706, received as a gift a "very likely slave," and believed that it was his job "to make him a servant of Christ." He took this mission to heart because, as Mather was known to pray upon seeing a black person, "Lord, wash that poor soul white in the blood of thy Son."[40] Mather tied the color of black humans' skin to the nature of their moral state before God, as did many other people who called themselves Christians. The evangelist George Whitefield argued that increasing the spread of slavery to the Georgia colony was a positive development, given all of the social and economic issues that their labor would provide for; yet

---

[37] Richard Dawkins, *The God Delusion* (Transworld, 2006), 300.

[38] Noel Rae, *The Great Stain: Witnessing American Slavery* (Overlook, 2018), 179.

[39] Rae, 180.

[40] Rae, 104.

he tied the practice of slavery to the moral mission that Christians had to convert Africans. Lisa Fields explains that while Whitefield thought slavery would ultimately lift up Africans in their relationship to God, "Whitefield preached that God could free Africans from sin, but lobbied to keep them enslaved to white men."[41] In many ways, the story of slavery in America is why many African Americans struggle to accept the Bible and the Christian faith. An early catechism for African slaves even taught the following:

> Who gave you a master and a mistress?
> God gave them to me.
> Who says that you must obey them?
> God says that I must.
> What book tells you these things?
> The Bible.[42]

All these things seem to simply reinforce a doctrine of inferiority and forced servitude on racial grounds. So might Christianity's detractors allege that Christianity simply leads to cultures where people will make slaves of one another. Since it is so well established in the Bible and in Christian practice, these detractors would say, there is no mistaking the Christian religion's propensity to enable a culture of slavery.

One must be clear-eyed about these historical facts and these allegations, yet we wholeheartedly disagree with the idea that Christianity

---

[41] Lisa Fields, "The Challenges of Racism Within Evangelicalism," in *Cultural Engagement: A Crash Course in Contemporary Issues*, eds. Joshua D. Chatraw and Karen Swallow Prior (Zondervan Academic, 2019), 168.

[42] Allen Dwight Callahan, *The Talking Book: African Americans and the Bible* (Yale University Press, 2006), 31–32. In this context, McCauley explains, "Early Black conversion entailed finding the real Jesus among the false alternatives contending for power in the culture." See Esau McCaulley, *Reading While Black: African American Biblical Interpretation as an Exercise in Hope* (IVP Academic, 2020), 78.

leads to cultures where enslaving other humans is affirmed or celebrated. The Bible itself is actually the key for seeing how God seeks to make slavery impossible among his people and, indeed, in the earth that he is redeeming. First, the Bible's teaching that all humanity is made in the image of God undercuts any sense that one group of humans has priority over other humans. "Then God said, 'Let us make man in our image, according to our likeness'" (Gen 1:26). The word "image" means that humanity represents God's authority. The word "likeness" has connotations of divinity, meaning that humanity is "godlike" in how they represent God's authority.[43] The Christian perspective on reality is that all of humanity, including all the cultures and ethnicities that exist, has divine authority and dignity before God. This is an ontological distinction, that is, one made with respect to the *being* or *existence* of human persons. The problem for equality among human persons is, therefore, not ontological, but moral, albeit in a different way than might be affirmed by slavery's apologists.

The doctrine of the fall indicates that humanity has broken with God's design and standard and our relationship to God, through sin. This is how slavery enters the world. When Adam and Eve sinned, God pronounced to Eve, "Your desire will be for your husband, yet he will rule over you" (Gen 3:16). The word *desire* here equates to something like a desire to dominate her husband; but instead of her dominating him, he will use his strength to rule over her.[44] This is not what God wishes, but the desire to dominate or rule over others is the natural result of human sin. God contends with this attitude in the children of Israel, who indeed, kept slaves. In his commentary on Deut 15:14–15, Esau McCauley explains, though, that God uses his relationship to Israel as a means to slowly eliminate the practice: "In Israel, no Hebrew slave could

---

[43] See John Goldingay, *Genesis*, Baker Commentary of the Old Testament: Pentateuch (Baker Academic, 2020), 45.

[44] See Goldingay, 83.

be enslaved for more than six years, and when the slave was freed, he or she was to be given resources to start a new life."[45] For Gentiles who were held in slavery, God's plan was twofold. First, Gentile slaves could escape from slavery with assurances that they would be safe and free: "Do not return a slave to his master when he has escaped from his master to you" (Deut 23:15). Second, God's plan was (and is) to use the mission of his people in the world to eliminate the practice. The prophet Isaiah tells us:

> And many peoples will come and say,
> "Come, let's go up to the mountain of the LORD,
> to the house of the God of Jacob.
> He will teach us about his ways
> so that we may walk in his paths."
> For instruction will go out of Zion
> and the word of the LORD from Jerusalem. (Isa 2:3)

This verse indicates that Israel's mission is to help Gentiles willingly come under God's leadership, effectively making Gentiles part of God's people, subject to the law, thus requiring that no slaves be kept. We see this same goal in Paul's letter to Philemon in the New Testament, where Paul commands Philemon to accept his escaped slave, Onesimus, "no longer as a slave, but more than a slave—as a dearly loved brother" (Phlm 16). About Philemon, McCauley explains, "God intended to use Paul's familial depiction of Christianity to put exactly that type of pressure on the church to redefine and abolish the institution [of slavery]."[46] This is in keeping with the teaching of Jesus, who commands us to welcome children in his name (Matt 18:5), to receive outsiders as neighbors (Luke 10:25–37), to love our neighbors as ourselves (Matt 22:39), and to do to others as we would have them do to us (Luke 6:31).

---

[45] McCauley, *Reading While Black*, 145.

[46] McCauley, 157.

This made sense to the earliest Christians. Gregory of Nyssa, for example, argued that one cannot own another human since all humanity belongs to God. Rebecca McLaughlin quotes Gregory and explains well the logic of the early church. "'How much does rationality cost?' he asked, 'How many obols for the image of God? How many staters did you get for selling the God-formed man?' Likewise, Gregory's contemporary theologians Augustine and John Chrysostom saw slavery as not ordained by God but a result of sin."[47] Even so, it simply took Christian institutions too long to universally recognize and condemn the practice of slavery; yet it was Christians who reclaimed the Christian tradition of equality and abolition to fight for the end of the practice. Charles Haddon Spurgeon did this when he called slavery "a crime of crimes . . . an iniquity that cries out for vengeance." He did this despite the fact that many fellow Christians ostracized him due to his views.[48] Frederick Douglass did this when he argued that "slaveholding religion" is not true Christianity at all. "I love the pure, peaceable, and impartial Christianity of Christ; I therefore hate the corrupt, slaveholding, women-whipping, cradle-plundering, partial and hypocritical Christianity of this land."[49] Harriet Beecher Stowe did this when she vowed to her sister-in-law to write what became *Uncle Tom's Cabin*, the book that awakened the Christian conscience of many Americans toward the evils of slavery. Historian James M. McPherson tells us, "Mrs. Stowe (or perhaps God) rebuked the whole nation for the sin of slavery. She aimed the novel at the evangelical conscience of the North. And she hit her mark."[50] Modern anti-slavery movements to this

---

[47] Rebecca McLaughlin, *Confronting Christianity: 12 Hard Questions for the World's Largest Religion* (Crossway, 2019), 184.

[48] Washington, *A Burning House*, 180.

[49] Frederick Douglass, *Narrative of the Life of Frederick Douglass, An American Slave* (Lerner, 2014), 97.

[50] James M. McPherson, *Battle Cry of Freedom: The Civil War Era* (Oxford University Press, 1988), 89.

day are often driven by deeply Christian concerns.[51] Consider the work of the human trafficking prevention and survivor aftercare organization Compassion First, whose website explains, "Just like the biblical parable of leaving the 99 for the one. We believe in the inherent value of each person. This is our worldview: no one is forgotten by God."[52]

Final Thoughts

So, does Christianity lead to racism, colonialism, and slavery? Sadly, aberrant "Christian" cultures have often said so, but Christians have rightly retrieved the biblical impetus toward abolition that was embraced by the earliest Christians. Ethnicity is a category embraced by Scripture, but race is not. The biblical view is that all humanity is made in the image of God, and Christianity has no room for favoritism for any group on religious grounds. The world Christian movement has acknowledged the sins that characterized colonialism and the iniquities of slavery and have retrieved the biblical message that each human derives their right to liberty from God. Even more, there is good news in the person and work of Jesus of Nazareth that we ought to consider when we confront these issues. In Jesus, we receive the message that whoever has been oppressed is actually in a special place to receive God's blessings:

> Blessed are the poor in spirit,
> for the kingdom of heaven is theirs.
> Blessed are those who mourn,
> for they will be comforted.

---

[51] See for example, the Evangelical Alliance of the United Kingdom's Anti-Slavery Groups, https://www.eauk.org/current-affairs/politics/modern-slavery/anti-slavery-groups.cfm.

[52] "About," Compassion First, https://www.compassionfirst.org/about. See Luke 15:1–7.

Blessed are the humble,
for they will inherit the earth. (Matt 5:3–5)

Those who have been the victims of racism and slavery are uniquely seen and loved by God. Those enslaved humans who were passed on as an inheritance to their enslavers "will inherit the earth." This same Jesus dignified an African man, Simon of Cyrene, to carry his cross (Matt 27:32). For context, the crucifixion, while an act of Jesus's atonement for our sins, is also his enthronement as King. As the writer of Hebrews tells us, "We do see Jesus—made lower than the angels for a short time so that by God's grace he might taste death for everyone—crowned with glory and honor because he suffered death" (Heb 2:9). During this act of redemption, Jesus brought an African man alongside himself to participate in his enthronement. Jesus died and rose from the dead to show that worldly oppression and our sinful rebellion against God, ourselves, and each other will not have the last word. When the Holy Spirit filled Jesus's Jewish apostles in Acts 2, the accompanying sign was that Jews and Gentiles who worshipped God from "every nation under heaven . . . Parthians, Medes, Elamites; those who live in Mesopotamia, in Judea and Cappadocia, Pontus and Asia, Phrygia and Pamphylia, Egypt and the parts of Libya near Cyrene; visitors from Rome (both Jews and converts), Cretans and Arabs" were heard "declaring the magnificent acts of God in our own tongues" (Acts 2:5, 9–11). In a picture of heaven in the book of Revelation, then, we see "a vast multitude from every nation, tribe, people, and language" worshipping Jesus because "Salvation belongs to our God, who is seated on the throne, and to the Lamb!" (Rev. 7:9–10). So shall it be for all God's children, a full embracing of all skin tones, backgrounds, and homelands. All are welcome to worship before the throne of God.

CHAPTER 9

Objection #9: Christianity Is Anti-LGBTQ

Math has never been my (Ike's) favorite subject. Despite attending great schools as a kid, I never developed much mathematical motivation. But teachers are a gift, and because I had some great math teachers in middle school, I placed into sophomore-level math as a high school freshman. That meant that when I was a sophomore, my math class was mostly juniors and even a few seniors. (Don't mistake me; there was an even higher class for math-enthused sophomores that put them on an Advanced Placement trajectory that I was not enrolled in.) It was in that math class that I met a friend I'll call Robert. Robert was the only other sophomore in the class, and he and I connected over being the only fifteen-year-olds in a room of upperclassmen. We worked on homework and a class project together and further bonded over liking some of the same movies.

Robert was a bit of an outcast, and he wasn't the most socially adept. But he was my friend, and when I sensed an opportunity to tell him about my faith, Robert was eager to learn more and eventually confessed his own faith in Jesus. Robert was different, though, and everyone knew it. I may have been his only male friend, and his manner and style were not common for the suburban, athletic culture in which we lived. That's why I wasn't really surprised when Robert "came out" to me and confessed that I was his crush. I think I responded with compassion and friendship; and though I'm sure there are things I could have done to handle the situation better, I think Robert knew that I cared about him only as a friend and that our friendship wasn't in jeopardy just because he was attracted to guys. Even so, Robert and I grew apart before he transferred to another school the following year.

Because of how our friendship changed and perhaps because of my own immaturity, I don't know if Robert was able to reconcile his faith in Jesus with his sexual attraction to guys. But I know this: For many who have same-sex attraction, they sense deep discord between Christian teaching about sex, gender, identity, and marriage and their own desires, attractions, and instincts. Many sense that identifying as LGBTQ puts them into direct conflict with Christianity. For many others who would not identify as LGBTQ, but who are sympathetic with those who do, they would argue that either Christianity is false in its teachings about gender, sexuality, identity, and marriage or that Christianity is simply false altogether. Moreover, given the perceived irrelevance of religious belief in the West, the apparent conflict between Christianity and those who identify as LGBTQ is seen by some as just another example of religious bigotry and hatred. In this chapter, we will examine why so many would say that Christianity is anti-LGBTQ; consider the ways in which the Bible presents issues of gender, sexuality, identity, and marriage; separate the myth from the facts about the accusation that Christians are bigoted and hateful toward those who identify as LGBTQ; and talk about how the gospel is uniquely suited for people like my friend Robert and the many others for whom these issues are important.

Considering the Objection

This topic is not just academic. Many feel that Christian doctrine and many Christian subcultures are hateful toward people who identify as LGBTQ. But where does this feeling come from? Matthew Vines tells a story of how he and his sister explained to their parents that their friend "Josh," who also grew up in a Christian family, had come out:

> Mom, who had known and loved Josh since he was born, was devastated. Dad questioned Josh's judgment.
>
> "How does he know he can never marry a woman?" Dad asked.
>
> "Well, he's gay, Dad," I said. "Why would he?"
>
> "I'm not convinced he couldn't overcome this. It just seems like he's decided not to try."[1]

The subtext of this exchange is that these parents, who are traditional Christians living in the United States, cannot understand what it means that Josh has come out as gay. Their faith and culture have made them unsympathetic to this Christian brother who has revealed a deep part of his sexual identity. Vines shares that Josh later left the faith.

Many Christians have experienced tension or conflict around this issue, whether from Christian subcultures or from the broader changing cultural context in which coming out as gay (or any other nontraditional sexual identity) is becoming more common and accepted. It has become a common understanding that most Christians are homo- or transphobic

---

[1] Matthew Vines, *God and the Gay Christian: The Biblical Case in Support of Same-Sex Relationships* (Convergent Books, 2014), 15. For a helpful review, see Tim Keller, "The Bible and Same Sex Relationships: A Review Article," *Redeemer Report* (2015), https://www.redeemer.com/redeemer-report/article/the_bible_and_same_sex_relationships_a_review_article. See also Robert A. J. Gagnon, *The Bible and Homosexual Practice: Texts and Hermeneutics* (Abingdon, 2002); and R. Albert Mohler Jr., ed. *God and the Gay Christian? A Response to Matthew Vines* (SBTS Press, 2014).

at worst or unaccommodating to LBGTQ-identifying persons at best, and one could see why. Just think of the hateful protests of Westboro Baptist Church, whose members show up at military funerals with hateful signs, proclaiming that "These soldiers are dying for the homosexual [*sic*] and other sins of America."[2] Moreover, research sadly suggests that LGBTQ-identifying people suffer in some ways when keeping ties with Christian communities. The *American Journal of Orthopsychiatry* found that among people who were members of more sexually traditional religious communities in the US, those identifying as lesbian, gay, or bisexual had worse mental health outcomes than LGB populations outside of those religious communities.[3]

Moreover, traditional Christian theology has nothing positive to say about sexual relationships outside of traditional marriage. A gay-identifying theologian confessed this to me (Ike) as a friend, acknowledging that the Bible's many laws and statements regarding sexuality make it clear that it is impossible to gather support from the Bible for same-sex, bisexual, or transsexual relationships. Consider the law given to the children of Israel in Lev 18:22: "You are not to sleep with a man as with a woman; it is detestable." Consider Paul's indictment of all humanity for its idolatry in Rom 1:26–27: "For this reason God delivered them over to disgraceful passions. Their women exchanged natural sexual relations for unnatural ones. The men in the same way also left natural relations with women and were inflamed in their lust for one another. Men committed shameless acts with men and received in their own persons the appropriate penalty of their error."

---

[2] LaVendrick Smith, "Westboro Baptist Plans to Take Its Controversial Protest to NC Soldier's Funeral," *Charlotte Observer*, June 24, 2017, https://www.charlotteobserver.com/news/local/article157638719.html.

[3] David M. Barnes and Ilan H. Meyer, "Religious Affiliation, Internalized Homophobia, and Mental Health in Lesbians, Gay Men, and Bisexuals," in *American Journal of Orthopsychiatry* 82, no. 4 (2012), DOI: 10.1111/j.1939-0025.2012.01185.x.

Think also of Paul's warning to the Corinthians: "Don't you know that the unrighteous will not inherit God's kingdom? Do not be deceived: No sexually immoral people, idolaters, adulterers, or males who have sex with males" (1 Cor 6:9). The above verses communicate the sinfulness of same-sex lust and sexual activity while explaining that such behaviors and attitudes are out of step with God's natural order. Therefore, they carry real consequences. Many LGBTQ-identifying persons have heard or read these verses and come to the simple conclusion that Christian theology is anti-LGBTQ. Many go further, claiming that Christians who believe in the Bible's teaching on these issues are homophobic or transphobic.[4]

So, is it really true that Christianity is anti-LGBTQ? Are Christians, who believe in the Bible, homophobic and transphobic? What does that mean for the many LGBTQ-identifying people who are raised in Christian homes and the many more loved ones whose lives faithful Christians touch on a daily basis through work, family ties, school, neighborhood activities, and other places in society? In what follows we will separate the cultural baggage from true, biblical faith and show how the Christian worldview, while uncompromising on the nature of humanity, marriage, sexual ethics, and the good life, has the intellectual and spiritual

---

[4] These claims, of homophobia and transphobia, are odd, given that phobias are typically regarded as fears, and nothing in the Bible or in a great deal of Christian practice suggests that most Christians are afraid of LGBTQ-identifying people. However, in our culture of expressive individualism, fear and hatred are often conflated if the people in question are sexual or racial minorities. As Carl Trueman argues, "Language has been transformed to serve the purpose of rendering illegitimate any dissent from the current political consensus on sexuality. Criticism of homosexuality is now homophobia; that of transgenderism is transphobia. The use of the term phobia is deliberate and effectively places such criticism of the new sexual culture into the realm of the irrational and points toward an underlying bigotry on the part of those who hold such views." See Carl R. Trueman, *The Rise and Triumph of the Modern Self: Cultural Amnesia, Expressive Individualism, and the Road to Sexual Revolution* (Crossway, 2020), 21. For an explanation of how "expressive individualism" has arisen in the West, see Charles Taylor, *A Secular Age* (Harvard University Press, 2007), 475–476.

resources to be of great hope for those who today identify as LGBTQ and for those who wish to love such souls in Jesus's name.

Of first importance is an affirmation of the doctrine of divine love. The Bible tells us that "God is love" (1 John 4:16b). Being loving is deeply tied to God's character, being first an expression of the divine persons of the Trinity (Father, Son, and Spirit) to one another and then offered to humanity from God himself. This is why Jesus has come into the world: "For God loved the world in this way: He gave his one and only Son, so that everyone who believes in him will not perish but have eternal life" (John 3:16). God's love for humanity is the best kind of love: deep, sincere, self-giving, fatherly, motherly (though the Bible doesn't refer to God as "Mother"), faithful, strong, and pure. This means that when anyone stands before God, he or she is standing before someone who loves them and who points them to the sacrificial love of God in Christ. This, of course, doesn't mean that God approves of every inclination, desire, or act of each person; but God does indeed love all humanity, even those who are far from him in sin.[5]

None of this means that we do not all, apart from salvation through Jesus, sit under divine wrath. In fact, the surprising story of the revelation of God's love is our alienation from God due to sin. Humanity has received the greatest gift of love in Jesus Christ, but we persist in our sin toward and hatred of God and his ways. The good news, though, is that God's love doesn't depend on us. "Love consists in this: not that we loved God, but that he loved us and sent his Son to be the atoning sacrifice for our sins" (1 John 4:10). Sin is serious, but God's love is that much more serious. That is, the love of God and the deadliness of sin require an atoning sacrifice, and this literally means the death of Jesus

[5] This does not negate the fact that, in the sense that God hates sin and wishes its destruction, God hates the unrepentant sinner. See Pss 5:4–5 and 11:5. God can give himself to us in redemptive love and still justly doom to destruction those who remain in sin.

on the cross. That's how big the love of God is and how serious the nature of sin is. Therefore, we must solemnly affirm the gravity of any sin that separates us from God. Because of God's holiness, we are rightly judged for our sins. The LGBTQ-identifying person and the straight-identifying person sit equally under just judgment from God for their sin.[6] But both may equally benefit from the world-changing, life-altering, and altogether satisfying love of God in Christ Jesus through repentance and faith. Praise God that sin and judgment are not the end of the story for those who put their faith in Jesus!

Second, the biblical understanding of the nature of humanity helps us to make sense of what the Bible does and does not say about LGBTQ issues. Biblical anthropology is the set of doctrines that examines what it means to be made human, including the Bible's teaching around human sexuality. Biblical anthropology begins with two incredible claims. The first is that humans are made in the image of God, and the second is that the creation of humanity is good. The key biblical passage is worth citing at length:

> Then God said, "Let us make man in our image, according to our likeness. They will rule the fish of the sea, the birds of the sky, the livestock, the whole earth, and the creatures that crawl on the earth." So God created man in his own image; he created him in the image of God; he created them male and female. God blessed them, and God said to them, "Be fruitful, multiply, fill the earth,

---

[6] Throughout this chapter, the reader may notice that we use terms like "LGBTQ-identifying person" or "straight-identifying person" rather than "LGBTQ person," "straight person," or "cisgendered person." This is simply because these categories are not biblical, and what we propose here depends on a Christian anthropology that does not view people as straight, gay, etc. Instead, in Christian anthropology, humans are male or female, and the *telos* of sexuality is marriage between a man and a woman. We do not seek to demonize people who think differently, but we do seek to provide biblical clarity on the issues to which these categories refer.

> and subdue it. Rule the fish of the sea, the birds of the sky, and every creature that crawls on the earth. . . ." God saw all that he had made, and it was very good indeed. (Gen 1:26–28, 31)

Unpacking the meaning of this is helpful. The Genesis account claims that being made in the image of God means that humans (1) represent God's authority in ruling over and caring for the creation. The doctrine of the image of God drawn from these verses affirms that (2) in significant ways, humans (while finite, fallible, and limited) are similar to God in personality, rationality, creativity, sociality, and in moral value. The image of God also offers to humanity (3) the gift of sexuality whereby we have the calling to be fruitful and multiply, filling the earth with humanity to fulfill our responsibilities to rule and care for the creation.[7] And God's act in creating humanity is (4) good, and humans retain goodness with respect to their existence as God's "remarkably and wondrously made" creatures (Ps 139:14). Just as all humanity is loved by God, all humanity retains the image of God. Inclusive of one's gender, skin color, or any other feature of their existence, all humanity is made in the image of God.

Biblical anthropology, however, confounds modern conceptions of what it means to be a human being. The doctrine of the image of God assumes that human identity is bestowed on us from above by virtue of humans having been designed and created by God. This means that God designed humans to be either man or woman. This also means that God has a purpose for human sexuality. Sex is a gift given in marriage for connection and pleasure, but firstly for the bearing of children and the cultivation of the earth. The command to humanity in Genesis 1 is to "be fruitful, multiply, fill the earth" (Gen 1:28). Of course, we live in a fallen world where some couples are unable to bear children naturally due to the general effects of the fall, but this does not negate the purpose of human sexuality.

---

[7] As Nancy Pearcey says, "It was this embodied, earthly, sexual creature that God described as reflecting his own divine image." See *Love Thy Body: Answering Hard Questions About Life and Sexuality* (Baker, 2018), 36.

Since sex is tied to the bearing of children, the Bible's view is that sex is something that should only happen between a husband and a wife in the context of openness to bearing children. This means that sex is forbidden outside of man-woman marriage (Exod 20:14; 1 Cor 6:18). Lust is forbidden altogether (Matt 5:27–30). Marriages must be sexually pure (Heb 13:4). Marriages must be open to having children (Gen 1:28). Divorce for any reason except for marital unfaithfulness is off-limits (Matt 19:1–9).[8]

Along with this countercultural view of sex and marriage, the Bible honors singleness. This isn't an afterthought, but something modeled by the Lord Jesus and the biblical heroes John the Baptist and Paul. It would have been the standard for a Jewish rabbi to be married and to have children, but Jesus chose not to marry. So living a celibate life in service to the Lord is something to be treasured and a unique way that single opposite-sex attracted and same-sex attracted Christians can more closely model their lives on Christ that cannot be shared by married Christians. Singleness is something that is to be prized and honored according to the Christian worldview:

> I want you to be without concerns. The unmarried man is concerned about the things of the Lord—how he may please the Lord. But the married man is concerned about the things of the world—how he may please his wife—and his interests are divided. The unmarried woman or virgin is concerned about the things of the Lord, so that she may be holy both in body and in spirit. But the married woman is concerned about the things of the world—how she may please her husband. (1 Cor 7:32–34)

[8] Since we live in a fallen world, there may be times in a marriage where our human limitations or some sexual, mental, or physical wounds might forestall openness to bearing children. For example, think of a couple where one member has been the victim of abuse. In such a situation, it may be best to forestall sexual intimacy within a marriage (and thereby be closed to the bearing of children) for a time to seek healing.

Paul didn't write this to put married people down, but to show the benefits of singleness. Christians have a hard time accepting this teaching, first because we rightly see marriage as a way to express our sexual desires in a God-honoring way, and second, because we are tragically unable to see that our modern, sex-obsessed culture has infected the Church, too. Truly, our culture is obsessed with sex. This is why most people's sense of self leads them to identify themselves according to their sexual desires. When we were church planters in a progressive, urban area, my (Ike's) wife and I hosted the parents of our daughter's friend for dinner. In a conversation about this issue, the woman objected to Christianity's limits on sex and its place for singleness, exasperatedly proclaiming, "But sex is such a huge part of life!" Indeed, for the dominant culture, sex truly is a huge part of life. For many Christians in the West, we must understand that we're living in a sex-obsessed culture that has little to no understanding or celebration of celibacy and singleness.

The picture of sex in the Bible is stranger and more countercultural than perhaps you thought at first. And it is obvious that the dominant culture in the West today simply does not share the Christian perspective on this issue. This is because the dominant culture of the West today does not see human identity and purpose as something imposed on us from above but as something that arises from within each individual and imposed on others. That is, God is not telling us who we are, so instead, people come to an internal awareness of who they are and who they want to be over time. Knowledge isn't from above, but from within. This helps to explain a common experience for LGBTQ-identifying persons, whereby they come to a gradual realization that deep inside, they have a true, sexual identity that needs to be expressed through nontraditional sexual activity.[9] We can easily see why this is so, for in the modern world, where God is a bit of an afterthought for most Westerners, "If nature does not

[9] The story of how this came to be is very helpfully explained in Trueman, *The Rise and Triumph of the Modern Self*.

reveal God's will, then it is a morally neutral realm where humans may impose *their* will."[10] This is precisely the case for many people (whom we dearly love) today: they have chosen to define their own sexuality from within rather than receiving a sexual identity from above.[11]

But think about what has happened here. Instead of one's identity being tied to one's nationality, interests, giftings, family, or religion, a key to identity in the West today is one's sexuality. This is odd since sex is something that we engage in for just a fraction of our lives. We have jobs and hobbies, kids and communities. We sleep and eat and rest and listen to music, watch television, and read books. And there are times for all of us when we abstain from sex due to physical limitations or illnesses. There are so many things that we could use to construct our identities; but in the modern West and given our sexualized individualism, we define our identities by who we want to have sex with.[12] This ought to be appalling to anyone who thinks that there are and ought to be scores of things more interesting about ourselves beyond who we're attracted to sexually. Of course, God does not define our identity this way. According to God, our identity is constituted as members of his creation, male and female, created good and in his image. We have talents and interests to

---

[10] Pearcey, *Love Thy Body*, 24.

[11] In the modern conception of the self, the problems that need to be solved are self-acceptance for the LGBTQ-identifying person, societal acceptance and celebration of any sexual expression that goes along with the sexual identity, and medical/psychiatric treatment to change someone's biology to fit their perceived sexual identity. However, all of this simply deepens the alienation that the LGBTQ-identifying person suffers.

[12] As Trueman argues, "All the groups represented in the LBGTQ+ do share a number of things in common. From the perspective of my earlier narrative, they are clearly psychological and sexual in terms of their understanding of selfhood. To identify oneself by one's sexual orientation or to identify one's gender by inner psychological conviction locates the LGBTQ+ within the world of expressive individualism and psychological man." See *The Rise and Triumph of the Modern Self*, 340.

create and cultivate within his universe. We have earthly families, and we are welcomed into membership in the divine family through Jesus. But the sad fact of modern identity politics is that humans are reduced to their sexual desires. The world says you are "straight," "gay," "trans," "bi," or whatever other label for the self that emerges from your inner sense. Your desires and internal feelings have manufactured *who you are*.

But where do those desires come from? Part of the biblical answer to the accusation that Christianity is anti-LGBTQ is to explain where LGBTQ sexual desire comes from. Many people feel that Christianity demonizes these people as somehow being willfully steeped in sin and rebellion. While it is true that for all of us, our sin is willful and rebellious, somehow LGBTQ-identifying persons and those sympathetic to them feel as if this issue is viewed as being particularly damning. But according to the Bible, same-sex attraction and gender identity are not particularly the liability of any individual person, but the result of humanity's sin generally. Here's what we mean.

In Romans 1, Paul paints the picture of the knowledge of God being shared widely and generally with all humanity. 'For his invisible attributes, that is, his eternal power and divine nature, have been clearly seen since the creation of the world, being understood through what he has made. As a result, people are without excuse" (v. 20). However, this isn't really good news because even though there is evidence of God readily apparent everywhere, humanity has rejected this revelation of God. "For though they knew God, they did not glorify him as God or show gratitude. Instead, their thinking became worthless, and their senseless hearts were darkened" (v. 21). Since humanity rejected God, they put other things in God's place, particularly idols of created things that look like humans and animals; they "exchanged the glory of the immortal God for images resembling mortal man, birds, four-footed animals, and reptiles" (v. 23). But the result isn't mere idolatry. Of course, people today worship all kinds of things—money, status, power, and as we've been exploring, the self—but idolatry has a cost.

> Therefore God delivered them over in the desires of their hearts to sexual impurity, so that their bodies were degraded among themselves. . . . For this reason God delivered them over to disgraceful passions. Their women exchanged natural sexual relations for unnatural ones. The men in the same way also left natural relations with women and were inflamed in their lust for one another. Men committed shameless acts with men and received in their own persons the appropriate penalty of their error. (vv. 24, 26–27)

So same-sex desires and sexual impurity come not from the sins of the few, those who happen to have those desires, but from the many, all of us who have rejected God and embraced the worship of idols. Idolatry causes broken sexuality. While this passage focuses on same-sex sexual desire and activity, Christianity claims additionally that humanity's fall into sin can confuse our natural (that is, God-given) sense of male or female human identity.[13] This is important because it lays at the feet of all humanity the responsibility for our sexual brokenness. We are the victims of our own sin. Of course, each person is responsible for his or her own sin, but the way that these sins have entered the world is through human idolatry and rebelliousness against the knowledge of God revealed in creation.

Since sexual brokenness is the fault of all humanity, this means that Christians must have nothing but compassion for all who have broken desires. After all, we are all guilty of idolatry; therefore, we all ought to have compassion for those who suffer idolatry's effects. In this way, Christians ought to be advocates of the LGBTQ-identifying person without advocating or condoning the sinful desires that LBGTQ-identifying people may struggle with or even celebrate. This means that

[13] This would extend to those who suffer physical abnormalities with respect to their genitalia or chromosomes.

we embrace, love, pray for, and live as ambassadors of the kingdom for the benefit of LGBTQ-identifying persons, all the while rejecting sin and falsehood. Some might say that the slogan "Love the sinner, hate the sin" is too simplistic, but we think that this kind of loving the sinner and hating the sin, modeled after Jesus's compassion and empowered by the Holy Spirit, is profoundly good news for those living in the land of the shadow of death.

Many Christians already live out the compassion needed here, and many more need to learn to do so. Imagine this situation: You gradually come to the belief that though you are biologically male, your inner psychology has delivered the message that you're really a woman. You look at your body, and it does not match how you feel. Add into this the possibility that you receive the message from the dominant culture that it would be good if you used (what are often painful and irreversible) chemical or surgical means to change your body. Surely the process by which this occurs is different for everyone, but imagine if it were you. You come to despise your male body, wishing it were a female body. With this come thoughts of self-loathing and deep frustration of not being at home in your own body. To help yourself with this picture, think about your own body image: For any of us who have ever thought that we weren't good looking or thin or strong or intelligent or funny enough, you might reasonably imagine a degree of what such transgender feelings might be like.[14] Christians ought to have nothing but compassion for someone in such a situation. We must see the person suffering in such a way as a dear one for whom Christ died, one whom we ought to love in Jesus's name. None of this means that we must agree that this person's inner feelings correspond to reality, however. In fact, it would be simply unloving

---

[14] Of course, everyone's suffering is their own, so it would be false to say that we know exactly how another feels in any situation. However, it is still true that our own feelings and experiences are helpful reminders to us that suffering is real, and suffering with respect to one's body and sense of self is lamentable.

and heartless to go along with the lie that this biological male *really is* a woman. The dominant culture sins by mixing sorrowful feelings with lies about gender identity that are deeply unloving. True compassion requires deep love and fellow feeling with a commitment to the truth.

Final Thoughts

This is precisely where the Christian worldview must marshal the good news of Jesus to meet LGBTQ-identifying persons where they are. The gospel of Jesus Christ provides a unique appreciation of the suffering and brokenness of LGBTQ-identifying persons and a holistic redemption that modern identity politics simply fails to offer. Consider again what it would be like to find oneself in the place of an LGBTQ-identifying person. Perhaps you've expressed what you consider to be a deep part of who you are to someone and were despised and rejected. Perhaps your family or religious community didn't understand you and cast you aside. Perhaps you grieve not being able to have naturally born children with your spouse. Perhaps you went through painful chemical and surgical procedures in the attempt to align your biology with your sexual identity. Perhaps you've been abused by those in your community who you thought would accept you. What we are describing here is a broad-brush exploration of the kinds of sufferings that LGBTQ-identifying persons have every day.

Now consider Jesus, who expressed his deepest longings and desires only to be despised and rejected by humanity (Isa 53:3). His family rejected him (Mark 3:21) as did many in his hometown synagogue (Luke 4:14–30). Jesus never married nor fathered children. His body was physically broken and scarred by a culture and people who thought they were doing a good thing by scourging and crucifying him. None of this is to say that the life of the LGBTQ-identifying person is morally equivalent to the life of Christ. After all, Jesus suffered for the truth. However, Jesus understands the feelings of rejection, isolation, and alienation from which these dear people suffer. In Jesus, we have a Savior who has experienced the depth of human sorrow and who offers us salvation and redemption, substantial healing from our pains in this life, and resurrection with glorified bodies in the new creation.

One of the most beautiful stories of this redemption takes place in the book of Acts, where Philip, one of Jesus's followers, is led by the Holy Spirit to encounter a eunuch from Ethiopia traveling on a desert road in southern Judea. Eunuchs often served in the courts of royal authorities. These were men who were castrated for the purpose of serving female royalty. It was painful and humiliating. As Craig Keener notes, "Many Mediterranean peoples mocked [eunuchs] as deficient in manliness," and the eunuch "would not have been accepted as a full convert to Judaism."[15] This eunuch was reading the scroll of the Hebrew prophet Isaiah, who had prophesied about the Messiah about 800 years previously. When Philip asks the eunuch if he understands the words of Isaiah, the eunuch replies.

> "How can I," he said, "unless someone guides me?" So he invited Philip to come up and sit with him. Now the Scripture passage he was reading was this: "He was led like a sheep to the slaughter, and as a lamb is silent before its shearer, so he does not open his mouth. In his humiliation justice was denied him. Who will describe his generation? For his life is taken from the earth." The eunuch said to Philip, "I ask you, who is the prophet saying this about—himself or someone else?" Philip proceeded to tell him the good news about Jesus, beginning with that Scripture. (Acts 8:31–35)

The passage quoted here is Isa 53:7–8. It explains how Jesus understands the person who suffers sexual brokenness. Jesus was a victim of intense pain from the violence perpetrated against him just as was the eunuch.

---

[15] "Conversion of an African Official," in Craig S. Keener, *The IVP Bible Background Commentary: New Testament* (IVP Academic, 2014), 344.

Jesus was humiliated and deprived of justice as was the eunuch. No one should suffer such cruel and unusual punishment. Jesus never had a wife or fathered children, which are both off the table for a eunuch. Given that Jesus is fully man (while still being fully God), he surely experienced human loneliness, much like the eunuch would have. The Bible is telling us that Jesus understands the kind of brokenness that LGBTQ-identifying persons suffer in a unique way.

Had Philip and the eunuch read just a bit further, which they likely would have since we are told "Philip proceeded to tell him the good news about Jesus, beginning with that Scripture" (v. 35), they would have come to Isaiah 54, which says "'Rejoice, childless one, who did not give birth; burst into song and shout, you who have not been in labor! For the children of the desolate one will be more than the children of the married woman,' says the Lord" (54:1). The promise for the person who is sexually broken is that there is something more beautiful ahead even if the normal results of sex (read: one's naturally born children) are not possible. Had Philip and the eunuch read just a bit further, they surely would have come across this: "For the Lord says this: 'For the eunuchs who keep my Sabbaths, and choose what pleases me, and hold firmly to my covenant, I will give them, in my house and within my walls, a memorial and a name better than sons and daughters. I will give each of them an everlasting name that will never be cut off'" (Isa 56:4–5). While the world wants to reduce people to their sexual identity, God says that people with sexual brokenness can have a *name* in his family. For all of our alienation and sexual brokenness, Jesus the Christ is in a unique place to offer the kind of healing, redemption, and home that the politics of sexuality could never offer. The truth is that the gospel is good news for the LGBTQ-identifying person, the good news that God has come in Christ to redeem them, save them, heal them, and consecrate them for a life of purified desire fulfilled in relationship with Jesus.

CHAPTER 10

Objection #10: Christianity Has Obstructed Scientific Progress

Despite rigorous scholarship on the historical interplay of science and Christianity in recent decades, it is not uncommon to encounter the spurious claim that Christianity has repeatedly challenged scientific progress. This accusation has contributed to the enduring "warfare thesis," and the general impression that the Christian worldview is incompatible with the scientific enterprise. This has been further ingrained in cultural consciousness by influential public intellectuals such as twentieth-century astronomer Carl Sagan and contemporary astrophysicist and science celebrity Neil deGrasse Tyson. While such figures may excel in their respective scientific fields, their understanding of the relevant history and philosophy surrounding the intersection of Christianity and science is often inaccurate. As we shall see, a careful consideration of the historical data and analyses by respected historians (both secular and Christian) reveals that the examples often cited as support for the warfare thesis have been caricatured; political dynamics, misguided personal agendas, and philosophical conflicts were often the real sources of tension.[1]

Considering the Objection

There are three infamous episodes that are typically cited by skeptics as paradigmatic of the warfare between science and Christianity: the so-called Dark Ages, the Galileo affair of the seventeenth century, and the Scopes trial of 1925. Each will be examined in turn.

The "Dark Ages"?

In his famous work *The Age of Reason*, American Founding Father Thomas Paine sharply critiques organized religion in general, and Christianity in particular:

> However unwilling the partizans [*sic*] of the Christian system may be to believe or to acknowledge it, it is nevertheless true, that the age of ignorance commenced with the Christian system. . . . It is owing to this long interregnum of science, and to no other cause, that we have now to look back through a vast chasm of many hundred years to the respectable characters we call the Ancients. . . . But the Christian system laid all waste; and if we take our stand about the beginning of the sixteenth century, we look back through that long chasm, to the times of the Ancients,

---

[1] Moreover, Christianity—both its institutions and devout adherents—played a significant role in the rise of modern science. In fact, decidedly Christian convictions motivated and philosophically justified the rational pursuit of knowledge about the natural world. As. C. S. Lewis famously put it, "Men became scientific because they expected Law in Nature, and they expected Law in Nature because they believed in a Legislator." C. S. Lewis, *Miracles* (HarperCollins, 2015), 169.

> as over a vast sandy desert, in which not a shrub appears to intercept the vision to the fertile hills beyond.[2]

By "age of ignorance," Paine means the medieval period of western Europe (approximately 476 to 1450) or a portion thereof.[3] In this passage, he perpetuates the claim that Christianity was an obstacle to the advancement of knowledge—including scientific progress—during these centuries. This idea stubbornly persists in contemporary culture, in part due to poorly researched science documentaries, flawed textbooks, underinformed educators, and literary tropes. However, widely respected historians have shown that not only was there significant intellectual activity during the medieval period that belies the common pejorative term "Dark Ages," but the church actually played a vital role in the preservation of knowledge and the rise of formal education during a time fraught with barbarism, political volatility, and the decline of urbanization.

There is no denying that the warfare and fragmentation that followed the fall of Rome resulted in a period of marked cultural decline. Western Europe lost much of its contact with the Greek East, and as a result, fluency in Greek and access to much of the classical tradition were greatly diminished. Widespread illiteracy among the general population contributed to the problem. Even during those fraught centuries, however, scribes in Christian monasteries worked diligently to preserve, develop, and teach an intellectual tradition based upon the precious scholarly resources available to them. This included a few Latin

---

[2] Thomas Paine, *The Age of Reason*, in *The Writings of Thomas Paine*, vol. 4, *1794–1796*, ed. Moncure Daniel Conway (1796), https://www.gutenberg.org/ebooks/3743.

[3] The term "Dark Ages" has been used to designate different lengths of time. In England, it typically refers to the years spanning 410 to 1066, and in continental Europe, 476 to 800 (the fall of Rome to the crowning of Charlemagne). But in the United States, it is commonly used as a pejorative for the entire Middle Ages (from Late Antiquity until the Renaissance). See James Hannam, "Dark Ages," in *Dictionary of Christianity and Science*, ed. Paul Copan et al. (Zondervan Academic, 2017), 151.

manuscripts translated from the original Greek and the writings of early church fathers, some of whose work reflected extensive education in Greek thought, including natural philosophy (the study of nature).[4] The church's efforts during this period were essential; historian James Hannam explains:

> During this period, it is not an exaggeration to say that the light of learning was preserved by the Catholic Church, which was the only institution of the late Roman Empire to survive its collapse. The church also ensured the continuation of Latin literacy. Almost all extant ancient Roman literature was copied and recopied by Christian monks who labored to preserve this pagan and secular heritage, together with exclusively Christian writing.[5]

Instead of hindering intellectual advancement, the Christian church worked to safeguard what they could and build upon it. Natural philosophy was deemed valuable and was thus included in these projects. For example, an influential Spanish scholar and bishop of the seventh century, Isidore of Seville, gathered together all the Latin sources he could find and synthesized the material into a work of natural philosophy known as the *Origines*.[6] The Venerable Bede, an English monk of the eighth century, wrote an important work of natural philosophy entitled *On the Nature of Things*. And tenth-century French monk Gerbert of Aurillac (who went on to become Pope Sylvester II), was a mathematician who

---

[4] For example, Calcidius's Latin translation of Plato's *Timaeus*, which was highly influential in the medieval curriculum; Boethius's translations of Aristotle's writings on logic; and the mathematical texts of Euclid and Nicomachus. For further discussion, see Melissa Cain Travis, *Thinking God's Thoughts: Johannes Kepler and the Miracle of Cosmic Comprehensibility* (Roman Roads, 2022), chap. 2.

[5] Hannam, "Dark Ages," 151.

[6] See Michael H. Shank and David C. Lindberg, "Medieval Latin Christendom," in *Science & Religion: A Historical Introduction* 2nd ed., ed. Gary B. Ferngren (Johns Hopkins University Press, 2017), 54.

worked to promote the mathematical sciences in his cathedral school, where he introduced astronomical tools such as the astrolabe and armillary sphere.[7] Gerbert is even credited with the invention of the first fully mechanical clock, which used a pendulum to keep time.[8]

The medieval church was also instrumental in the proliferation of institutional education and the rise of the first universities. When Charlemagne came to power in the latter part of the eighth century, massive education reform began. During what is now known as the Carolingian Renaissance, he instituted cathedral and monastic schools and invited prestigious scholars to join his court, many of whom were appointed as bishops and abbots who oversaw the schools.[9] Natural philosophy—notably astronomy—was an important element in this Christian educational program, but there was no "revolutionary leap forward," according to historian of science David Lindberg:

> The importance of Charlemagne, his reforms, and the scientific achievements of the Carolingian period is to be found not in novelty, but in the recovery and preservation of important portions of the classical tradition, the establishment of schools, the spread of literacy, and (in the case of astronomy) attempts at geometrical representations of various planetary phenomena. All of this laid the foundation for a true and nearly full recovery of the classical tradition in the eleventh, twelfth, and thirteenth centuries.[10]

---

[7] Shank and Lindberg, 54.

[8] See George Ryan, "The Pope and the Pendulum: The First Mechanical Clock Was a Medieval Catholic Invention," uCatholic.com, March 27, 2019, https://ucatholic.com/blog/the-pope-and-the-pendulum-the-first-mechanical-clock-was-a-medieval-catholic-invention/.

[9] See David Lindberg, *The Beginnings of Western Science*, 2nd ed. (University of Chicago Press, 2007), 196–197. See also Olaf Pedersen, *The First Universities: Studium Generale and the Origins of University Education in Europe* (Cambridge University Press, 1997).

[10] Lindberg, 197–98.

In subsequent centuries, the fruits of this revival included the rise of urban cathedral schools as well as a variety of public schools that were open to anyone who could pay the tuition.[11] These schools experienced an explosion of growth, and by the twelfth century, the first universities were formed: in Bologna by 1150, in Paris by 1200, and in Oxford by 1220.[12]

Thanks to the work done by the church to protect, recover, and expand learning during the volatile medieval period, general literacy increased, many schools were instituted, and higher education emerged. The university curricula, which was heavily influenced by Aristotelian thought, included studies in natural philosophy, which set the stage for the scientific revolution of the sixteenth and seventeenth centuries.[13] As Cambridge University historian Seb Falk puts it in the epilogue of his book, *The Light Ages*, "Rather than a synonym for backwardness [the term 'medieval'] should stand for a rounded university education, for careful and critical reading of all kinds of texts, for openness to ideas from all over the world, for a healthy respect for the mysterious and unknown."[14] Had it not been for the heroic efforts of the medieval church, this renaissance of learning would likely have begun much later and taken far longer.

The Rise of Modern Science

Although astronomical studies were not emphasized in the medieval university arts curricula, such instruction was typically available to all interested students.[15] Aristotle's geocentric cosmology, with the earth fixed at the center and surrounded by revolving, concentric crystalline spheres

---

[11] Lindberg, 205.

[12] Lindberg, 219.

[13] The term "scientific revolution" has fallen somewhat out of favor in the contemporary history of science literature, but it is still common parlance in many circles.

[14] Seb Falk, *The Light Ages* (W. W. Norton, 2020), 297.

[15] See Lindberg, *The Beginnings of Western Science*, 267.

containing the moon, Mercury, Venus, the sun, Mars, Jupiter, and Saturn, had been gradually syncretized with Ptolemy's mathematical model of observed planetary motions. The result was a geometrically unwieldy composition of orbits and epicycles meant to "save the appearances" (make sense of naked-eye astronomical observations) while retaining perfect circular motion. The church, which had adapted major portions of Aristotle's philosophy for theological ends, readily embraced this cosmology, which harmonized well with a literalistic reading of biblical passages such as Eccl 1:5, which speaks of a rising and setting sun.[16]

The church-endorsed Aristotelian-Ptolemaic model was the intellectual inheritance of Polish astronomer Nicolaus Copernicus (1473–1543). A devout Christian, he regarded geocentrism as aesthetically distasteful and mathematically incoherent, so he constructed a heliocentric model that, in his view, better reflected God's supreme wisdom and glory. Published in *The Revolutions of the Heavenly Spheres*, the Copernican model was not based on any new observations; and (contrary to popular belief) it was no more accurate than Ptolemy's in terms of predicting future planetary positions. However, moving the sun to the center and situating the earth in its orbit reflected Copernicus's philosophical convictions about the mathematical elegance of the cosmos. In his book's prefatory dedication to Pope Paul III, he explained that the great system of the universe was harmoniously and rationally framed for the sake of mankind by "the Best and Most Orderly Workman of all."[17] The great appeal of his model was the "fixed symmetry of its parts," a mathematical unification in which the diameters of the planetary orbits are scaled in relation to one another such that changing the size of one orbit proportionally resizes the orbits of the others. Copernicus explains

---

[16] Other examples of verses that seem to suggest an immobile earth are 1 Sam 2:8b and Ps 104:5. Biblical scholars today recognize that such passages were intended as metaphorical or phenomenological language.

[17] Nicolaus Copernicus, *Revolutions of the Heavenly Spheres* in Great Books of the Western World, vol. 15 (Encyclopaedia Britannica, 1990), 508.

that "this correlation binds together so closely the order and magnitudes of all the planets and of their spheres or orbital circles and the heavens themselves that nothing can be shifted around in any part of them without disrupting the remaining parts and the universe as a whole."[18] He argued that this reflected the aesthetic sensibilities of a divine Workman far better than the Ptolemaic scheme, which he believed lacked appropriate rational harmony. Thus, Copernicus's theological and philosophical views facilitated progress toward the discovery of the true arrangement of the planets. He did not see any conflict between his model and Christian doctrine; he recognized that interpreting Scripture in light of a cosmological system was misguided.

The scientific revolution gained critical momentum when the Copernican model was embraced and championed by Johannes Kepler and Galileo Galilei. Kepler, a devout Christian in the Lutheran tradition, became convinced of Copernicanism while studying at the University of Tübingen, where his most influential professor argued (unofficially, of course) that the Copernican system accounted for celestial phenomena in a more mathematically coherent and harmonious way. "It was undoubtedly the beautiful harmonic regularities 'so pleasing to the mind' that appealed strongly to Kepler's sense of the aesthetic and induced him to become such an enthusiastic Copernican," writes eminent historian of astronomy Owen Gingerich.[19] Indeed, Kepler's entire life's work was driven by his search for the harmony of the world—the mathematical archetypes that offer God's image-bearers a glimpse into the divine mind. He regarded the calling of natural philosophers as the priestly exegesis of the book of nature—God's general revelation of himself to rational creatures. In a letter to an associate he wrote, "I had the intention of becoming a theologian. For a long time I was restless: but now see how God is, by

---

[18] Copernicus, *Revolutions of the Heavenly Spheres*.

[19] Owen Gingerich, *The Eye of Heaven: Ptolemy, Copernicus, Kepler* (American Institute of Physics, 1993), 307.

my endeavors, also glorified in astronomy."[20] It was this fervent devotion and a fundamentally mathematical understanding of the material world that led him to his three laws of planetary motion. Remarkably, he made his discoveries without the advantages of modern mathematics, anything like an established empirical method, or even access to a telescope.

Unlike some academics and theologians of his time, Kepler saw no conflict between heliocentrism and Scripture; he was essentially an accommodationist.[21] His widely read introduction to *Astronomia Nova* (1609) includes his case for their compatibility, and it was the only portion of his corpus translated to English prior to the 1870s. In this opening essay, he explains that when Scripture refers to common, observable phenomena "concerning which it is not their purpose to instruct humanity," they "make use of what is generally acknowledged among humans, in order to weave in other things more lofty and divine."[22] In other words, Scripture accommodates the reader by speaking of the natural world in a manner consistent with its appearance to the average observer. When it describes the sun as "ascending" or "descending" or even "standing still" (Josh 10:12–13), it is merely using language appropriate to an earth-bound person's perspective. Kepler insists that biblical statements about observable phenomena—such as the sun's daily journey across the sky—reveal theological truths rather than facts of natural philosophy.[23]

The so-called Galileo affair is perhaps the most often cited example of the alleged warfare between science and Christianity. Like Kepler,

---

[20] Carola Baumgardt, *Johannes Kepler: Life and Letters* (Philosophical Library, 1951), 31.

[21] The accommodation principle, stated simply, is that God's revelation is written in language that the original audience, in their cultural and historical context, would have understood. It is not a challenge to the doctrine of inerrancy.

[22] Johannes Kepler, *Astronomia Nova*, trans. William H. Donahue (Green Lion, 2015), 29.

[23] For further discussion, see Travis, *Thinking God's Thoughts*, 146–47.

Galileo was a committed heliocentrist. After vastly improving the magnification strength of the "perspiculum" (telescope) in late 1609, he was able to make a series of observations that undermined the Aristotelian-Ptolemaic notion of immutable heavens containing perfect spheres all revolving around the earth: phenomena such as moons orbiting Jupiter, Venusian phases, sunspots, and topographical irregularities on the lunar surface. Galileo described these observations and others in *The Sidereal Messenger* (1610) and *History and Demonstrations Concerning Sunspots* (written in 1612, published in 1613). In 1611, he went to Rome, where the pope, cardinals, and other dignitaries attended the banquets and ceremonies given in honor of Galileo and his astronomical discoveries.

Contrary to popular understanding, this new empirical evidence did not constitute definitive proof of heliocentrism; Galileo's observations were also compatible with the Tychonic geo-heliocentric model, in which the planets revolved around the sun, and the sun revolved around the earth.[24] Nevertheless, Galileo openly declared that Copernicanism was *the* correct model of the universe, not merely a viable hypothesis. Consequently, he experienced vehement opposition—first from Aristotelian academics and then from like-minded leaders in the church, who interpreted some passages of Scripture as teaching a fixed earth and moving sun (geocentrism). Galileo's response was to critique this literalistic hermeneutic in two widely circulated letters: the first to his disciple Benedetto Castelli, a Benedictine monk and professor of mathematics at Pisa (1613) and the second (which was an expansion upon the first) to the Grand Duchess (dowager) Christina (1615). Both of these rhetorically superb letters argue for the truth of holy Scripture *and* the testament of creation—the "two books" philosophy of divine revelation: "For the Holy Scripture and nature both equally derive from the divine Word, the

---

[24] Moreover, Galileo's cosmology was geometrically problematic, since he intentionally ignored Kepler's first law of planetary motion (elliptical planetary orbits), which was published in the *Astronomia Nova* (1609).

former as the dictation of the Holy Spirit, the latter as the most obedient executrix of God's commands."[25] This was all well and good; however, Galileo goes on to say that natural philosophy should be consulted for guidance on the proper interpretation of biblical passages that relate to natural phenomena:

> I do not wish to imply that one should not have the highest regard for passages of Holy Scripture; indeed, after becoming certain of some physical conclusions, we should use these as very appropriate aids to the correct interpretation of such Scriptures and to the investigation of the truths they must contain, for they are most true and agree with demonstrated truths. . . . I do not think one has to believe that the same God who has given us senses, language, and intellect would want to set aside the use of these and give us by other means the information we can acquire with them, so that we would deny our senses and reason even in the case of those physical conclusions which are placed before our eyes and intellect by our sense experiences or by necessary demonstrations.[26]

Thus, it was not merely Galileo's heliocentrism that concerned ecclesial authorities; it was more the fact that he dared to boldly tread in their staunchly-guarded territory—the interpretation of Scripture. He argued that the few passages that, on the surface, seemed to indicate geocentrism should be understood as reflecting the perspective of the earthbound observer.[27] In other words, though true and divinely inspired, the phenomenological language was meant to accommodate the understanding of ancient readers.

---

[25] Galileo Galilei, Letter to Castelli (1613), in *The Essential Galileo*, ed. and trans. Maurice A. Finocchiaro (Hackett, 2008), 104.

[26] Galileo Galilei, Letter to the Grand Duchess Christina (1615), in *The Essential Galileo*, 117.

[27] Recall that Kepler had the same view.

In 1615, a Dominican friar filed a formal complaint against Galileo, which resulted in a year-long investigation by the Roman Inquisition. However, since the letters that sparked the fury had been informally circulated, and Galileo's published work did not explicitly endorse Copernicanism or promote his views on using natural philosophy to interpret Scripture, he was not summoned to Rome. At the end of that same year, he traveled there voluntarily to defend his views on heliocentrism. In early 1616, Cardinal Robert Bellarmine warned Galileo about this activity and forbade him to hold or defend his ideas about a moving earth. Galileo agreed to heed this warning. Several years later, in 1623, an admirer of Galileo's work became Pope Urban VIII, and the warning from Bellarmine suddenly seemed less threatening. Galileo decided to write a fictional dialogue that implicitly promoted Copernicanism by casting it in a more favorable light compared to geocentrism. In *Dialogue on the Two Chief World Systems* (1632), the Aristotelian character is named Simplicio, which sounds like "simpleton" in Italian. Simplicio's argument for a stationary earth was the very one favored by the pope himself, which added more fuel to the fire. The timing of this tongue-in-cheek strategy could not have been worse; the volatility of the counter-Reformation combined with Galileo's inflammatory rhetorical tactics and undiplomatic attitude finally brought him to a standoff with the Roman Inquisitors. Citing a special injunction of 1616 that prohibited Galileo from discussing his cosmology *in any way whatsoever* (a document of which Galileo said he was unaware), formal charges of heresy were made and a trial commenced.

Ultimately, Galileo took a plea bargain and was convicted of a lesser charge: strong suspicion of heresy. He was forced to verbally retract his statements about a mobile earth and the interpretation of Scripture. Contrary to popular myth, there was no torture or imprisonment involved; Galileo spent the last several years of his life under house arrest, but this was spent in luxurious villas, carrying out what was arguably the most important scientific work of his career. Interestingly, the Catholic church was partially responsible for the false impressions of the affair. The only trial documents that were publicized at the time used language that implied a much harsher examination and sentence than were actually carried out. As eminent historian Maurice Finocchiaro explains, Pope Urban "wanted Galileo's case to serve as a negative lesson to all Catholics and to strengthen his own image as an intransigent defender of the faith."[28] Thus, the documents that disproved the imprisonment thesis remained concealed for 150 years, and those contrary to the torture thesis were not made public for 250 years.[29] Unfortunately, the Catholic church did not formally absolve ("rehabilitate") Galileo until 1992, by declaration of Pope John Paul II, even though admission of the error had been made in the nineteenth century.

Galileo's prosecution by the Catholic church is frequently cited as an example of the episodic warfare between science and Christianity, often with false claims about imprisonment, torture, or even execution. As we have seen, this is a gross mischaracterization of documented historical facts. To be sure, there are important lessons to be learned from the Galileo affair. It involved, on both sides, fallible human beings behaving badly. Personal pride and political pressures of the time (among other issues) contributed to what became, unfortunately, a perfect storm. In addition to correcting the pervasive myths about Galileo's case, it is important to recognize that heliocentrism was not a threat to any primary Christian doctrine. Rather, it conflicted with some of the near-sacred Aristotelian philosophy that had influenced both the academics and biblical interpreters of Galileo's time.

Darwin's Theory and the Scopes Trial of 1925

Finally, we come to the issue that took center stage in the science and faith conversation in the late nineteenth century and remains there

---

[28] Maurice A. Finocchiaro, "Myth 8: That Galileo was Imprisoned and Tortured for Advocating Copernicanism," in *Galileo Goes to Jail and Other Myths About Science and Religion*, ed. Ronald L. Numbers (Harvard University Press, 2009), 72.

[29] Finocchiaro, 73.

today: biological evolution. Have Christians of any tradition, motivated by theological convictions, ever attempted to thwart progress in this area of research and education? Various subgroups within Christianity have reacted differently to evolutionary theories, motives have been misconstrued, and confusion has surrounded the concepts and terminology involved. We can, however, give a concise response meant to avoid misrepresentation, with the caveat that far more could be said about both the relevant historical events and the contemporary conversation.

When Charles Darwin published his theory of evolution by natural selection in *On the Origin of Species* in 1859, the reactions from the Christian world varied significantly. Some viewed it as a scientific description of the natural outworking of God's premiere creative activity, and saw no insurmountable theological or hermeneutical difficulties. The co-discoverer of the mechanism of natural selection, Alfred Russel Wallace, considered it a thoroughly teleological (goal-oriented) process and believed that design was wonderfully evident in the biological world. Asa Gray, a Harvard botanist and devout Christian, avidly championed Darwin's theory in America, but viewed it as supportive of teleology in nature—much to Darwin's dismay. Meanwhile, others saw Darwin's naturalistic objective as part and parcel of his scientific theory, which of course meant that it was perceived as dissonant with Christian doctrine about divine creation and God's sovereignty over the world. Some welcomed this allegation of incompatibility; Thomas Henry Huxley, known as "Darwin's Bulldog," happily proclaimed that the idea of purpose and design in nature "received its deathblow at Mr. Darwin's hands."[30] This exacerbated the confusion and tension surrounding the origins conversation.

In the post-Civil War United States, American Protestantism began to polarize in terms of differing attitudes toward "modernism." This created fertile ground for debates over Darwinism—its validity as a theory

[30] Thomas H. Huxley, "Criticisms on 'The Origin of Species'" in *Collected Essays by T. H. Huxley*, vol. 2 (Greenwood, 1968), 82.

as well whether it was a threat to Christian doctrine—to flourish. The dispute was part of a broader conflict between theological conservatives and liberals (modernists), the latter of whom were influenced by the German higher criticism that had infiltrated biblical scholarship. Yet, even within the conservative camp, responses were not homogenous. Some were opposed to Darwinian theory on theological grounds, equating it with atheism; some opposed the theory but thought that proponents should have the freedom to make their scientific case; and still others explored ways to establish harmony between Christian theology and biological evolution. Important evidence of this diversity can be found in the landmark publication *The Fundamentals: A Testimony to the Truth* (1910–1915), which contains theological essays written by conservative evangelical Protestants concerned with preserving the doctrines of biblical authority and inerrancy. Several of the contributors demonstrated open-mindedness toward the idea of a fully teleological evolutionary creation. For example, Scottish theologian James Orr and Princeton theologian B. B. Warfield drew a distinction between Darwinism as a theory of biological development and Darwinism as a naturalistic philosophical paradigm.[31] The key point here is that *The Fundamentals*, which was distributed to hundreds of thousands of pastors, missionaries, and lay leaders, was intended to serve as a defense of conservative Christianity against the encroaching theological liberalism, yet it contained a variety of positions on biological history and biblical creation.

The growing acceptance of evolutionary theory by the modernists nevertheless made it a main target of those within a militant subgroup of Christian conservatives. Under the banner of the World Christian Fundamentals Association (founded in 1919), debates were organized,

---

[31] For further discussion on this point, see Melissa Cain Travis, "Religion and Science, Reconstruction to World War II," in *American Religious History: Belief and Society Through Time*, 3 vols., ed. Gary Scott Smith (ABC-CLIO, 2020), 2:63–69.

and activists began lobbying for legislation against evolution education with an evangelistic fervor. In March 1925, the Butler Act was passed in the state of Tennessee, outlawing the teaching of evolutionary theory in all public education institutions. The brand new American Civil Liberties Union (ACLU) saw this as an opportunity for a freedom of speech test case, so they ran ads in Tennessee newspapers hoping to recruit a teacher willing to boldly break the law and face formal prosecution. With pragmatic hopes of drawing attention and money to their economically failing town, various elite men of Dayton, Tennessee, convinced physics teacher and football coach John Scopes, an agnostic who had briefly served as a substitute biology teacher, to volunteer. Notorious defense attorney and pro-evolution agnostic, Clarence Darrow, represented Scopes. The renowned politician and devout Christian, William Jennings Bryan, who had run for president three times as the Democratic Party's nominee and served as secretary of state under Woodrow Wilson, assisted the prosecution. Media interest exploded; the town was flooded with reporters, spectators, and souvenir vendors. The trial was the first to be broadcast over live radio, which heightened national awareness.

What ensued in Dayton was a media circus, to put it mildly. The issue at hand—the constitutionality of prohibiting the teaching of evolution in public education—was completely overshadowed by the real main attraction: the heated celebrity showdown between Bryan and Darrow over whether it was rational to believe (literalistically construed) passages of Scripture. Darrow made a caricature of the conservative stance on biblical reliability and interrogated Bryan with questions designed to paint Christian beliefs as absurd. These inflammatory tactics frustrated and flustered Bryan; but court transcripts reveal that, contrary to popular historical myth, he performed quite well in the debate. Unsurprisingly, the national media portrayed Darrow as the rational victor and Bryan as the humiliated loser, even though Scopes was convicted and ordered to pay a fine of $100. The Butler Act and similar laws in other states were eventually overturned.

The Scopes trial became the stuff of legend, and mischaracterizations were immortalized in both theater and film. The case continues to be offered as an example of Christianity opposing progress in science education and the metaphorical martyrdom of a courageous champion of science (John Scopes). The historical documentation does not support this interpretation; the truth of the matter is that a faction within the ranks of Christian conservatism carried out a misguided political crusade that intensified a preexisting polarization in the American public. Dayton businessmen, the ACLU, and the media capitalized on this dynamic, and the theological and philosophical nuances essential to the science and faith conversation were the tragic casualties. The crucial points here are that (1) the actual details of the trial and related events were extremely complex, (2) it was a subgroup within early twentieth-century Christian fundamentalism (before that term came to be used in its contemporary pejorative sense) that fought for legislation that stifled the teaching of evolutionary theory, and (3) the main public interest in the trial was the clash between two high-profile men with conflicting worldviews rather than the constitutionality of the Butler Act.

Final Thoughts

The historical periods and episodes discussed in this chapter are often used as examples of the church—in a monolithic sense—opposing scientific progress and education. As has been shown, this is inaccurate. The medieval church championed the preservation of knowledge and, eventually, the expansion of education. The rise of modern science owes much to the philosophical and theological convictions of giants such as Johannes Kepler and Galileo Galilei, who were convinced that the investigation of nature only heightened our reverence for its Creator. While conflict did arise, it was not due to an intrinsic incompatibility between Christianity and natural philosophy, but rather disputes over hermeneutics and ecclesial authority during an extremely volatile period of church history. Myths arose, in part due to concealment of information, and developed a life of their own, leading to persistent mischaracterization. Early reactions to Darwinian theory were very mixed among Christian scholars, and ideological clashes plagued the interdisciplinary conversation. A polarization within Christianity between modernists and conservatives, rooted in German higher criticism, spawned the early twentieth-century evolution debates that led to the famous Scopes trial, which was far more nuanced than popular portrayals reveal.

Unfortunately, the relationship between science and Christianity has often been hindered by politics and abuse of church authority. Mistakes have certainly been made and should be acknowledged, and the church can still learn from these historical missteps. Charity and humility would almost certainly have mitigated the interpersonal conflicts discussed above. Today, promoting a better understanding of the relevant philosophical, scientific, and theological issues will greatly improve the intellectual rigor of the conversation and perhaps help the church find fresh and effective ways to reach scientifically minded skeptics. As God's image-bearers, we are able to investigate the created order and thereby perceive part of the deep rationality of nature. Indeed, Scripture teaches that God is uniquely revealed in what he has made; when we explore the natural world, we encounter evidence of his majesty (Psalm 19; Acts 14:17; Rom 1:18–20). Scientific investigation is one way humankind can contemplate the wonders of the cosmos and delight in the power and ingenuity of its Creator.

CHAPTER 11

Objection #11: Christianity Is Anti-Science

"Science and religion," writes evolutionary biologist and atheist Jerry Coyne, "are competitors in the business of finding out what is true about our universe. In this goal religion has failed miserably, for its tools for discerning 'truth' are useless. These areas are incompatible in precisely the same way, and in the same sense, that rationality is incompatible with irrationality."[1] Coyne concedes that not all religious people are science-deniers (by which he means those who reject evolutionary theory); but he sees science and religious belief as epistemological opposites, two domains with conflicting beliefs about how we attain knowledge and what can properly be an object of knowledge. This idea is often expressed at the popular level with sentiments such as, "Science is based on evidence, but religion is based on blind superstition," or as atheist

[1] Jerry A. Coyne, *Faith vs. Fact: Why Science and Religion Are Incompatible* (Penguin, 2015), xvi.

neuroscientist Sam Harris likes to put it, "The contest between faith and reason is zero-sum."[2]

When Christianity is rejected as "anti-science," the complex historical interaction (discussed in chapter 10) may be in view. In other cases, the accusation may simply reflect a naturalistic philosophy, which excludes anything outside the natural order and the laws that govern it. It could also mean that the detractor is skeptical, to one degree or another, of truth claims that are not drawn from scientific data—a view of knowledge called scientism. At the popular level, the anti-science objection is typically a response to certain interpretations of the Genesis creation narrative, but this involves an overgeneralization that ignores the fact that there are several different views on how to properly integrate biblical and scientific knowledge. The in-house debate over interpretive issues is far too complex for a brief treatment, but fortunately, it is sufficient for present purposes to examine scientific findings about the birth of the universe and the origin of humankind and ask whether there is genuine conflict with the relevant Christian doctrine. As we shall see, the truth is quite the opposite.

Considering the Objection

Philosophical Issues

Christianity affirms the existence of immaterial agents that have the ability to interact with the physical world: God, angels, demons, and human souls. Naturalism, by contrast, regards belief in such things as anti-scientific. As naturalists see it, a properly scientific worldview has no room for anything besides the physical stuff of the universe, which is constrained by the laws of nature. This philosophy is a lens through which the world is viewed; and when it is applied to scientific investigation, it

---

[2] Sam Harris, "The Politics of Ignorance," *Huffington Post* (August 2, 2005).

strictly limits the kinds of conclusions that can be drawn. The term for this approach to science is methodological naturalism; and its proponents insist that only naturalistic causes should ever be considered when a scientist hypothesizes explanations for events like the origin of the universe, life, and consciousness. There is an a priori rejection of the possibility that nature may bear signs of a transcendent mind or that human beings are more than material bodies.

Methodological naturalism has two primary weaknesses. First, it attempts to draw a hard line of demarcation between what counts as science and what does not. On the surface, this may seem straightforward, but it is a notoriously difficult problem in the philosophy of science. As J. P. Moreland explains:

> Methodological naturalists say that we can come up with certain conditions that are both necessary and sufficient for "science" to be practiced. Once those features are identified, we can draw a big bright red line down the middle of the page: everything that has those features is on one side and is labeled "science," and everything that doesn't match that combination of characteristics is "something other than science." . . . There is just one problem with that proposal: *no one has ever been able to draw such a line*. It simply does not exist.[3]

If there is no agreed-upon set of necessary and sufficient conditions for categorizing something as scientific, then to rule out design only where nature is concerned seems arbitrary. Why should we simply *assume* that we will never find any indication of design rather than remain open-minded? This sets a boundary that may very well prevent discovery. If there *is* a Creator behind the existence of all things whose intelligence is purposefully imprinted upon aspects of the natural world in discernable

---

[3] J. P. Moreland, *Scientism and Secularism: Learning to Respond to a Dangerous Ideology* (Crossway, 2018), 163.

ways, the methodological naturalist will be blind to this fact; he or she has rejected this possibility in principle, not for scientific reasons. As philosopher of science Del Ratzsch puts it, "If part of reality lies beyond the natural realm, then science cannot get at the truth without abandoning the naturalism it presently follows as a methodological rule of thumb."[4] The scientist genuinely concerned with the unconditional pursuit of truth should at least remain *open* to detecting signals of design in nature.

It should be noted that there are theists, including some Christians, who argue that methodological naturalism must be employed without exception in scientific practice. This position is typically motivated by a desire to avoid the dreaded God-of-the-gaps mistake—positing supernatural causation to account for a phenomenon merely because a naturalistic explanation has not yet been identified.[5] This is akin to the "science-stopper" claim, which says that attributing a characteristic of nature to a transcendent Creator halts the search for naturalistic causes and thus prevents scientific progress. However, the person who is open to design is not arguing that we must resort to a supernatural explanation in any particular case for which a natural one has not been identified. Rather, he or she is pointing out that blind, undirected processes have well-known limitations in terms of what they can produce and that we sometimes observe attributes of nature that exceed those limits.

While design in nature cannot be proven with 100 percent certainty (very little of reality can), there are cases in which we are justified in having a good measure of confidence in such inferences. Here's why: Scientific

---

[4] Del Ratzsch, *Science & Its Limits: The Natural Sciences in Christian Perspective* (IVP Academic, 2000), 105.

[5] For an excellent discussion of the problem methodological naturalism poses for theistic evolution (which some Christian proponents of methodological naturalism are attempting to defend), see Stephen Dilley, "How to Lose a Battleship: Why Methodological Naturalism Sinks Theistic Evolution," in *Theistic Evolution: A Scientific, Philosophical, and Theological Critique*, ed. J. P. Moreland et al. (Crossway, 2017), 593–631.

investigation involves positing causes that are known to have the effect in question. For example, intelligent agency is the *only* cause ever observed to have produced specified complexity—meaning-laden order like that found in human language, mathematical systems, and computer software coding. If a far more sophisticated instance of such complexity is discovered in nature, then hypothesizing an intelligent agent as the source is entirely rational. Note that those who oppose wholesale methodological naturalism by no means object to ongoing research in any case where intelligent design is suspected, yet scientific discovery has never weakened a proper design inference. Quite the contrary; in some cases, expanding knowledge has even strengthened the case for design, sometimes dramatically.[6]

Naturalism is what philosophers call a metaphysic–a belief about *what* exists. Questions such as "what constitutes knowledge and how do we obtain it?" are answered according to one's epistemology, or theory of knowledge. Many naturalists ascribe to scientism, which says that the hard sciences, such as physics, biology, and chemistry, are the only (or at least the far superior) path to knowledge. In its strong form, scientism regards scientific methodology as the only completely valid way of pursuing truth, and thus a belief is only rationally justified when it has legitimate scientific support. In its weak form, scientism allows for some truths that are not gleaned from science, but still regards such truths as inferior and far less authoritative. This means that in any instance of conflict between a scientific and nonscientific truth claim, the former always trumps the latter.

Strong scientism is ultimately incoherent because it is self-refuting. It stands upon philosophical assertions that cannot be tested or supported by science, and this contradicts its own principles about the conditions

---

[6] A fantastic example of this is the specified complexity of genetic coding, which is now understood to be far more intricate and multilayered than when the DNA design inference was first made. This point will be discussed at length in chapter 12.

required for rational justification of a belief. "The only objective truths are scientific truths" is not itself scientifically supported, so it cannot qualify as objective truth. Moreover, the necessary axioms of science, its methodological presuppositions, and ethical guidelines for scientists are not scientific knowledge, nor are they rationally justified by science, so how could they have any truth value, according to strong scientism? There cannot even be a scientific enterprise if strong scientism's precepts are consistently applied. As philosopher of science Del Ratzsch puts it, "The price of holding out for science as the only legitimate basis for belief is the illegitimacy of science itself, and that seems too high a price."[7]

Resorting to the weak form of scientism does not help matters. While it allows for some other types of knowledge, those are deemed less certain by nature and thus never carry the weight of scientific truth. The reason this is detrimental to the edifice of science, Moreland explains, is that "the conclusions of science (i.e., the structure) cannot be more certain than the presuppositions of science (i.e., its foundation)."[8] Those who champion science are forced to accept its axioms and presuppositions as *at least* equal with scientific beliefs, which means that science cannot be the sole or superior source of truth. Ratzsch explains:

> Not only can science not validate its own foundations (implying that there are areas outside the competence of science), but if we do accept science, including its foundations, there must be some other sort of grounds for accepting at least some beliefs. This implies that science cannot be the only legitimate basis for believing something. Those who claim that science is competent for dealing with all matters or that science is the only legitimate method for dealing with any matter are seriously confused.[9]

---

[7] Ratzsch, *Science & Its Limits*, 94.

[8] J. P. Moreland, *Theistic Evolution: A Scientific, Philosophical, and Theological Critique* (Crossway, 2017), 56.

[9] Ratzsch, *Science & Its Limits*, 93.

It seems that science is inescapably subject to philosophy, without which it could not exist. In other words, because the assumptions on which science depends are philosophical rather than scientific, philosophy has the magisterial role. Thus, even weak scientism is fundamentally incompatible with science.

Cosmic Intelligibility and the Argument from Reason

Perhaps the biggest irony of the "anti-science" accusation is that science would be impossible if the universe did not come from a transcendent rational mind with whom we have a level of intellectual kinship (in theological terms, a Creator in whose image we are made). This is often referred to as the problem of cosmic intelligibility. For science to be possible, two key circumstances are necessary: the physical world must be intrinsically rational, and human beings must have precisely the kind of cognitive faculties necessary for advanced logical and mathematical reasoning. As we are about to see, cosmic intelligibility requires immaterial realities and interconnections that do not submit to scientific investigation.

The rationality of the universe is demonstrated by a peculiar fact: mathematics maps onto the material world with astounding precision. During the scientific revolution, giants such as Kepler, Galileo, and Newton transformed natural philosophy with their discovery and mathematical formulation of various physical laws. This intrinsic rationality made perfect sense within the Christian paradigm, which sees nature as the material manifestation of divine intelligence. Natural philosophers who discerned this mathematical order were, as Kepler so memorably phrased it, "sharing in God's own thoughts."

During the mid twentieth century, Hungarian nuclear physicist and Nobel laureate Eugene Wigner became fascinated with the intelligibility of nature. Wigner considered himself agnostic; he found arguments for the existence of God unconvincing but happily attended a Protestant church with his wife and children. Yet, despite his lack of religious conviction, Wigner was captivated by the question of why mathematics is such a powerful tool in the natural sciences. In 1960 he published an essay entitled "The Unreasonable Effectiveness of Mathematics in the Natural World," a philosophical commentary that continues to generate reflection and debate. Wigner argued that "the enormous usefulness of mathematics in the natural sciences is something bordering on the mysterious" and that "there is no rational explanation for it."[10] What he seems to have meant by "rational" in this context is "scientific," since any viable explanation for this deep connection between the abstract and the material must be metaphysical. He was also struck by the level of cognitive complexity required for the incredibly advanced mathematics used by the physicist. "Certainly it is hard to believe," he wrote, "that our reasoning power was brought, by Darwin's process of natural selection, to the perfection which it seems to possess."[11]

Since Wigner's time, the remarkable resonance between mathematics, the material world, and the human mind has intrigued many high-ranking intellectuals, including physicists, philosophers, mathematicians, and theologians. Physicist Roger Penrose, another agnostic Nobel laureate, has puzzled over this strange harmony for decades. He calls it the "three worlds, three mysteries problem." The first mystery is the applicability of mathematics in the natural sciences. In response to those who argue that this state of affairs is nothing more than human beings making up mathematical systems to fit what we observe in nature, or analyzing empirical evidence within a previously devised mathematical framework, Penrose writes:

---

[10] Eugene Wigner, "The Unreasonable Effectiveness of Mathematics in the Natural Sciences," reprinted in *The World Treasury of Physics, Astronomy, and Mathematics*, ed. Timothy Ferris (Little, Brown, 1991), 527. This essay is also freely available online.

[11] Wigner, 528.

> It makes no sense to me that this concurrence . . . between the workings of the natural world at its most fundamental levels (here the very structure of space and time) and sophisticated mathematical theory . . . is merely the result of our trying to fit the observational facts into some organizational scheme that we can comprehend; the concurrence between Nature and sophisticated beautiful mathematics is something that is "out there" and has been so since times far earlier than the dawn of humanity, or of any other conscious entities that could have inhabited the universe as we know it.[12]

The second mystery is how the world of conscious rationality could have emerged from the material world. He asks, "How does consciousness arise in a world which seems to be governed by entirely impersonal mathematical operations?"[13] How could blind matter, behaving according to mathematical laws of nature, "wake up" and discern those operations? Penrose's third mystery is how human minds (which he takes to be somehow synonymous with the material brain) are able to conjure up mathematical concepts from an immaterial realm. After all, how could something immaterial, like a mathematical concept, have a physical effect in a human brain?

The problem that mathematical reasoning (or logical reasoning of any kind) poses for any naturalistic explanation of the human mind is central to the argument from reason against naturalism, a powerful argument that has been developed in various ways since its rise in popularity in theological and philosophical circles, largely through the work of C. S. Lewis. In the second edition of *Miracles*, Lewis argues that rationality

---

[12] Roger Penrose, "Mathematics, the Mind, and the Physical World," in *Meaning in Mathematics*, ed. John Polkinghorne (Oxford University Press, 2011), 45.

[13] Penrose, 42.

defies naturalistic explanation because any such account assumes the causal closure of the universe (nothing immaterial directs or otherwise intervenes) and therefore what we call "reasoning" boils down to brain matter behaving according to the laws of physics rather than the abstract laws of logic.[14]

Lewis draws an important distinction between what he calls a Cause and Effect reason for a belief, which involves "a dynamic connection between events" and a Ground and Consequent reason, which arises from "a logical relation between beliefs or assertions."[15] In the latter case, a conclusion (B) is drawn from a prior belief (A) because the thinker *sees* that B logically follows from A. The person must be conscious of *why* B follows from A, and *for that reason* conclude B. However, if naturalism is true, any thought whatsoever is entirely the result of Cause and Effect reasons; the neurons firing during thought A are the physical cause of the firing neurons that produce thought B (the inevitable effect). Logical grounding is completely irrelevant to the process, which is merely a physical chain of events. Lewis asks, "How could such a trifle as a lack of logical grounds prevent the belief's occurrence or how could the existence of grounds promote it?"[16] What is needed for genuine reasoning is direct conscious awareness of the logical relationship between one thought (A) and the thought that follows as a result (B), and this understanding must truly be the *cause* of B. This would be impossible if the mind were nothing more than a series of physical brain states.

Philosopher Stewart Goetz has developed Lewis's argument in the following way:

---

[14] The fact that we still do not have a comprehensive account of physics is irrelevant here, as is quantum indeterminacy.

[15] C. S. Lewis, *Miracles* (HarperCollins, 2015), 22.

[16] Lewis, 24.

1. If naturalism is true then we do not reason.
2. We reason.
   [Therefore]
3. Naturalism is false.[17]

This deductive form of the Lewisian argument takes human reasoning as a given. Since, as explained above, naturalism would exclude true reasoning, naturalism cannot be true. If it were, we could not reason to that conclusion, and thus the claim "naturalism is true" is ultimately self-defeating. In his characteristically pithy manner, Lewis levels this critique at the naturalistic account of human reason by saying that such an explanation "discredits our processes of reasoning or at least reduces their credit to such a humble level that it can no longer support Naturalism itself."[18]

Christian theism does not suffer from these fatal difficulties concerning the existence and reliability of human reason. It conceives of human beings as made in the image of God, the *Logos*, the paradigm of rationality. We are creatures with immaterial souls that interact with our physical brains, and thus we can consciously and freely reason according to Ground and Consequent causation. According to Christian theism, Lewis explains, "Reason—the reason of God—is older than Nature, and from it the orderliness of Nature, which alone enables us to know her, is derived . . . the human mind in the act of knowing is illuminated by the Divine reason. It is set free, in the measure required, from the huge nexus of non-rational causation; free from this to be determined by the truth known."[19] The Logos is the necessary and ultimate cause of the intelligibility of nature.

Christianity, unlike any fully naturalistic account of reality, explains the existence and success of the natural sciences. It accounts for the deep rationality of nature as well as the corresponding intellectual capacities

---

[17] Stewart Goetz, "The Argument from Reason," *Philosophia Christi* 15, no. 1 (2013): 51.

[18] Lewis, *Miracles*, 22.

[19] Lewis, 34.

that allow human scientists to discover it. The more we have discovered about the cosmos, the more robust the case for a Creator has become, as we shall see in this chapter and the next.

A Finite Universe

When Albert Einstein was developing his general theory of relativity (published in 1915), he assumed a static, past-eternal universe.[20] The assumption that the universe does not change in size over time manifested in his system of equations as a mathematical constant represented by the Greek letter *lambda* (Λ). Einstein viewed this so-called cosmological constant as a reasonable way to avoid an odd ramification—an expanding or contracting universe. In the 1920s, Alexander Friedmann and Georges Lemaître (a Catholic priest) independently produced solutions to Einstein's theory that predicted an expanding universe. Yet, Einstein refused to relinquish his cosmological constant and accept a non-static universe until he was faced with compelling empirical evidence. Such evidence was produced by American astronomer Edwin Hubble in 1929 at the Mount Wilson Observatory. By measuring the wavelengths of light coming from distant galaxies, Hubble observed that the further away the galaxy, the redder its emitted light. This "red shift" indicated that other galaxies are receding from the Milky Way in every direction, accelerating in proportion to their distance.

Meanwhile, Lemaître was interested in how general relativity would play out in the physical world. He realized that if cosmic expansion were extrapolated backward in time, one would arrive at a singularity, the seed from which the universe sprang. He referred to this as the "primeval atom," an unfathomably dense state from which matter and spacetime itself burst forth. In an interview years later, Lemaître recalled that when he had discussed his theory with Einstein, the latter's response was,

---

[20] The purpose of Einstein's work was to achieve a comprehensive mathematical model of the universe.

"No, not that, that suggests too much the creation."[21] Despite subsequent attempts in the ensuing decades to construct a viable steady-state (static) cosmology, an expanding universe became the standard model. In a 1949 BBC radio program, Sir Fred Hoyle used the term "Big Bang," and after it appeared in a scientific publication several years later, it stuck.[22]

Further empirical support for a temporally-finite universe came in 1964 at Bell Laboratories, when Arno Penzias and Robert Wilson detected the cosmic microwave background radiation—the heat echo of the Big Bang—which the model had predicted. Since then, as instrumentation and telescopes have advanced, measurements have become even more precise. Cosmologists have continued to search for possible alternatives to an ultimate beginning, but without success. Theoretical physicist Alexander Vilenkin, who is renowned for his work in the field, is convinced that such a theorem is impossible. "We have no viable models of an eternal universe," he says, and we have "reason to believe that such models simply cannot be constructed."[23]

Now, if something began to exist at some point in the past, it must have had a cause, and this is the central idea behind the *kalām* cosmological argument for the existence of God. Cosmological arguments, as a general category, have a long intellectual history, but the scientific evidence against a past-eternal universe provides support for the second premise in the *kalām* version:

1. Whatever begins to exist has a cause.
2. The universe began to exist.
3. Therefore, the universe had a cause.

---

[21] John Farrell, *The Day Without Yesterday: Lemaitre, Einstein, and the Birth of Modern Cosmology* (Thunder's Mouth Press, 2005), 100.

[22] Helge Kragh, "How Did the Big Bang Get Its Name? Here's the Real Story," *Nature* 627 (2024), 726–28, DOI: 10.1038/d41586-024-00894-z.

[23] Alexander Vilenkin, "The Beginning of the Universe," *Inference* 1, no. 4 (October 2015).

Proponents of this argument explain that any cause of the universe, which includes space-time and all matter, must be an immaterial, eternal agent who possesses the will and power to create. This description is perfectly harmonious with the traditional conception of God. Note that premise 2 was defended philosophically long before the rise of modern cosmology. Medieval theologians who were targeting the Aristotelian idea of an eternal universe contended that an infinite past is impossible. This philosophical support is still used in the contemporary version of the *kalām*, but the addition of scientific support has greatly increased the argument's popularity.[24]

Challenges to the *kalām* are typically aimed at premise 1. For example, Vilenkin claims that "no cause is needed"; he is convinced that a universe can "pop out of nothing," or rather, from the random (i.e., uncaused) decay of a radioactive atom (which is technically not "nothing").[25] The causal connection that would exist between this hypothetical atom and the universe would make it *part of the universe itself.* To say that the atom existed from eternity in another space-time and then at some point spontaneously decayed and triggered the Big Bang beginning of another universe with an independent space-time seems to be grasping at unverifiable straws. Not to mention, it does not escape the philosophical problem of an infinite past.[26]

As our understanding improves, the scientific case for an ultimate beginning grows ever more robust. Attempts to escape the problem this poses for naturalism are not only highly speculative, they also face logical difficulties. A timeless, immaterial mind who was the first cause of all things is a simpler and more intellectually satisfying solution.

---

[24] William Lane Craig is the premier developer and defender of the *kalām* and has interacted extensively with the various rebuttals.

[25] Vilenkin, "The Beginning of the Universe."

[26] See discussion in William Lane Craig, *The Kalām Cosmological Argument* (Wipf and Stock, 2000), 65–111.

Human Origins and the Historical Adam and Eve

Without a doubt, the topic receiving the most attention in the current science and faith conversation is the question of a historical Adam and Eve. This is not surprising, since the issue has direct bearing on Gospel-related doctrines such as original sin. It is a common misconception that the historical Adam and Eve debate is merely about evolution versus special creation. There are positions that affirm, or are agnostic about, evolutionary models of biological origins yet believe Adam and Eve were real people. Within this category of views, some regard them as the universal common ancestors of humanity, while others believe that there were hominids outside the garden of Eden with whom Adam and Eve's offspring interbred. Of those who hold to a no-evolutionary view, some place the primal couple hundreds of thousands of years in the past while others believe they lived approximately 6,000 to 10,000 years ago. Then there are some who affirm the special creation of Adam and Eve yet are open to the evolution of hominids with whom image-bearing human beings interbred after the fall.[27]

A key point here is that the theological question concerning the existence of Adam and Eve is technically independent of questions related to biological origins. The former is a historical issue that science simply cannot address. For this reason, some conservative scholars who argue for the theological necessity of a real Adam and Eve are open to considering the most recent data and models from fields such as paleoanthropology (fossil(s) evidence) and population genetics when elaborating their view on humanity's biological origins. Many theologians and Bible scholars believe that some essential Christian doctrines require a historical Adam and Eve. Paul's words in Romans 5 about one man's sin bringing about universal human mortality are indicative of his belief that there was indeed

[27] For an in-depth treatment of the debate, see Kenneth D. Keathley, ed., *Perspectives on the Historical Adam and Eve: Four Views* (B&H Academic, 2024).

an original act of disobedience carried out by a real person (not a symbolic literary figure). The corresponding solution to the fall and the gift of eternal life came through another man's (Christ's) obedience. This is just one reason why a historical Adam and Eve is required. It seems that the task at hand is to answer the "anti-science" accusation from that starting point.

The conflict that some perceive between modern science and the biblical Adam and Eve is based upon evolutionary theory in one way or another. The objector may wrongly assume that if humans have an evolutionary history, then Adam and Eve *must* be purely fictitious, and therefore Christianity is false. In such a scenario, we need only explain why this is not necessarily so (*even if* we reject evolutionary theory wholesale). Andrew Loke, a Christian theologian and philosopher, explains that "to demonstrate that there is no contradiction between the teaching of the Bible and evolutionary biology, one only must show that it is *possible* that both are true. One can show this by offering a *possible* model of the relationship between both."[28] To reiterate, one need not *accept* evolutionary theory to make this argument, and merely showing that there is no logical contradiction between the two claims can be helpful.

Some who dismiss Christianity's teachings on human origins as "anti-science" may mean something more scientifically specific: the belief that genomic studies have eliminated the possibility of a single pair who were the biological progenitors of the human race. As early as the 1990s, geneticists were attempting to extrapolate backward and estimate the smallest population of early humans since the alleged divergence of human-chimp lineages from a common ancestor. Some evolutionary genealogical models developed during the 2010s seemed to indicate a minimum population size of ten thousand individuals. The belief was that our present genetic diversity could not have resulted from a population bottleneck any smaller than this, which meant that one pair of ancestors was deemed scientifically

---

[28] Andrew Loke, "The Genealogical Adam and Eve Model," in *Perspectives on the Historical Adam and Eve: Four Views*, 108.

impossible. Evolutionary biologist, author, and popular antagonist of religion Jerry Coyne put it this way in 2011:

> Unfortunately [for the Abrahamic faiths], the scientific evidence shows that Adam and Eve could not have existed, at least in the way they're portrayed in the Bible. Genetic data show no evidence of any human bottleneck as small as two people: there are simply too many different kinds of genes around for that to be true. There may have been a couple of "bottlenecks" (reduced population sizes) in the history of our species, but the smallest one not involving recent colonization is a bottleneck of roughly 10,000–15,000 individuals that occurred between 50,000 and 100,000 years ago. That's as small a population as our ancestors had, and–note–it's not two individuals. . . . *Of course* there was no literal Adam and Eve: the genetic data show unequivocally that humanity did not descend from a single pair that lived in the genus *Homo*.[29]

However, even at the time, these conclusions were not universally accepted. Some, such as biologist Ann Gauger and mathematician Ola Hössjer, have challenged the methodologies and assumptions used to construct the models from which such estimates were drawn. They concluded that a single pair of human ancestors living sometime around five hundred thousand years ago is consistent with the data, and that with only minor modifications to their revised model, the possibility arises that the pair lived as recently as one hundred thousand years ago.[30]

More recently, a 2023 paper published in the prestigious journal *Science* discussed data gleaned from newer, higher-resolution modeling

---

[29] Jerry Coyne, "Adam and Eve: The Ultimate Standoff Between Science and Faith," at whyevolutionistrue.com (June 2, 2011).

[30] Ola Hössjer and Ann Gauger, "A Single-Couple Human Origin is Possible," *BIO-Complexity* 2019, no. 1, DOI:10.5048/BIO-C.2019.1.

software. The researchers' conclusion was that there could have been a population bottleneck as small as 1,200 people that occurred several hundred thousand years earlier than the time frame mentioned in previous studies.[31] This is a drastic reduction in the previous minimum population estimates, and only time will tell if this downward trend continues. The authors of the 2023 paper noted that further methodological improvement or an altogether different approach will be necessary to increase the accuracy of the estimates. It is likely that this kind of modeling, with all the assumptions it must include and how far it must delve into the deep past, simply cannot detect any short, severe population bottlenecks that may have occurred. The bottom line is that the possibility of Adam and Eve as progenitors of humanity has not been definitively ruled out; in fact, recent data has only increased the scientific plausibility of two original biological ancestors.

Final Thoughts

What we have seen is that the "anti-science" accusation against Christianity is entirely unwarranted. The conflict lies not between Christianity and science, but between Christianity and naturalistic philosophical biases, such as scientism and methodological naturalism, which are often imposed upon scientific practice and the construction of models. Free inquiry must be upheld in the pursuit of truth about the world, and this means following the evidence wherever it happens to lead. In the case of cosmic origins, a metaphysical boundary is encountered; to seek an ultimate explanation for the existence of all things is to move beyond the chain of physical events, which cannot stretch back into an infinite past. Scientific discoveries of the past century have revealed that such a cause

[31] Wangjie Hu et al., "Genomic Inference of a Severe Human Bottleneck During the Early to Middle Pleistocene Transition" *Science* 381, no. 6661 (August 2023): 979–84, DOI:10.1126/science.abq7487.

must transcend both the material and temporal. It must account for the laws of nature and its comprehensibility, which involves the astonishing interconnections between mathematics, matter, and mind. Christianity provides a satisfying account of things; as Col 1:17 says, "He is before all things, and by him all things hold together." Theology provides what science, because of its inherent limitations, cannot: a metaphysical explanation. We need both for a holistic understanding of reality.

The issue of human origins is different from that of cosmology because it involves an investigation into the scientific possibility of what historic Christianity teaches about humanity—that we are all descendants of one original pair of parents, the first creatures made in the image of God. Bold claims about a biological Adam and Eve having been rendered impossible by the data were incredibly premature; and as methods have improved, so has the case for the feasibility of a population bottleneck of two individuals in the remote past. It seems likely at this point that we will not gain much more scientific insight, since these sorts of past-extrapolations into primordial history necessarily depend upon assumptions and theory-laden model construction.

We certainly still have work to do when it comes to helping Christians overcome fear, gain philosophical and theological discernment, and appreciate the value of scientific discovery. Efforts to improve our understanding of the structure and workings of nature should be championed by Christians, especially. After all, increasing our knowledge of the world God has created is to delight in his endless ingenuity and artistry—it is, as Kepler acknowledged, an act of worship.

CHAPTER 12

Objection #12: Evolutionary Theory Has Ruled Out a Creator

Decades ago, when Christian *ichthus* (fish) emblems on cars became popular, I (Melissa) encountered a bumper sticker with the now-common Darwinian parody—a fish with legs—alongside the slogan, "We have the fossils. We win." At the time, I knew what the sticker was meant to imply: that the evidence for evolutionary common descent (the hypothesis that all living things are genetically related because they share a universal ancestor) is irrefutable, and thus Christianity's doctrine of creation cannot be true. In other words, there is an inherent contradiction between the two. I knew next to nothing about how one might answer such a claim, or if it *could* be reasonably answered. Was the fossil record kind of like a Rorschach test, where one's philosophical predisposition determined one's conclusions? Or was I terribly under-informed about how well the paleontological data supported Darwinian theory? It turns out that the fossil and biochemical evidence suggests a far more intriguing history of life, and the more we learn, the greater the challenges faced by naturalistic accounts.

As we saw in chapter 11, there are various perspectives on how to reconcile the biblical creation account with scientific data, and divine creation as such does not crucially depend upon one specific interpretation of the fossil record. Some mistakenly believe that if evolutionary common descent is true, then a creator is unnecessary for explaining biological history; and thus naturalism stands. It turns out, however, that two intertwined facts present serious difficulties for naturalistic accounts of the existence, complexity, and diversity of life: (1) the fossil record does not reflect a steady, tree-like divergence of increasingly sophisticated lifeforms from a universal common ancestor, and (2) advances in biochemistry have gravely undermined any naturalistic understanding of both the origin and diversification of life (and certain attributes of the fossil record compound this problem). Even if evolutionary common descent is granted for the sake of the argument, the idea that it could have been driven by blind, unguided processes is, to put it mildly, untenable.

Considering the Objection

The Implications of the Fossil Record

In his 1859 magnum opus, *On the Origin of Species*, Charles Darwin's project was to account for the diversification of life forms over the entire course of biological history. Central to his theory of evolution by natural selection was the concept of descent with modification—the hypothesis that random variations advantageous to an organism's survival and reproduction are preserved by natural selection and spread throughout a population. As these changes add up over time, there is a treelike divergence of lineages as well as extinction of the less fit (represented by the terminal side branches on his famous tree diagram). He argues that we can extrapolate backward from this idea to formulate a theory of biological evolution:

> By the theory of natural selection all living species have been connected with the parent-species of each genus, by differences not greater than we see between the varieties of the same species at the present day; and these parent-species, now generally extinct, have in their turn been similarly connected with more ancient species; and so on backwards, always converging to the common ancestor of each great class. So that the number of intermediate and transitional links, between all living and extinct species, must have been inconceivably great. But assuredly, if this theory be true, such have lived upon this earth.[1]

Expressing his belief that this process began with a universal common ancestor, he wrote that "probably all the organic beings which have ever lived on this earth have descended from some one primordial form, into which life was first breathed."[2]

In light of his theory, Darwin was puzzled by the conundrum presented by the fossil record. If common descent by a process of natural selection is a true account of biological history, "why does not every collection of fossil remains afford plain evidence of the gradation and mutation of the forms of life? We meet with no such evidence, and this is the most obvious and forcible of the many objections which may be urged against my theory. Why, again, do whole groups of allied species appear, though certainly they often falsely appear, to have come in suddenly on the several geological stages?"[3] Vast numbers of fossilized transitional

---

[1] Charles Darwin, *On the Origin of Species* (W. Clowes and Sons, 1859), 281–82.

[2] Darwin, 484. There is debate over whether Darwin used biblical allusions like this in a genuine way or simply metaphorically.

[3] Darwin, 463.

forms, moving from the simpler in lower geologic layers to the more advanced and diverse in the higher is what would be expected on Darwin's theory; but that is not the exhibited pattern. Rather, the overall trend is the abrupt appearance of species that exist for a time and then go extinct. Darwin speculated on why this is so, and concluded that the imperfection of the fossil record was the problem (fossilization failure or merely undiscovered fossils), one that would hopefully diminish to some degree as new deposits were discovered and a better understanding of the connections between fossilized forms was gained (the now so-called artifact hypothesis). While he admitted that the nature of the record presented a serious difficulty for his theory, he did not regard it as fatal.

Well over a century and a half has passed since the publication of Darwin's *Origin*, and his theory has been substantially revised. First and foremost, it was integrated with Gregor Mendel's work on the principles of biological inheritance (most high school biology textbooks discuss his famous experiments with pea plants). Since Mendel, a great deal has been discovered about the biochemical mechanisms involved with reproduction and transmission of biological traits. This includes the phenomenon of genetic mutations and how they affect the form and function of an offspring. The fields of embryology and paleontology have also become important facets of evolutionary theory's Modern Synthesis, known colloquially as neo-Darwinism. This is not to say that there is some sort of grand scientific consensus on the details of evolutionary history (far from it); in fact, there is even disagreement over what the Modern Synthesis entails. Neo-Darwinism (the term that will be used going forward) can essentially be thought of as an umbrella term for a myriad of sub-theories that seek to account for the empirical evidence as well as piece together a coherent picture from the available data.

What of Darwin's concern about the lack of evidential support for his theory in the fossil record? Since his time, the sheer amount of fossil data has dramatically increased, yet the paleontological case for unguided common descent has not improved. Quite the contrary; the pattern of discontinuity, with abrupt explosions of new kinds of flora and fauna, is even more pronounced; and as paleontological research progresses, this data trend continues. This does not bode well for a neo-Darwinian understanding of biological history. As German paleontologist Günter Bechly explains, "If gaps and discontinuities in the fossil record were just artifacts, they should more and more dissolve with our greatly increasing knowledge of the fossil record. But the opposite is the case. The more we know, the more acute these problems have become."[4] Bechly quips that if Darwin were still alive, "he would likely agree that the evidence simply does not add up, since he was much more prudent than many of his modern followers."[5]

The Cambrian explosion (nicknamed "evolution's big bang") is perhaps the most widely known instance of the sudden appearance of a variety of creatures, and it is one with which Darwin himself was familiar.[6] The Cambrian layers in the geological column attest to the extraordinarily sudden appearance of anatomically complex organisms that together represent all of the major animal body plan categories. As philosopher of science Stephen C. Meyer explains, "During this explosion of fauna, representatives of about twenty of the roughly twenty-six total phyla present in the known fossil record made their first appearance on earth."[7] The portion of the Cambrian period during which these novel animal forms first appeared is believed to have lasted no more than ten million years. This may seem like an unfathomably enormous duration of time; but in terms of an evolutionary timescale, this amounts to the blink of an eye.

---

[4] Günter Bechly, "Does the Fossil Record Demonstrate Darwinian Evolution?" in *The Comprehensive Guide to Science and Faith: Exploring the Ultimate Questions About Life and the Cosmos,* ed. William A. Dembski, et al. (Harvest House, 2021), 348.

[5] Bechly, 348.

[6] Darwin used the older designation, Silurian, for this geological period.

[7] Stephen C. Meyer, *Darwin's Doubt: The Explosive Origin of Animal Life and The Case for Intelligent Design* (HarperOne, 2013), 31.

It is not merely the abruptness of the Cambrian explosion that defies the neo-Darwinian account, but also the sophistication of these creatures and the lack of evidence for Precambrian evolutionary precursors. The plentiful fossil evidence for simpler life forms preceding the Cambrian fauna is, on its own, insufficient support for a neo-Darwinian model. On the theory that unguided descent with modification has occurred, a reasonable scientific prediction would be that the Precambrian fossil record should contain a wide variety of specimens that are only moderately less complex, with body plans and other features that could have given rise to those observed in the Cambrian strata. What has actually been found does not even come close to fulfilling this prediction. In the late twentieth century, eminent paleontologist and evolutionary biologist Stephen Jay Gould remarked that Darwin had been "vindicated by a rich Precambrian record."[8] Gould was referring to the fact that plenty of evidence for Precambrian life has been discovered since Darwin's time. Still, he acknowledged a difficulty:

> The peculiar character of this evidence has not matched Darwin's prediction of a continuous rise in complexity toward Cambrian life, and the problem of the Cambrian explosion has remained as stubborn as ever—if not more so, since our confusion now rests on knowledge, rather than ignorance, about the nature of Precambrian life. . . . The later history of Precambrian life stands strongly against his assumption of a long and gradual rise in complexity toward the products of the Cambrian explosion. . . . Step way way back, blur the details, and you may want to read this sequence as a tale of predictable progress: prokaryotes first, then eukaryotes, then multicellular life. But scrutinize the particulars and the comforting story collapses.[9]

---

[8] Stephen Jay Gould, *Wonderful Life: The Burgess Shale and the Nature of History* (W.W. Norton, 1989), 57.

[9] Gould, 58, 60.

The main point here is that a large number of distinct new body plans made their debut during the Cambrian window, with little or no warning in the fossil record of the preceding geological era. But this is only part of the problem. Highly sophisticated organs seem to appear out of nowhere, without any fossil precursors. Trilobites, the marine arthropods that have become iconic of this geologic period, are an excellent example. In addition to their complex body plan, which included mouth parts, a digestive system, and articulated appendages, they had amazing compound eyes that provided a 360-degree field of vision.[10] There is simply no evidence of a gradual evolution of these impressive structures; as one University of Cologne zoologist notes, trilobites "are equipped *from the very beginning of their appearance in the fossil record* with elaborate compound eyes" (emphasis mine).[11] If these advanced sensory organs were the result of a step-by-step accumulation of genetic mutations, there is no record of it. More recent discoveries of trilobites preserved in volcanic ash have revealed their marvelous complexity in unprecedented detail, providing higher-resolution evidence of the abrupt appearance of highly complex body plans.[12]

In an attempt to solve the Cambrian mystery, some have resorted to a retrieval of Darwin's tactic—the artifact hypothesis. Perhaps there are no Precambrian fossils that could be reasonably interpreted as evolutionary precursors to the Cambrian menagerie because of the imperfections of the record. Maybe the transitional fossils will eventually be discovered. Perhaps conditions were not conducive to fossilization, or the bodies of the organisms were not large or rigid enough for preservation. These are

---

[10] Not every variety of trilobite, despite their compound eyes, had quite this broad a field of vision.

[11] Brigitte Schoenemann, "An Overview on Trilobite Eyes and Their Functioning," *Arthropod Structure & Development* vol. 61 (March 2021), DOI:10.1016/j.asd.2021.101032.

[12] Abderrazak El Albani et al., "Rapid Volcanic Ash Entombment Reveals the 3D Anatomy of Cambrian Trilobites," *Science* 384, no. 6703 (June 2024), 1429–35, https://doi.org/10.1126/science.adl4540.

the suggested explanations for the glaring absence of transitional forms. However, the fossilization failure idea seems less and less likely as knowledge increases. In the late 1990s and early 2000s, for example, Chinese paleontologists were able to examine samples of Precambrian strata using powerful magnification. Paul Chien describes what he and his team discovered when they examined slices of the rock under the microscope:

> In many of the thin rock slides, we found many microscopic round fossilized objects . . . A large percentage of the spheres appeared to be the fossils of sponge cells and embryos with characteristic spicules. . . . [In further studies] I photographed these sponge eggs and early embryos at much higher resolutions. After carefully cracking them open and using a scanning electron microscope, I could identify cellular structures inside the cells, such as the nuclei and granules of egg yolk.[13]

He then explains why this discovery poses such a problem for one aspect of the artifact hypothesis:

> Some have tried to rescue evolutionary theory by claiming that there might have been many precursor animals leading up to the Cambrian, and it's just that Precambrian conditions were not very good at preserving those fossils, so those precursors are missing from the fossil record. But if the conditions for fossil preservation were so poor, why did they manage to preserve soft, delicate sponge eggs and early embryos, and preserve them extremely well, including the nucleus in eggs and embryo cells? Given this, why have no precursors to the Cambrian animals yet been found?[14]

---

[13] Thomas Y. Lo et al., *Evolution & Intelligent Design in a Nutshell* (Discovery Institute Press, 2020), 141–42.

[14] Lo et al., 143–44.

Since the discovery of the fossilized embryos, geologists and paleontologists have further investigated the Precambrian rock composition; some have concluded that it would have provided equally or even *more* favorable conditions for fossil formation compared to the Cambrian strata.[15]

As mentioned above, the Cambrian event was not the only instance of an explosion in biodiversity. For example, there was an abrupt appearance of a wide variety of marine invertebrates roughly 470 million years ago (the "great Ordovician biodiversification event") that has been referred to as "life's second big bang."[16] Fossils of flowering plants, major bird groups, insects, land animals, and even the genus *Homo* attest to a similarly rapid appearance on the biological scene; and the list goes on. Rather than evidence of a gradual divergence of species over eons of time, the fossil record exhibits a trend of abrupt appearance, stasis (existing for a time, significantly unchanged), and then extinction. While it is certainly apparent that the level of biological complexity and diversity increased over time, the record is not indicative of the gradualism and transitional fossil series that would be predicted on a neo-Darwinian account of common descent. As biologist Jeffrey H. Schwartz puts it, "We are still in the dark about the origin of most major groups of organisms. They appear in the fossil record as Athena did from the head of Zeus—full blown and raring to go, in contradiction to Darwin's depiction of evolution as resulting from the steady accumulation of countless infinitesimally minute variations."[17]

---

[15] See Meyer, *Darwin's Doubt*, 68.

[16] Bechly, "Does the Fossil Record Demonstrate Darwinian Evolution?" in *The Comprehensive Guide to Science and Faith*, 349. Note that the standard chronology used in the scientific community is granted here. However, those who take a young-earth view of creation can make full use of the argument articulated in this section by simply setting aside the dating issue altogether.

[17] Jeffrey H. Schwartz, *Sudden Origins: Fossils, Genes, and the Emergence of Species* (John Wiley & Sons, 1999), 3.

Some have attempted to solve the difficulty presented by these explosions of biodiversity by rejecting a pillar of neo-Darwinism and suggesting that most divergences in evolutionary lineages happened by *non-gradualistic* mechanisms. This, they believe, helps explain why the fossil record exhibits sudden leaps forward in complexity and diversity with insufficient (or zero) evidence of transitional forms. For example, in the 1970s, Stephen Jay Gould and his colleague Niles Eldredge proposed a model known as *punctuated equilibria* that postulated periods of evolutionary stasis occasionally interrupted by rapid macroevolutionary change involving small populations of organisms. Speciation occurred too rapidly and perhaps in a location too far removed from the parent population for the fossil record to capture much evidence of intermediate forms. This was a controversial departure from the consensus, to say the least.

In his 2019 book, *Extinction and Evolution: What Fossils Reveal About the History of Life*, Eldredge continues to insist that punctuated equilibria is the correct interpretation of the fossil data, while affirming that "evolution really occurs essentially the way that Darwin said it does."[18] What he means is that natural selection is a real phenomenon, only it functions predominantly for maintaining stasis and only achieves speciation in small, isolated populations. "Through it all," he writes, "the fundamental pattern of stability, 'punctuated' by occasional fits of evolutionary change, rings clear as the most basic of all messages the fossil record has to tell us on the very nature of the history of life."[19] Meyer disagrees; he argues that punctuated equilibria does not offer a sufficient explanation for events like the Cambrian explosion for a variety of reasons; but the most serious challenge comes from a realm that is invisible to the naked eye: biochemistry.

---

[18] Niles Eldredge, *Extinction and Evolution: What Fossils Reveal About the History of Life* (Firefly Books, 2019), 76, 84.

[19] Eldredge, 85.

Evolutionary Change and Biological Information

Whatever fossil evidence may be discovered in the future, the problem with relatively sudden and dramatic biodiversification events like the Cambrian explosion is not merely the lack of candidates for evolutionary precursors. Directly related to this dynamic is an even more serious challenge to a naturalistic evolutionary account: the massive amount of novel biological information required for new cell types, new functions, new structures, and new animal body plans. Naturalistic evolutionary mechanisms cannot explain the origin of this information; it is not that the problem simply has not been solved scientifically, it is that the very nature of the information involved is categorically different from what any blind process could be expected to achieve. A short summary of the relevant biochemistry will be helpful here.

DNA, which contains the so-called "language of life," is a double-helical molecule that resembles a coiled ladder. It is constructed of two "backbones" made of sugars and phosphates and connected by chemical "rungs" called nucleotide base pairs. The four different bases are adenine (A), guanine (G), cytosine (C) and thymine (T), and they always pair the same way: As with Ts and Gs with Cs. Thus, where an A occurs on one backbone, it will be bonded to a T on the parallel backbone. The resulting sequence of bases on one side is complementary to the sequence on the other; so if the sequence of bases down a single strand of the double helix is known, the sequence of the other strand can be deduced. Along the DNA molecule, the sequence of base pairs constitutes a digital code, the information necessary for the construction, operation, and reproduction of an organism. Protein construction begins with a process called transcription, in which the DNA molecule is "unzipped" and a gene segment (section of code) on one strand is used as a template for the synthesis of a single-stranded molecule called RNA, which also contains A, C, and G, but uses uracil (U) in the place of T. Next, in a process called translation, the RNA code dictates the formation of a specific amino acid chain (called a polypeptide), and then this chain folds into a specific protein molecule with an intricate geometrical shape. The shape of the protein product determines the job it can perform.

One crucial point here is that the ordering of the bases in the DNA segment determines the particular protein that is produced. This so-called sequence specificity is analogous to computer coding or the ordering of letters in the words of human language. Biological evolution requires new cell types, and as Meyer explains, "building novel cell types typically requires building novel proteins, which requires assembly instructions for building proteins—that is, genetic information. Thus, an increase in the number of cell types implies an increase in the amount of genetic information."[20] Remember those Precambrian sponges? Meyer points out that even those simple organisms likely required about ten different kinds of cells, but what about moving from that level of complexity to that found in the Cambrian record? "During the Cambrian period," he writes, "a veritable carnival of novel biological forms arose. But because a new biological form requires new cell types, proteins, and genetic information, the Cambrian explosion of animal life also generated an explosion of genetic information unparalleled in the previous history of life."[21] The million-dollar question that arises is whether unguided processes, like natural selection acting upon random mutations, could have generated the required genetic information for all the new Cambrian structures and body plans.

Biochemist Michael J. Behe has explored the capabilities of unguided evolution in detail over many years. A central figure in the intelligent design movement, he has concluded that while the neo-Darwinian mechanism—random mutation coupled with natural selection—is wonderfully capable of driving environmental adaptation to new ecological niches and producing other small-scale evolutionary changes, it is

---

[20] Meyer, *Darwin's Doubt*, 162.

[21] Meyer, 163.

inherently self-limiting: "The same factors that make it work well on a small scale ensure that it doesn't go very far."[22] It turns out that "*the great majority of even beneficial positively selected mutations damage an organism's genetic information*—either degrading or outright destroying functional coded elements" (emphasis his).[23] In other words, mutations are typically detrimental to the organism. As Behe explains, the most sophisticated experiments in evolutionary biology have revealed that a species "will never have greater genetic wealth than what it inherited."[24] This limitation spells big trouble for the Cambrian event, which involved an explosion in constructive biological information. Evolving one new functional protein from a preexisting type of protein would be, by itself, incredibly improbable, given the necessary sequence specificity of the amino acids in the polypeptide chain. While a single genetic mutation causing an amino acid substitution can be tolerated in some instances, protein functionality is greatly diminished or completely destroyed if more than one amino acid in the sequence is changed. The diversification recorded in the Cambrian strata would have required the rapid evolution of thousands of new types of proteins composed of unique amino acid sequences, but this is only part of the problem. Meyer explains:

> The Cambrian animals exhibit structures that would have required many new types of cells, each requiring many novel proteins to perform their specialized functions. But new cell types require not just one or two new proteins, but coordinated systems of proteins to perform their distinctive cellular functions. The unit of selection in such cases ascends to the system as a whole. Natural selection selects for functional advantage, but no

---

[22] Michael J. Behe, *Darwin Devolves: The New Science About DNA That Challenges Evolution* (HarperOne, 2019), 172.

[23] Behe, 183.

[24] Behe, 197.

> advantage accrues from a new cell type until a system of servicing proteins is in place.[25]

What Meyer means here is that in a naturalistic scenario, the right *set* of mutations needed for one new *system* of proteins would have needed to accumulate without the benefit of natural selection. Without this mechanism of preservation, he argues, the odds of this occurring even once are "so small as to render the chance origin of the information needed to build a new cell type fantastically improbable (and implausible) given the most optimistic estimates for the length of the Cambrian explosion."[26] Even if, against all odds, so-called neutral evolution could occur over and over (and over), in just the right directions, none of the mechanisms that have actually been observed to produce microevolutionary change operate fast enough to be a viable explanation of the macroevolutionary change exemplified by the Cambrian fossils. There simply was not enough time for this to occur.

The situation for a naturalistic explanation for the array of new Cambrian body plans gets even worse. We now know that the information encoded into DNA is not the only kind of biological information required for the development of an animal body plan. Epigenetic information, which is stored in cell structures themselves, is also essential. Developmental biologists have discovered that structural information—the information imparted by a specific arrangement of matter—is required for building an animal body plan. Both the unfertilized egg and embryonic cells contain such information, which is crucial to the proper hierarchical organization necessary for the construction of a specific body plan. Protein properties alone are insufficient. Meyer sums it up this way: "Other sources of information must help arrange individual proteins into systems of proteins, systems of proteins into distinctive cell types, cell

[25] Meyer, *Darwin's Doubt*, 206.

[26] Meyer, 206.

types into tissues, and different tissues into organs. And different organs and tissues must be arranged to form body plans."[27] How would this structural information evolve over time and lead to new body plans? The hypothesis that epigenetic information could mutate from generation to generation is not viable for at least a couple of reasons. First, the structures that serve as the "code" for this kind of information are impervious to the causes that produce mutations in genes, and second, alteration of these structures will most likely result in either the death of the embryonic organism or sterility (dead ends for evolutionary change).[28]

Because of the dire problems faced by neo-Darwinian theory, such as the Cambrian explosion, some evolutionary biologists have begun to doubt the veracity of the theory and call for the development of naturalistic alternatives. The obvious and simplest solution—intelligent agency operating at some level over the course of biological history—is avoided for philosophical reasons (see chapter 11). To reiterate, to hypothesize intelligent design is neither to deny nor affirm common descent; Behe and others have emphasized the fact that the idea of purposeful design is logically separate from the question of common descent.[29] Bechly puts a fine point on it: "Overall, the best explanation of the available fossil data may be some form of common descent but certainly not an unguided gradual process of transition, but rather, abrupt transitions and saltational changes that require intelligent design."[30]

The Origin of Life Problem

The debate over the origin of novel biological information, both genetic and epigenetic, will undoubtedly continue. There is, however, a problem

---

[27] Meyer, *Darwin's Doubt*, 276–77.

[28] Meyer, 285.

[29] Behe, *Darwin Devolves*, 157.

[30] Bechly, "Does the Fossil Record Demonstrate Darwinian Evolution?," 347.

for naturalism that is even more fundamental: the origin of the biological information necessary for the initial emergence of life. Supposing that a single-celled universal common ancestor of all living things existed in the remote past, neo-Darwinian mechanisms presuppose living organisms capable of reproduction. Where did all the essential biochemical information come from in the first place? In his *Origin*, Darwin did not address the origin of life question, but of course he considered it. In his personal correspondence, he cautiously speculated that, given the right conditions, a simple protein compound could have formed in some "warm little pond" and undergone "still more complex changes" that eventually led to the first living organism.[31] He never would have imagined the biochemical intricacies of protein chemistry, genetic coding, epigenetic information, and cellular reproduction.

Contemporary researchers are well versed on these matters and thus approach the problem at the most basic level: the origin of the biochemical information that a self-replicating genetic molecule would have to possess and how it could have chemically evolved into a living cell. Unfortunately, popular science journalism is often misleading about the progress that has been made in origin-of-life studies. James Tour, a renowned synthetic chemist with well over six hundred research publications to his credit, and who has been named as one of the top fifty most influential living scientists in the world, makes no bones about it:

> Contrary to the hyperbole of press reports, any synthetic molecularly derived structures that have been touted as being cell-like are in reality far from it. . . . Scientists have no data to support molecular 'evolution' leading to life. The research community remains clueless. Many scientists and professors who are outside

---

[31] Charles Darwin, Letter to Joseph Hooker, February 1, 1871, University of Cambridge, Darwin Correspondence Project, https://www.darwinproject.ac.uk/letter?docId=letters/DCP-LETT-7471.xml.

> boutique origin-of-life circles have been led astray by researchers' claims and the subsequent press, thinking that far more is known about life's origin than really is known.[32]

Indeed, the difficulty of the problem is vastly understated, leading many to mistakenly assume that a feasible scientific (read: naturalistic) account is right around the corner. It is not merely that there is a great deal of research left to do; rather, the problem is an utter lack of plausible evolutionary pathways leading from nonliving matter to even the simplest (in theory) living organism. The more we have learned about the biochemistry of life, including the inner workings of a cell, the worse the problem has become, and it all traces back to the question of the origin of information.

As explained earlier, genetic molecules (DNA and RNA) contain sequences that exhibit specified complexity—the protein product ultimately depends upon the ordering of the nucleotide bases; the function of the protein is determined by the sequence of the amino acids that have been strung together, and this sequence is dictated by a gene encoded on a DNA molecule. It has been well established that even a short section of DNA containing the code for one simple yet functional protein could not have evolved by chance alone. For one thing, DNA does not have chemical properties that facilitate any specific ordering of the bases along the backbone. Moreover, evolution requires replication, and DNA replication requires specialized proteins, which themselves are information based. This interdependence presents a classic chicken-and-egg problem. Not to mention the fact that protein complexes are required to get from DNA to a protein product.

---

[32] James M. Tour, "We're Still Clueless About the Origin of Life" in Charles B. Thaxton et al., *The Mystery of Life's Origin: The Continuing Controversy* (Discovery Institute Press, 2020), 323.

The currently popular hypothesis for the formation of a self-replicating molecule is the so-called RNA-world scenario, the idea that the prebiotic earth was populated with RNA segments capable of both self-replication and protein assembly. This multi-purpose RNA molecule, called a ribozyme, would have carried digital information, catalyzed some biochemical reactions, and self-replicated. Through some sort of chemical selection, these molecules would have evolved into more complex versions with broader functionality. This hypothesis faces many difficulties, not the least of which is the fact that the unguided organization of such molecules would virtually qualify as a miracle. Laboratory simulations have demonstrated that in light of realistic early-earth conditions, the synthesis of RNA building blocks would have been extremely difficult or even impossible. Also, the assembly of the building blocks (should they somehow arise) presupposes sequence specificity in the first RNAs, and that too must be explained.[33] Researchers have had very limited success with producing the building blocks, coaxing them into RNA molecules, and then directing their "evolution" into ribozymes possessing a tiny amount of functionality—the ability to catalyze a single chemical bond.[34] Notice that even this modest achievement was made with a great deal of intervention by intelligent agents who knew the necessary end goal. Naturalistic evolutionary scenarios have no such foresight. Even if researchers one day manage to synthesize a ribozyme with the necessary capabilities, this is a very far cry from forming even the simplest imaginable living cell with a minimal amount of complex protein machinery and genetic coding.

If a solution to the origin of life problem is dependent upon the capabilities of unguided chemical processes to produce the first biological information, there is little reason to hope for real progress. If, however, we follow a classic rule of scientific investigation and postulate a cause that is

---

[33] Stephen C. Meyer, "Evidence of Intelligent Design in the Origin of Life" in *The Mystery of Life's Origin: The Continuing Controversy.*

[34] Meyer, 450.

known to have the effect in question (information), uniform experience tells us that the only observed option is intelligent agency. We need not know *how* this agency produced the information in living organisms to reasonably conclude that it *did.*

Final Thoughts

The person who claims that evolutionary theory has made a creator unnecessary for explaining biological history and the origin of life itself is woefully underinformed about the actual data. As we have seen, the fossil record does not attest to a gradualistic divergence of animal kinds from common ancestors; it suggests a series of explosive diversification events that were not anticipated by preceding fossil evidence. As paleontological data has mounted, this pattern has not diminished, it has been amplified. Adequate transitional forms and reasonable precursors for complex biological structures are missing. The far more serious problem, though, is the information explosion that had to coincide with the appearance of the many new organs and body plans, such as those of the Cambrian period. A plausible solution has been elusive, to put it mildly. This situation has sparked debate in the scientific community about whether the neo-Darwinian paradigm needs significant revision or even wholesale replacement.

Although these are significant challenges to a naturalistic account of biological history, they pale in comparison to the one presented by the origin of life, which is fundamentally about the origin of biological information. Naturalistic hypotheses have fallen far short in terms of accounting for the specified complexity of a genetic molecule, which is merely one problem of a multitude involved with getting all the way to a living cell. Origin of life research, which has had unremarkable success, involves precisely orchestrated conditions and intervention by intelligent agents who have a specific goal in mind. This is not analogous to life emerging "in the wild."

Evolutionary theory has most assuredly not ruled out a Creator. On the contrary, as our knowledge about the biological world has expanded, especially over the last century, evidence of a mind behind nature has become even more striking. God gives us glimpses of his infinite intellect and power through what he has made (Rom 1:20), and through the natural sciences we continue to uncover wondrous new facets of this revelation. The study of nature, unbound from artificial limitations, is something to be encouraged and celebrated with thanksgiving.

CONCLUSION: AN INVITATION

In the preceding pages, we attempted to answer the most important accusations that people offer against the Christian faith. One ought not to shy away from answering one's critics, and Christianity has nothing to hide from its accusers. Since the accusations offered against Christian faith are so serious and affect people in such deeply existential and emotional ways, Christian love demands the responses offered here. Here is what we have covered.

When looking to the possibility of building a good and meaningful life, it becomes clear that Christianity provides a solid foundation for meaning and goodness where naturalism fails. While the problem of evil is profound and existentially troubling, Christianity has the intellectual and spiritual resources to provide solid answers to our deepest pains. The Christian perspective on reality entails that we are all hypocrites in various ways, and it is directly into this world of ugly hypocrisy that Jesus comes to bring righteous judgment and ultimate healing. There have been grave abuses in Christian ministries, yet the Christian picture of reality provides a unique set of resources to judge abuse and to care for the victims of abuse. Many Christians have been and are misogynistic, but Christian theology is deeply affirming of women in ways that continue to enrich the modern world. There is nothing in Christianity that seeks to oppress the thriving of women through the pro-life perspective; in fact, being pro-life is actually an embodiment of the universal human rights movement.

Violent Crusades and gruesome Inquisitions loom large in our culture's imagination and cannot be dismissed as rogue groups of self-proclaimed Christians behaving badly. But Christianity teaches tolerance, freedom of religion, peacemaking, and the intrinsic worth of every human being. These values have shaped our intuitions about how we ought to treat those with whom we disagree. While Christian history is indeed filled with stunningly evil examples of racism and other kinds of ethnic hatred and injustice, biblical Christian religion shows a concern for justice, ethnic equality, and a care for the lowest in society that many Christians have splendidly observed. While the Bible's picture of sexuality is at odds with the dominant culture in the West, the gospel of Jesus Christ provides a unique appreciation of the suffering and brokenness of LGBTQ-identifying persons and a holistic redemption that modern identity politics simply fails to offer.

When we examine issues of science and faith, we find that the warfare thesis is a caricature of the rich history of Christian support for scientific progress. Indeed, there is no conflict between Christianity and science, but instead a surprisingly deep conflict between naturalism and science. The claim that evolutionary theory has made a Creator unnecessary for explaining biological history and the origin of life itself is woefully underinformed.

Along the way, we defend and commend the Christian faith and life. Still, we wish to invite you to embrace the Christian faith. This book has covered important issues in history, culture, science, philosophy, and theology. Why should someone who is diligently seeking clarity on these difficult issues then consider becoming a Christian? Truthfully, we spend our whole lives trying to embody the answer to that question, yet we offer three simple reasons to accompany our invitation: (1) because it's true, (2) because it's hard, and (3) because God is actually the one inviting you.

First, we welcome you to embrace Jesus and faith in him because it is true. Science shows us that there is a Creator, a God who designed and made the universe. You may recollect the *kalām* cosmological argument that we defended in chapter 11.

1. Whatever begins to exist has a cause.
2. The universe began to exist.
3. Therefore, the universe had a cause.[1]

Belief in this cause of the universe is further corroborated by the moral argument that we made with reference to hypocrisy in chapter 3. You'll recall that only God can be the grounding for an objective moral standard like "hypocrisy is unacceptable." Here is the argument:

1. If God did not exist, then hypocrisy could be acceptable, all things being equal.
2. However, hypocrisy is not acceptable, all things being equal.
3. Therefore, God exists.

One could add to the list of moral values and duties things like "murder and rape are always wrong." Without an objective lawgiver, whose judgments apply to all peoples and at all times, such moral injunctions are meaningless artifacts of our cultural or social upbringing. However, that is not the case. Murder is not just out of step with current culture; murder is wrong.[2] So the Christian belief that God exists is true, but it is not sufficient to show that Christianity is true.

---

[1] See William Lane Craig, *The Kalam Cosmological Argument* (Wipf and Stock, 2000). See also Douglas Groothuis and Andrew I. Shepardson, "Cosmological Arguments," in *The Knowledge of God in the World and the Word: An Introduction to Classical Apologetics* (Zondervan Academic, 2022).

[2] For a lengthier defense of the moral argument, see C. S. Lewis, *Mere Christianity* (HarperCollins, 1952), bk. 1, chaps. 3–4; Shepardson and Groothuis, *The Knowledge of God in the World and the Word*, chap. 6; J. P. Moreland and William Lane Craig, *Philosophical Foundations for a Christian Worldview* (IVP Academic, 2017), chap. 26.

Christianity's truth claims are uniquely supported by the person and work of Jesus Christ, a Jewish rabbi whose ministry in Roman-controlled Palestine began a revolution of salvation and love in the first century AD. We can trust the sources about Jesus in the New Testament because we have thousands of early manuscripts to compare to be able to accurately reconstruct the message of the New Testament. The stories about Jesus are corroborated by secular historians of the day like Josephus, Tacitus, Suetonius, and others. The writings about Jesus show internal signs of authenticity: the gospels' recordings of Jesus's difficult sayings; stories in which the disciples who would later lead the Christian movement embarrassed themselves with poor behavior or lack of faith; and by the keystone of the Christian message, the resurrection of Jesus, being announced by women whose testimony wouldn't have been acceptable in court.[3] About the resurrection, scholars Gary Habermas and Michael Licona employ a "minimal facts" approach, based on "data that are so strongly attested historically that even the majority of non-believing scholars accept them as facts." These are Jesus's death by crucifixion, the empty tomb, the disciples' belief that Jesus appeared after his death, the conversion of Paul (who was a persecutor of Christians), and the conversion of the skeptic James.[4] The best explanation of these facts is that Jesus rose from the dead. We commend further investigation by any seeker or questioner.

Most important, Jesus claimed to be God (see John 8:58–59) and predicted his death and resurrection to his followers: "The Son of Man is going to be betrayed into the hands of men. They will kill him, and after he is killed, he will rise three days later" (Mark 9:31). "Son of Man"

---

[3] For a defense of the New Testament, see Craig L. Blomberg, *The Historical Reliability of the New Testament: Countering Challenges to Evangelical Christian Beliefs* (B&H Academic, 2016). See also "The Bible's Trustworthiness," in Groothuis and Shepardson, *The Knowledge of God in the World and the Word.*

[4] Gary R. Habermas and Michael R. Licona, *The Case for the Resurrection of Jesus* (Kregel, 2004), 75.

is a divine title from the Old Testament book of Daniel, which predicts a heavenly figure who "was given dominion and glory and a kingdom, so that those of every people, nation, and language should serve him. His dominion is an everlasting dominion that will not pass away, and his kingdom is one that will not be destroyed" (Dan. 7:14). If he claimed to be God, and accurately predicted his death and resurrection, this shows that the chief elements of the Christian message are true. There is much more to add to the truthfulness of Christianity. For the diligent seeker we recommend looking at the cumulative case for Christianity presented in books like Douglas Groothuis's *Christian Apologetics*, William Lane Craig's *Reasonable Faith*, or Groothuis and Shepardson's *The Knowledge of God in the World and the Word*.

The second reason we invite you to embrace Christianity is because it is hard. The Christian message confronts us with some difficult truths about ourselves, and it calls us to a way of life that is challenging (and beautiful). A difficult truth that Christianity offers is that humanity and the world we inhabit are broken by sin. God made the world good and made humans good, but instead of using our freedom to cultivate creation, we have all turned away from God, seeking our own pride, pleasure, and independence rather than relationship with him. Sin means a broken relationship with God, the self, and others. It means that we miss the mark of God's perfect moral standard, and that we have transgressed his laws. God has allowed us to experience the consequences of our sin, and this is why the world is filled with suffering. This is exceedingly difficult news for anyone who wishes to view themselves or the rest of humanity as basically good. We retain the ontological goodness of our humanity, but our moral goodness is dramatically broken through our sin. The Bible recounts this difficult truth in this way:

> There is no one righteous, not even one.
> There is no one who understands;
> there is no one who seeks God.

> All have turned away;
> all alike have become worthless.
> There is no one who does what is good,
> not even one.
> Their throat is an open grave;
> they deceive with their tongues.
> Vipers' venom is under their lips.
> Their mouth is full of cursing and bitterness.
> Their feet are swift to shed blood;
> ruin and wretchedness are in their paths,
> and the path of peace they have not known.
> There is no fear of God before their eyes. (Rom 3:10–18)

This likely offends most people's pride, as it does our own, but this is precisely the point. If you fail to lament the state of the world, if you fail to see your own desire to sin, and if you cannot acknowledge your own brokenness, then you have simply doubled down on sin through your own pride. This is hard.

The solution, though, is exceedingly beautiful. The Christian message is that in Jesus of Nazareth, God has come to the world to usher in an age of healing and peace. Jesus shows us the way to be truly human by living a life of love and self-sacrifice, by giving preference to the poor and abused and by judging the evil in the world. He offers a salvation that we are free to accept or reject. In Jesus, we see God taking the hard consequences of sin onto himself to provide forgiveness. His death takes on the just penalty for sin. His resurrection shows that death will not have the last word and that God has the power to make all the dead things in creation come alive again. This is hard, too, because it entails that all of our striving to make the world better is not enough. We need help from above. We need a solution that is bigger than our own efforts. This offends our pride. Still, the way of life that we are welcomed into by Jesus's death and resurrection is one in which we also die to our own way of thinking and living and choose to live for the glory of God and the love of all humankind. This is hard because it requires a complete reorientation of one's life and goals to God's life and goals. This life will contain suffering as we seek to live this way, but it also contains great joy as we remain connected to our source of life.

Jesus's death and resurrection are not the end of the story either. He has ascended to heaven, seated at the right hand of God the Father. And having sent the Holy Spirit to aid us in our transformation and work, he is returning to bring a new creation into existence where death and suffering will die. This is the good news of Jesus. It is hard because it means that one must look outside of oneself for salvation. But it is beautiful because it is comprehensive, pure, and true.

Finally, the invitation to embrace Christianity is ultimately from God himself. Jesus invites you, "Come to me, all of you who are weary and burdened, and I will give you rest. Take my yoke upon you and learn from me, because I am lowly and humble in heart, and you will find rest for your souls. For my yoke is easy and my burden is light" (Matt 11:28–30). He invites you to learn how to be truly human again and to find rest in his presence. He calls, "If anyone wants to follow after me, let him deny himself, take up his cross, and follow me. For whoever wants to save his life will lose it, but whoever loses his life because of me will find it" (Matt 16:24–25). He does not offer an easy life, but in casting off your old way of living, you will find a renewed life in him. He is the fulfillment of your deepest needs, your purpose, and your true desires. He offers, "Let the one who is thirsty come. Let the one who desires take the water of life freely" (Rev 22:17). We welcome you to find the love and peace of God through Jesus Christ our Lord. Amen.

GENERAL INDEX